The Ideology of Home Ownership

The Ideology of Home Ownership

Homeowner Societies and the Role of Housing

Richard Ronald
OTB Research Institute
Delft University of Technology, The Netherlands

© Richard Ronald 2008

All rights reserved. No reproduction, copy or transmission of this publication may be made without written permission.

No paragraph of this publication may be reproduced, copied or transmitted save with written permission or in accordance with the provisions of the Copyright, Designs and Patents Act 1988, or under the terms of any licence permitting limited copying issued by the Copyright Licensing Agency, 90 Tottenham Court Road, London W1T 4LP.

Any person who does any unauthorised act in relation to this publication may be liable to criminal prosecution and civil claims for damages.

The author has asserted his right to be identified as the author of this work in accordance with the Copyright, Designs and Patents Act 1988.

First published in 2008 by
PALGRAVE MACMILLAN
Houndmills, Basingstoke, Hampshire RG21 6XS and
175 Fifth Avenue, New York, N.Y. 10010
Companies and representatives throughout the world.

PALGRAVE MACMILLAN is the global academic imprint of the Palgrave Macmillan division of St. Martin's Press, LLC and of Palgrave Macmillan Ltd. Macmillan® is a registered trademark in the United States, United Kingdom and other countries. Palgrave is a registered trademark in the European Union and other countries.

ISBN-13: 978–1–4039–8945–1
ISBN-10: 1–4039–8945–1

This book is printed on paper suitable for recycling and made from fully managed and sustained forest sources. Logging, pulping and manufacturing processes are expected to conform to the environmental regulations of the country of origin.

A catalogue record for this book is available from the British Library.

A catalog record for this book is available from the Library of Congress.

10 9 8 7 6 5 4 3 2 1
17 16 15 14 13 12 11 10 09 08

Transferred to Digital Printing 2009

Contents

List of Figures	vii
List of Tables	viii
Preface	ix

1 Housing and the Rise of Home Ownership ... 1

2 Unravelling Home Ownership Ideology ... 16
   Introduction ... 16
   Theorizing housing and society ... 17
   Home ownership and ideology ... 24
   Social structure, discourse and ideology ... 36
   Conclusions ... 46

3 Homeowner Ideologies ... 48
   Introduction ... 48
   Housing discourses and ideologies ... 49
   Privatism and individualism ... 62
   Consumption and individualization ... 67
   Normalization and subjugation ... 74
   Conclusion ... 81

4 Housing, Globalization and Welfare States ... 83
   Introduction ... 83
   Housing systems and welfare regimes ... 84
   Competitive states and asset-based welfare ... 95
   Home ownership and the neo-liberalization
     of welfare ... 108
   Conclusion ... 115

5 Anglo-Saxon Homeowner Societies ... 118
   Introduction ... 118
   A British nation of homeowners ... 119
   An American home ownership dream ... 138
   The Great Australian Dream ... 152
   Conclusion ... 161

6 East Asian Homeowner Societies 163
Introduction 163
A Japanese nation of homeowners 168
Home ownership in Hong Kong 180
'Public' owner-occupied housing in Singapore 191
Conclusion 203

7 Comparing Homeowner Societies 206
Introduction 206
Convergence and divergence in the
  Anglo-Saxon model 207
Identifying convergence in the
  East Asian model 219
Comparing home ownership regimes 232

8 The Future of Home Ownership and the Consequences of Tenure 239

Bibliography 255

Index 277

List of Figures

1.1	International house-price increases 1997–2005	3
1.2	Mortgage debts to GDP ratios	4
5.1	UK home ownership rates 1914–2005	123
5.2	UK nominal house-price increases measured as an index, 1993 = 100	129
5.3	Tenure trends of young households in the UK	134
5.4	US home ownership rates 1910–2006	143
5.5	Australia home ownership rates 1911–2001	156
6.1	Nominal housing prices of homes with GHLC loans within a 70km radius of central Tokyo 1987–2003	176
6.2	Tenure rates for permanent residential housing in Hong Kong	183
6.3	Home ownership rate of houses by dwelling type in Singapore	191

List of Tables

5.1	Home ownership rates by race in the United States	144
6.1	Housing tenure in Japan	171
6.2	Singapore housing indicators	196
7.1	Key aspects of Anglo-Saxon home ownership systems	212
7.2	Key aspects of East Asian home ownership systems	220
7.3	Divergent features of East Asian and Anglo-Saxon home ownership models	234

Preface

This book considers the phenomenal growth of owner-occupied housing tenure across societies in recent decades, asking why and how has home ownership become so significant in so many different contexts? A central concept in my approach is 'home ownership ideology', which implies that tenure practices are not benign but support a particular alignment or interaction of social and power relations. A complementary concept is that of 'homeowner society', which suggests that social relations in some societies are specifically orientated towards the tenure and that owner-occupied housing systems play a special role in the development pathways of some countries. The purpose of looking at home ownership and society in this way is to develop understanding of the role of housing systems and housing cultures in emerging social structures. Although there has been a growing obsession with home ownership following its growth across societies in terms of tenure rates, and the global augmentation of home-property values, there has not been a parallel awareness of its wider social impact.

The academic material in the book is drawn from theoretical and empirical data from various disciplines which intersect in a field that can be loosely described as 'housing studies'. Research in this area has generally considered the structure of housing systems, differences between societies, and shifts in policy and practice in terms of the most tangible of variables such as tax concessions and tenure subsidies. This book takes a broader view. It considers the construction or constitution of home ownership orientated tenure systems in terms of policy practices, housing discourses and socio-political contexts. The aim is to identify similarities in tenure processes between advanced societies in order to illustrate the augmented impact housing is having on individual households as well as the structure of social systems. I also seek to identify differences in the role of home ownership in different countries in order to demonstrate its salience as a dimension of society.

I address a number of societies that have been associated with traditions and strong preferences for owner-occupied housing. This primarily includes a group of Anglo-Saxon societies including Britain, Australia and the United States. I also consider more unfamiliar cases of homeowner society in the literature including Singapore, Hong Kong and Japan. These countries do not have the highest rates of owner-occupation in the industrialized world as many South and East European societies, for example, have home ownership rates well above 80 per cent. I argue however, that there are discernable patterns among groups of homeowner society that underlie regimes of ideological relations.

Like many books, since the time of conception to the time of publication, considerable changes have unfolded in both the research field as well as in the material reality of housing markets and socio-economic situations. This book was put together following a decade of rapid house price inflation in most Western societies. This stimulated considerable social and economic restructuring in terms of national economies and the risks and debts taken on by individual house-purchasers. Over the same period, housing systems and markets in the 'Tiger' economies of East Asia were fundamentally destabilized by global economic fluctuations, and have only begun to recover very recently.

The actual writing of the book was done in three very different contexts. Initial studies were carried out in Nottingham, England and there is an unavoidable slant throughout the text towards examples from the United Kingdom. The second national context was Japan where I carried out comparative research on East Asian homeowner societies at Kobe University. The final stages of completion have been accomplished at the OTB research Institute for Housing, Urban and Mobility Studies, at Delft University of Technology in the Netherlands. These three societies contrast starkly in terms of housing systems and cultures of housing consumption and provide good examples for considering the context and objectives of the book.

In Britain house-prices have boomed in the last decade. Consequently, the majority of homeowners, with little real effort, appeared to make considerable capital gains. This consolidated the status of the tenure socially and, furthermore, created a general sense of smugness among owner-occupiers that they were property investment experts. Whether house price levels are sustainable or not is yet to be seen. A likely long-term implication of house price inflation is that those who were still moving up the housing-ladder when the market kicked off, while currently euphoric from the gains made on their existing small home, may end up paying two or three times more for housing during their lifetimes. A more fundamental implication is that many households, especially younger ones, are now effectively excluded from their preferred tenure.

In Japan, the 1980s housing-market was at the heart of the economic bubble which proved to be one of the greatest examples of unsustainable over-speculation in history. During the 1990s most house values dropped by almost half and there has only recently been notable recovery, and then only in specific central-urban-areas. Japanese homeowners are not so smug, but they do have a commitment to home ownership as the best form of housing and a good family investment. Indeed, it seems the polarization of preferences around owner-occupation during the 'golden era' of housing market increases established a tenure order that even the most drastic market losses cannot diminish.

While there has been a long commitment in the Netherlands to providing social-rental housing, the owner-occupied sector has grown by more than 10 per cent in the past 20 years and house prices have rocketed. The Netherlands is in danger of becoming a type of homeowner society and government policy is certainly not against this outcome, especially in terms of the tax deductions homeowners receive. Nevertheless, the social-rental sector remains relatively un-stigmatized and there seems no contradiction between renting a home and a secure family life.

These three contexts provided a radically stimulating environment for considering and investigating home ownership ideology. They specifically illustrate that while housing units, systems, practices and traditions are considerably different, home ownership itself is becoming an increasingly evident and significant aspect of global modernity. This is not to say that all places are getting more similar as a result of irresistible global forces; it is ratherto reaffirm that how each local context interacts is influenced by the organization of housing, which is becoming an increasingly important means by which households and governments can redistribute risks and deal with growing levels of insecurity and competitiveness driven by the global economy. Home ownership, as an individual hedge against risk, has thus become central to the ideology, and governments argue that increasing choice and access to owner-occupied housing is imperative. However, commodification of, and over-investment in housing has made the home a source of insecurity and a direct conduit for fickle international financial markets.

The book hopes to shed some light on these processes, or at the very least stimulate thinking about the ideological implications of tenure. I have received considerable help in putting this text together. The following individuals deserve my appreciation, but should be in no way held responsible for any misunderstandings, muddling or misrepresentations that appear in the book. First of all, great thanks go to my OTB colleague Marja Elsinga, who has provided fundamental insights and given up substantial amounts of her time to help on this project. I must also thank Yosuke Hirayama of Kobe University, Kath Arthurson of Swinburne University, James Lee of Hong Kong City University, and Michael Oxley and Marietta Haffner of OTB who provided supportive comments on

xii *Preface*

draft chapters. I should also acknowledge my other colleagues in Housing Systems at OTB who provided stimulating discussions on housing and tenure, especially Janneke Toussaint and Kees Dol. There are also friends and former colleagues who need mentioning for similar reasons. These include Gabriel Mythen and Luke Goode, of Liverpool and Auckland Universities, and Adam Barnard, Stuart Young, Neil Maycroft, Gerry Strange, Tony Burns and Jim Shorthose of TDF in Nottingham. Finally, I would like to demonstrate my appreciation for the love and support of my partner Violeta, to whom I dedicate the book.

RICHARD RONALD

1
Housing and the Rise of Home Ownership

It is impossible to deny how dominant home ownership has become across advanced societies in recent decades. Anglo-Saxon societies like Britain and the United States have, arguably, been most strongly associated with preferences for home ownership and rapid increases in houseprices, although post-war growth of home ownership has also been exceptional in countries like Japan, Australia, Spain, Singapore and Norway, among many others. There have even been market transformations across societies like the Netherlands and Sweden that, 30 or so years ago, had majority rental sectors and strong public housing policies. The advancement of home ownership has been largely considered 'natural', or at least has been constituted as natural in public and academic discourses. However, overall owner-occupied tenure levels have principally increased in most societies during specific periods of deep government subsidy and policy stimulation.

At the national level, housing was, not too long ago, a relatively marginal feature of social and economic policy. In many societies now, especially those who have suffered (or enjoyed) the worst (or best) of house-price inflation, national economies are overwhelmed by the aggregate wealth built up in private housing property, as well as by the debt – and the dependency on servicing this debt – bound up with mortgage markets. Indeed, macroeconomic steering mechanisms such as interest rates are now, arguably, as much determined by government desires to keep homeowners secure as by economic imperatives. Individually too, getting on the homeowner housing-ladder has become a central preoccupation and a primary frustration for many households, especially younger ones with low-to-middle incomes, while others already on the ladder have appeared to have made fanciful gains from their homes. This has been particularly evident in English speaking societies where owner-occupied property markets dominate, but also, increasingly, across a broader group of European societies.

Concomitant with market and tenure changes, perceptions, values and discourses have polarized. In societies where home ownership has boomed the status of the homeowner has become a social ideal. Owner-occupation has become embedded with routes to adulthood and autonomy and bound up with discourses of choice and freedom. The owner-occupier has been elevated as a better type of citizen, neighbour and even parent. The reverse has also been true. Renters and renting have become heavily stigmatized. It is not only an inferior tenure but also constitutes a poorer type of home. In some societies the realm of the public rental housing estate has been marginalized and its residents demonized. This social polarization is clearly ideological as in many continental European societies the idea of spending one's life and bringing up a family in a rented 'home' is very normal. Moreover, public and private-renters may even be envied by those tied down to their homes and mortgages.

This book addresses the changing role of home ownership across a number of societies that appear to have been deeply affected by changes in their housing systems. A particular focus is ideological as the restructuring of housing systems appears to meet up with broader social changes characteristic of advanced industrial societies in recent decades. The proliferation of home ownership has fundamentally restructured not only housing systems but also the housing 'dimension' of the social structure. The argument is that although housing has always been embedded in relations among families, communities, labour markets and the state, the growing household dependence on housing property and mortgage debt, and state reliance on housing markets as drivers of economic and social stability have placed housing more centrally in social relations. This shift aligns specifically, I suggest, with the intensification of globalization and is associated with the restructuring of governance, the redistribution of risk and intensified experiences of individualization. Another focus is divergence between home ownership systems and the nature of homeowner societies. Housing systems and housing markets are constituted fundamentally differently in each society with subsequently uneven outcomes derived from ostensibly similar global processes. In this introduction, I establish the main contexts of investigation, the main themes of the book and the central issues I seek to explore.

The rise of home ownership

Research has struggled to keep up with recent transformations in housing sectors. The house-price-bubble of the last decade has been hailed as the biggest bubble in history with an estimated increase in the total value of residential property in developed economies from $40 trillion to $70 trillion in the first five years of the century (*Economist*, 2005). House-price augmentation has been largely comprehensive (Figure 1.1) although its growth across Europe – especially in countries not historically associated with home ownership preferences – is particularly revealing. Housing-equity and housing-debt have become increasingly central to the structures of national economies as well as household portfolios of wealth and debt (Figure 1.2). The average home ownership rate in the EU has reached 64 per cent and housing-equity now constitutes more than 40 per cent of total GDP. At the same time, mortgage debt has tripled in a decade, becoming equal to around one-third of EU GDP. Essentially, housing systems and finance have been increasingly deregulated, and there has been a landslide of capital from other sectors into housing (see Doling, 2006; Horsewood and Neuteboom, 2006).

Evidence to suggest that housing systems are being transformed in each society is substantial, although little is yet understood about the social outcomes and long-term impacts. For many households, house-price increases have been the cause of euphoria. The perceived augmentation of individual wealth has been associated with the expansion of

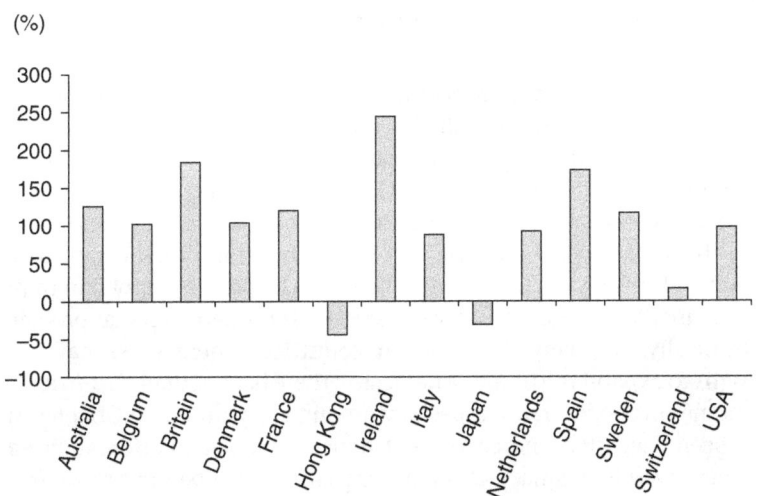

Figure 1.1 International house-price increases 1997–2005

Sources: ESRI, Japan Real Estate Institute, Knight Frank, Nationwide, Nomisma, NVM, OFHEO, Swiss National Bank.

4 The Ideology of Home Ownership

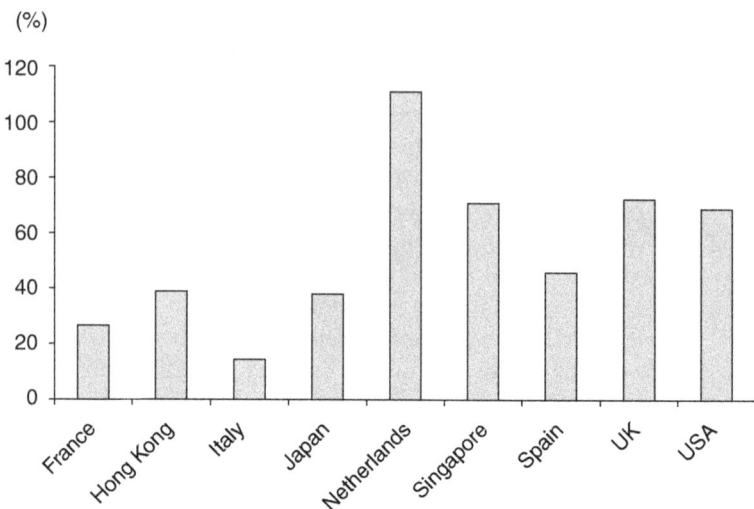

Figure 1.2 Mortgage debts to GDP ratios
Sources:
Hong Kong – Renaud, 2004.
Japan – Ministry of Land, Infrastructure and Transport, 2007.
Singapore – Phang, 2007.
USA – OFHEO, 2004.
European countries – European Mortgage Federation, 2005.

borrowing, as well as increased refinancing in order to reinvest in the housing market, which has driven up prices further. In some countries (for example, Britain, Spain, Australia) the government has intervened with subsidized home ownership schemes in order to ensure an inflow of younger homeowners, which has also contributed to the flow of cash into the sector, again pushing up prices. The in-affordability of owner-occupied housing has increasingly been constituted as a problem in public and media discourses and associated with numerous social problems.

Ironically, in many Anglo-Saxon countries, where there have been designs to expand the homeowner sector, there have actually been declines in home ownership rates, especially among the young (see Chapter 5). It has been suggested, moreover, that housing market in-affordability and the perceived inadequacy of rental alternatives may be preventing family formation and undermining fertility rates (Mulder, 2005). Meanwhile, older homeowners have expanded property portfolios and accrued considerable housing wealth. In East Asian countries, alternatively, house-prices have been rather volatile. This has also stimulated economic instability and has similarly generated rifts between generations (Forrest and Lee, 2004; Hirayama and Ronald, 2007). Essentially, across societies, inequalities in housing market access have become more central to social inequalities and emergent patterns of socio-structural transformation.

What is common across societies, despite the inequalities and frustrations created by the market, is an overwhelming commitment to home ownership which runs through the fabric of society. 'House-price euphoria' may have been an important driver, but cannot account for the radical shifts in housing policies and preferences or the resilience of such preferences following market cycle busts. Moreover, it appears that shifts in housing patterns are playing an important role in restructuring relationships between households, labour markets and state social-security nets. The consideration of home ownership in this book suggests that the ideological structures of tenure relations are becoming more dynamic and embedded in power relations.

Nations of homeowners

In many developing countries, home ownership rates are often high because of weak legal systems, underdeveloped land-use and the rural-family base of economic production. Industrialization and urbanization tend to stimulate the growth of rental housing, necessary to support growing populations of workers, and the development of recognizable 'systems' of housing which involve a complex coordination of diverse areas of planning, legislation, financing, construction, marketing, distribution and consumption, among other things. For the industrial societies of Europe, North America and East Asia there has been considerable divergence in approaches to housing with some societies extending the number of homeowners and others building strong rental housing regimes. The central concern in this book are the industrialized, post-industrialized, or, more generally, 'advanced' societies that appear to have adopted an approach to housing, politically, economically and socially focused on owner-occupation.

Past explanations of tenure changes in advanced industrialized societies have largely forwarded the view that home ownership rates are an aspect of economic development. Approaches have thus emphasized convergence, seeing home ownership rates as reflecting augmentation in levels of GDP per capita. Schmidt (1989) identifies in the literature a general assumption that policies are dominated by economic prerogatives, rather than political or ideological ones, so that countries are seen to move along a common trajectory of development. The suggestion that owner-occupation rates grow with GDP follows the argument that the high cost of ownership is relative to incomes which is dependent on national prosperity. However, this argument soon for the very simple reason that some of the richest advanced societies have the lowest home ownership rates (Germany, 43 per cent; Switzerland, 35 per cent) and some of the poorest the highest (Greece, 83 per cent; Spain, 85 per cent). Indeed, there are fundamental problems in asserting a single home ownership trajectory due to the diversity of housing histories, systems and structures, cultures and ideologies among owner-occupation orientated societies.

Economic convergence models fail to take into account two critical factors. First, localized features make different housing tenures more or less advantageous (Scanlon and Whitehead, 2004). Housing system features always form in unique combinations in each society, meaning that home ownership inevitably mediates or represents different sets of advantages and rights regarding different kinds of properties distributed in different kinds of spatial and regional arrangements. Owner-occupation is also framed against the set of rights and advantages provided by alternatives to owning, which ultimately make home ownership more or less accessible or preferable. Moreover, tenure itself is a slippery concept and the meanings, rights and obligations of 'owning' a home vary radically from society to society. For example, in Singapore the majority dwell in 'public-owner-occupied housing' which is essentially constructed and mortgaged by the state and leased for 99 years. Even within Europe, the concept of owner-occupied tenure varies radically between the freeholds of Britain, the cooperatives of Scandinavia and the privatized municipal flats of Eastern Europe.

Second, socio-ideological forces are central in the proliferation of home ownership. It has been suggested that in some countries national belief systems have sanctified the status of the homeowner. This is encapsulated in phrases like the 'great American Dream' and an 'Englishman's home is his castle'. Other societies demonstrate similar charged idiomatic notions. For example, the Flemish are born with 'bricks in their bellies' and in a Japanese home there is 'one castle, one country, one master'. Saunders (1990) suggests that the engrained cultural orientation towards home ownership in English speaking countries has influenced the development or logic of settlement and housing. Owner-occupied housing in these societies has been bound up with a cultural tradition of individualism and historically related to land and property ownership. This ideology has often been promoted or reinforced by government policy making home ownership more attainable and the benefits greater. For Kemeny (1981, 1992) the status of home-owning is related more to the constitution of either a collectivist or an individualist ideological orientation. Individualist societies are prone to subsidizing and promoting owner-occupation with this form of residency increasingly becoming embedded. In this way the preference for, and ideology of, home ownership, considered natural by Saunders, is manipulated for Kemeny.

Barlow and Duncan (1994) link the domination of home ownership in countries like Britain and the United States, which in their view is 'ideologically symbolic', with economically liberal capitalist regimes. The ideological orientation towards owner-occupation is further related to a stigmatization of social and rental housing (Gurney, 1999b; Ronald, 2006). The pro-home-buying economic subsidies that are subsequently preferred under these regimes give ideological advantages an economic dimension (Doling, 1997). This is in contrast to the ideologically symbolic status of tenure in other capitalist regime types, where more collective or egalitarian values may prevail in the organization of housing. In Denmark and Sweden state housing has been viewed as an alternative open to all, in part, to achieve high overall standards. In these countries therefore, tenure may have been equally ideologically charged with a commitment based on a social democratic project of bringing about a collective ideal. However, this does not simply translate from ideology to tenure. Home ownership can be provided within more egalitarian frameworks which illustrates that demand for the tenure can come from different trajectories (Poggio, 2006). For example, Norwegian governments have pushed home ownership as a form of social housing, with subsidies distributed in order to achieve greater social equality (see Gulbrandsen, 2004).

This book addresses various ideological orientations towards home ownership among groups of societies where there the tenure has been strongly embedded in housing policies, housing preferences and discourses. The very notion of a 'homeowner society' suggests that social relations in some societies are specifically orientated towards owner-occupied housing systems which play a special role in the development pathways of some countries. In basic terms, home ownership has advanced considerably in the economically liberal, English speaking societies of Australasia, North America and the British Isles, while North European societies tended to develop stronger rental housing sectors, although there is considerable variation. South European nations on the Mediterranean rim are associated with more traditional family housing practices and some of the highest rates of home ownership (see Allen et al., 2004). Eastern Europe also contains some nations with super-high home ownership rates, although this phenomenon is largely attributable to the rapid sell-off of state-owned rented housing blocks after the transfer from state-socialism almost two decades ago (see Tosics and Hegedus, 1998). Newly industrialized countries in East Asia have also seen a rapid growth in home ownership rates along since the 1950s and 60s (see Forrest and Lee, 2003).

The growth of home ownership in these societies is not simply a natural phenomenon but has been stimulated, constituted and reinforced by government practices, social discourses and the expansion of market relations. Furthermore, there are outcomes for the distribution of wealth and life-chances, as well as the structure of relations between individuals, markets and the state. My assertion is that constellations of power relations and social conditions around home ownership vary between different groups of countries that can be classified as 'homeowner societies'. I focus in this book on two specific groups of homeowner societies where ideological relations and the social production of housing preferences have, arguably, been most evident. The first group is constituted of cases of Anglo-Saxon homeowner societies, the second from East Asia.

Home ownership ideology

The very use of the term of 'home ownership ideology' implies that tenure practices are not benign but support a particular alignment or interaction of social and power relations. Ideology is a slippery term and refers in one sense to practices which maintain social solidarity or support social control, and in another, a world view or system of integrated values through which subjects make sense of the world (Goodman and Refsing, 1992, p. 9). A more discursive view of ideology would see the two as more integrated with the everyday meanings and practices embedded in the flow of discourses which regulate flows of power in society. In housing research, such an approach has been most effectively represented by social constructionism (see Jacobs et al., 2004) which asserts that social reality is constituted by the systems of meaning located in everyday discourses. This has provided some important insights into the meanings of housing and home ownership consumption, but has been less effective in defining relationships between structural features and housing discourses.

The understanding of the ideological impact of home ownership which dominated approaches in the 1970s and 80s was largely hegemonic. It saw working-class homeowners as victims of false-consciousness and the promotion of home ownership by the political right as a strategy to build a conservative hegemony. The theoretical assumption has been that home ownership stimulates market practices, reinforces household dependency on wage labour and private property relations, and promotes political conservatism (Kemeny, 1981; Ball, 1986; Berry, 1986; Marcuse, 1987), the idea being that growing levels of home ownership support the hegemonies of capital in power conflicts between the political left and right. However, the notion of home ownership ideology has, surprisingly, been poorly developed theoretically and empirically (Ronald, 2004), even though writers normally allude to it as a self-evident phenomenon.

One of my concerns in addressing home ownership ideology is to move beyond a simple hegemonic ideological model. Since the 1990s the discursive consideration of markets has been elevated by the advancement of globalization and neo-liberalization. Globalization has been a driver of neo-liberalized relations and practices that assert the centrality of free trade, privatization and undistorted market processes as a means to advance economic growth and individual liberty (see Waters, 1995; Weiss, 1998; Peck and Tickell, 2002). While the increased privatization and marketization of housing across societies has been implicated in global neo-liberal processes (Doling and Ford, 2003), the ideological aspects have not been developed. An important consideration for this book therefore is the relationship between advancing neo-liberal technologies of governance, and housing practices and discourses. This is developed in terms of discursive ideological practices and relations between housing, families, the market and the state, across societies.

My approach differentiates home ownership ideology and homeowner ideolog*ies*: the former concerning networks of social power relations and the latter referring to discourses and meanings which constitute objects and subjects, and relations between them. I develop a more discursive notion of ideological processes where housing practices and discourses constitute particular forms of housing objects and individual investor or consumer subjects, which align with varying degrees of neo-liberalization of social life in different social contexts.

Housing tenure and Anglo-Saxonism

Kemeny's initial observations illustrated the comprehensive impact 'monotenural housing systems' have on a society. He suggested the domination of owner-occupation in societies like Britain and Australia had comprehensive privatizing effects on society as a whole, influencing urban form (suburban rather than urban), public transport, lifestyles, gender roles, systems of welfare and social security.

an overwhelming emphasis on home ownership created a lifestyle based on detached housing, privatized urban transport and its resulting 'one-household' (and increasingly 'one-person') car ownership, a traditional gendered division of labour based on female housewifery, and the full-time working male, and a strong resistance to public expenditure that necessitated the high taxes needed to fund quality universal welfare provision. (2005, p. 60)

In most English speaking societies home ownership has come to represent an ideal. At the institutional level this ideal has arguably become an imperative. Policies and discourse essentially construct home ownership as the default position with renting for those either waiting to become homeowners or those on the margins of society. Indeed, housing discourses in English speaking societies often differentiate between the 'homes' of owner-occupiers and the dwellings of renters (Gurney, 1999b). If there is a hierarchy of tenure, renting sits just above homelessness and marks a graded boundary of social exclusion. The language of Anglo-Saxon housing research has also reduced tenure to concepts of either renting or owning, or public or private, despite the diversity of systems. For example, types of renting are often reduced to private or public with the former involving market provision and second the state. Social housing constitutes a form of social safety-net and in Anglo-Saxon societies normally denotes types of renting involving subsidies to support low-income households. However, social housing is a complex notion and can involve, particularly in continental Europe, a mix of private and public provision and a diverse combination of tenures including owner-occupation (Kemeny, 1995; Czischke, 2005).

While there has been some resistance to this tyranny of home ownership (Kemeny, 1981; Berry, 1986; Marcuse, 1987), there has been a fundamental lack of challenge to the ethnocentric, or even 'tenure-centric', bias in the consideration of tenure. Academic discourses on owner-occupation in the international (English language) literature have largely been voiced by those from Anglo-Saxon societies. One of the intentions of this book is to look at home ownership from within and without an Anglo-Saxon cultural gaze, in order to expand the conception of tenure. Essentially, the Anglo-Saxon understanding of home ownership, housing systems and tenure relations provides a starting point. However, I also look to home ownership outside this model, and specifically to East Asian examples where this tenure ideal is equally embedded but mediated and practiced in radically different ways.

The role of housing

Housing is more often than not considered in terms of an aggregate of units which function as shelter for individuals or groups. However, housing constitutes a rather dynamic element of the social structure and performs a plethora of functions. Houses as homes constitute indispensable spaces in which loving relationships are developed, nurtured or dissolved. Indeed, 'home' is the centre of individual and family life, and forms a spatial domestic ideal. Homes provide a refuge from the world, a place of personal investment and play, and the backstage of personal life. The house, as the container of the home, is thus best conceived as a kind of relationship between people and their environment (Dovey, 1985, p. 33). Houses are also exchanged and consumed. The commodification of housing and its circulation in a market means that wealth can be accumulated, stored and transferred between individuals and across generations. Houses can thus also constitute assets and investments. They are normally the biggest or only investment a household has. Housing consumption takes many forms but may also represent membership of a group or social class, a feature of lifestyle consumption, or a pivotal point for identity formation and self expression (see Rybczynski, 1986; Lawrence, 1987; Allen and Crow, 1989; Madigan and Munro, 1996; Gurney, 1999a,b; Clapham, 2005). Ultimately, housing is far more than shelter, and how it is organized in any society has fundamental impacts on other areas of social life and elements of the social structure.

The most central way housing can be understood as a feature of the social structure is in its role in mediating welfare. For Kemeny (1992) housing is so deeply embedded in welfare and the social structure that it is difficult to disentangle (p. 80). Housing constitutes a welfare good in itself in terms of shelter, but also forms the basis of how households use and share other welfare goods. It acts as a store of resources in terms of use, asset and exchange, and spatially constitutes the point of exchange of goods and welfare services between family members. Resources can be carried across generations or be transformed into cash to buy other goods. Housing also situates the household in a market where people compete for and trade housing goods, which establishes more or less dependent relationships with the state, the family or the market for the satisfaction of welfare needs. Nevertheless, housing has not been so well integrated into theories of welfare systems and welfare states (see Lowe, 2004). Many approaches exclude housing from analyses of welfare structures as there are problems of measurement or because housing is often too commodified to be considered within the welfare state.

Essentially, despite their importance to the actual mediation of welfare, housing systems have historically been considered the 'wobbly pillar' of welfare states (Torgersen, 1987). Nevertheless, increasing privatization and commodification of housing in terms of market forms of provision and consumption have begun to intensify and extend the significance of housing systems in welfare relations. Housing policies, specifically those associated with the promotion of owner-occupation have recently been associated more with government moves to reduce social safety-nets and withdraw public welfare provision.

My concern with the role of housing in homeowner societies specifically concerns recent national and international transformations in housing systems, with the rapid augmentation of home ownership and house-prices, which appear to promote and underpin a restructuring of welfare relationships and the advancement of neo-liberal forms of governance. The privatization of goods and services has long been associated with the 'roll-back' of the welfare state in market-liberal societies like Britain and the United States (Peck and Tickell, 2002). However, the ostensible growth of individual property assets among a growing majority of national populations has arguably provided a platform for governments to reconsider the structure of welfare provision and obligations. Increasingly, it is being encouraged through policies and suggested in state discourses, that responsibility for welfare provision should be placed on the individual, rather than the state. Individuals are reminded that they can afford to purchase services through the market by 'drawing upon the wealth that they have accumulated through home ownership' (Groves et al., 2007, p. 193). This new system of welfare has been described as 'asset-based' (see Regan, 2001; Sherraden, 2003) and represents a fundamental and historic shift in the welfare logic of advanced societies.

Evidence of such transformations in the role of housing and welfare is more limited. However, I address in the course of this book the nature and scope of this aspect of neo-liberalization across groups of societies. It is argued that shifts in housing systems and the expansion of owner-occupied sectors support transformations in ideological relations in which housing is increasingly constituted as a private-market good rather than a social-merit good. This underpins the broader commodification of social relations, with market practices constituted as the best and most appropriate means of welfare provision, and state mediation the least. This inevitably supports the reduction of public spending and the transfer of economic and social risks from the state to individuals, which underlie a more globalized model of a competitive and market-orientated neo-liberal state.

Scope and aims

The focus of this book is both theoretical and empirical. In terms of theory, the aim is to contextualize and re-centre some of the debates on the ideological character of housing relations and the social significance of tenure. Conceptualizing the function of housing systems in emerging patterns of governance and welfare capitalism is also emphasized. Empirically, the task is more challenging. Ideology has been notoriously difficult to capture, especially in the context of tenure (Richards, 1990). Essentially, 'evidence' is constituted by drawing contextual frameworks of development of home ownership ideology in different societies which emphasize social, economic and political features. Policy developments are drawn upon specifically and, where possible, discourses which provide insights into discursive social and state practices. There is also a comparative element to the approach, which is rare among ideological analyses. The aim is to assert a middle-range comparison which is scientific to the extent than non-quantifiable variables will allow (see Oxley, 2001; Somerville and Bengsston, 2002).

In terms of the framework concerning the ideology of home ownership and its dynamic role in homeowner societies so far set out, three central questions which guide consideration and analysis can be established.

- How is housing related to social and power relations, and what are the ideological effects of tenure systems?
- How is housing integrated, or not, with social systems and welfare regimes?
- How has home ownership ideology been constituted in the societies considered, how does it vary between societies, and what are the implications of these differences in social processes and patterns of social development?

If there is a research field in which this book stands, it is the one normally identified as 'housing studies'. This is a rather loose category and involves various disciplines and approaches to housing phenomena. It is also an area identified as being fundamentally un-reflexive and slow to respond to developments in other research fields and academic disciplines (Kemeny, 1992). Addressing home ownership ideology provides a means to stimulate thinking in this area by drawing attention to some prevalent assumptions and the socially reactionary nature of housing research. It further constitutes a reflexive dimension for the (re)consideration of policy development in both intellectual and practical housing fields.

The approach in this book is inevitably constrained by the nature of the data considered and the limitations of comparative analyses which attempt to make general assertions about whole countries and even groups of nations. The data drawn upon is eclectic, making use of policy documents, homeowner discourses and secondary analysis in varying measures. The intention is to forward analytical insights that may enhance understanding rather than demonstrate the 'truth' about housing systems and ideology or assert causal relations between tenure features and social development.

Structure of the book

The book can be divided into two main parts. The first is more theoretical and the second empirical and comparative, although there are elements of empirical analysis in the former and theoretical development in the latter. In Chapters 2 and 3 a conceptual understanding of the relationship between housing and society is developed as well as the main features of homeowner ideologies as found in the Western housing literature. In Chapter 4, the focus is on emerging debates concerning the relationships between housing and 'welfare regimes' that have dominated understanding of welfare states and divergences between societies in recent years. Housing systems and tenure have been poorly integrated in past debates, but have developed a new salience in light of competitive global shifts which have forced governments to readdress labour market protection and welfare provision. The undermining of welfare states and the erosion of de-commodified forms of consumption has put greater pressure on individual property assets and the wealth built up in owner-occupied housing in particular.

In Chapters 5 and 6, the focus is on social contexts, policy developments and housing and political discourses in different societies. The pattern of home ownership policy development and the emergence of home ownership ideology in Britain, the United States and Australia is examined in Chapter 5. Similar relationships between housing and society are addressed in Chapter 6 for Japan, Hong Kong and Singapore. These two groups of societies are compared in Chapter 7, where they are more clearly identified as groups of Anglo-Saxon and East Asian homeowner societies in which housing has played different roles in social development and the constitution of ideological relations. Finally, in Chapter 8, I contemplate international trends in housing and society. Within Anglo-Saxon homeowner societies fundamental market problems are likely to develop following a decade of unsustainable market increases. Across homeowner societies more generally, similar patterns of social inequality between groups of owners and renters, and between different generations, driven by the uneven distribution of housing property wealth, are already emerging.

2
Unravelling Home Ownership Ideology

Introduction

Home ownership has long been considered in terms of its ideological significance. This association arguably originates in the late nineteenth century with Engels who suggested that individual home ownership leads to the embourgeoisement of the working class and diminishes autonomy in the political sphere. Indeed, there is considerable evidence, as I shall identify in the course of this book, to suggest that states and political groups have historically recognized the significance of promoting working-class home ownership as a means to promote an individualist ethos and resist the growth of collectivist forms of social organization. Much of the debate on the socio-political salience of home ownership until the 1990s focused on tenure relations in these terms.

In the past few decades, however, social commentators have observed fundamental social shifts characterized by greater social fragmentation, differentiation, privatization and marketization, the restructuring of employment, production, welfare and risk. Such theories have subsequently focused *inter alia* on various aspects of globalization, shifts in post-Fordist modes of production and postmodernity (for example, Giddens, 1991; Beck, 1992; Fukuyama, 1999). An underlying argument in this book is that such shifts have changed the nature and role of home ownership, both in the structure of social relations and in ideological practices of power and legitimation. Home ownership has taken on a new salience in mediating relations among individuals, families, jobs and welfare, the market and the state. The traditional association of home ownership with bourgeois ideology is thus no longer adequate in capturing the complex relationships between private housing consumption and socio-ideological practices.

The aim of this chapter, as a precursor to an analysis of diversity and transformation in the role of tenure relations, is to unravel key debates and theoretical concerns regarding the impact of tenure and housing systems on social organization and power relations. It specifically sets out to develop a working understanding of ideology and how it relates theoretically and practically to the structure and practice of home ownership. Despite the influence of housing policy, the significant costs of housing subsidy, and the substantial capital, cultural and status advantages many homeowners receive, the role of home ownership in society was not examined coherently until the late 1960s. Even then, debates were not central in the social sciences. At the same time, influential theories of social power and the state, prevalent in debates in sociology and political science, were not reflected in the housing literature (Kemeny, 1992). It was not until the 1980s and 1990s, following the considerable impact on households and national economies of house-price bubbles and their subsequent implosions, that home ownership really began to draw attention in sociological, economic and political debates.

The chapter begins by considering home ownership in theories of housing and society. The first section deals with housing consumption as a dimension of social class relations. It also considers the outcomes of housing consumption on patterns of social inequality traditionally thought to be determined by production relationships (that is, position in the labour market rather than position in the housing market). The section concludes by considering some implications of postmodern theories of identity consumption for home ownership ideology. The second section of the chapter addresses the notion of ideology directly, identifying problems associated with the conceptualization and investigation of ideological processes in housing. The relationship between home ownership ideology and political attitudes is also considered. The final section turns to the issue of methodology and problems associated with the study of housing discourses in relation to housing policy, state power and social change, as well as international comparison.

Theorizing housing and society

Housing and social class

From the late 1960s to the late 1980s housing was primarily considered in relation to processes of production and consumption with often neoclassical economic conceptions of 'rational actors', and Weberian or Marxist conceptions of society. Initially, a debate emerged in the housing literature between approaches which asserted, on one side, that housing tenure divisions were increasingly influential in determining life chances and, on the other, approaches that maintained that traditional social class relations were fundamental to patterns of social inequity and subjugation, where housing simply reinforces these divisions at an ideological level.

Arguably, the work of Rex and Moore (1967) marked a key change in the consideration of housing tenure, and in particular the relationship between housing and broader socio-structural issues. The introduction of the concept of 'housing classes' or 'housing groups', although not fundamental to Rex and Moore's position, initiated a divergent approach to understanding the role of tenure in the social structure. It was suggested that housing tenure was theoretically significant as a means of identifying social divisions and that social groups could be adequately separated and classified in terms of shared housing experiences. This meant that 'housing classes', alongside occupational classes, could become a critical marker of life chances.

Crudely speaking, homeowners as a group (or 'housing class') were argued to share common experiences through their housing consumption. By focusing on an individual's access to desired housing resources, a hierarchy of housing classes could be identified from owner-occupier to private tenant, the important point being that these divisions cut across those arising from the world of work. The concepts used to identify groups in this way developed from the original 'housing classes' of Rex and Moore, to include classifications such as 'housing status groups', 'domestic property classes', and 'consumption sector cleavages' (Haddon, 1970; Saunders, 1978, 1990; Dunleavy, 1979, 1980, 1987; Pratt, 1982).

In Saunders's (1978, 1979) initial concept of 'domestic property class', the most salient division in society was between owners and tenants. The potential exchange value, rights and control were definitive privileges for owner-occupiers who experienced significant wealth accumulation through property ownership. Saunders inevitably recognized that this model was neither exhaustive nor complete. Nevertheless, his arguments continued to elevate the role of housing in explaining social inequality.

Saunders (1990) later developed the concept of a 'consumption sector cleavage' in which he asserted that consumption was increasingly determining social structural developments and social inequalities in late modernity. His criticism of Marxists, who conceived social relationships in terms of production relationships and thus a dichotomy between owners and non-owners, was that the complex divisions and social striations of contemporary societies were ignored. Saunders's conception of consumption as a framework of inequality identified three key factors in a household's capacity to consume: the ability to earn, rights to state services and the capacity of self-provision. The basis of emerging social divisions, following a process of social re-stratification, thus lay in a central division between those who could afford to satisfy their needs through private consumption and those forced to rely on the provision of state services and goods. Those who consumed privately from market facilities were argued to enjoy greater benefits than those consuming public goods. Access to private housing as a means to accumulate wealth and bolster private patterns of consumption thus becomes the most salient aspect of home ownership rather than the divisions it draws between social groups.

The idea of housing classes superseding traditional social classes received considerable opposition, especially from those on the left. Kemeny argues (1992) that housing group paradigms decontextualized housing from social relations to form the basis for a new single factor explanation of social inequality. While housing is important in explaining social divisions, a 'crudely formulated tenure division' between private homeowners and state sector tenants is limited to two forms of tenure, (public and private), which ignores the complexity of housing and its wider social ramifications. Indeed, private renters are often more disadvantaged than public ones in terms of costs and security of tenure, while many low-income homeowners are less mobile in employment markets and more vulnerable to economic fluctuations than renters. A specific criticism of Saunders concerned the excessive focus on the relative significance of housing market position vis-à-vis labour market position. The social advantage of home ownership is not simply material as more intricate connections exist between owner-occupation, ethnicity and gender within social stratification (Pratt 1982, 1986; Winter, 1994). For example, the conceptualization of consumption fails to take into account types of consumption provided by informal family networks and unpaid female labour (Warde, 1992).

For Marxists the significance of housing and tenure divisions was theorized as an *ideological* division (Clarke and Ginsberg, 1976; Kemeny, 1981; Berry, 1986), as it symbolically and materially reinforced capitalist property relations, false consciousness and the reproduction of a labour force dependent on wage labour. Private home ownership was argued to foster a concern for dwelling and its contents, and promoted home-centred lifestyles, which encouraged ideologies and practices of individualism and privatism. This stands in contradiction to the public-centred life and more collective and inclusive systems of social organization. Moreover, homeowners become locked into the capitalist system through the mortgage debt they have encumbered in order to buy a house. This ensures the compliance of the worker who, through his or her mortgage, is bound to wage labour. Critically, the effect of home ownership is that it invests the individual into private property relations, tying them to the prevailing structures and ideologies of capital. Consequently, differences in housing consumption simply reinforce existing social power relationships.

Home ownership and social inequality

A central question in understanding the social role of home ownership became whether or not housing tenure represents an independent source of inequality sufficient to affect the distribution of social power. Evidence of patterns of social inequality determined by access to owner-occupied housing has rarely been clear-cut or conclusive. Data have suggested, however, that economic inequalities grounded in the employment market are largely perpetuated or exaggerated through the housing market and not independently reshaped through property ownership (Thorns, 1981, 1989; Forrest, 1983; Hamnett, 1999). What is more important, is that it appears that home ownership, while not eroding inequalities between social classes has become more important to the structure of economic differences and features of social relationships.

Economically, the impact of home ownership has been substantial and increases in house-prices in recent years have meant, in many societies, that housing property has constituted the most significant means of individual investment and asset accumulation. While it has appeared to be a road to capital accumulation for a broad class of citizens, it has also been a primary mechanism by which households have accumulated debts and economic risks (see Ford et al., 2001; Doling, 2006; Horsewood and Neuteboom, 2006).

In analyses over the last 25 years of occupation, household income, tenure and capital gains, it appears that those in managerial and professional occupations have made the largest gains (for example, Thorns, 1989; Hamnett, 1999; Kurz and Blossfeld, 2004). Moreover, not only has owner-occupation brought greater financial benefits to middle-class homeowners than to working-class ones, capital gains made from owner-occupancy have disproportionately advantaged those at the top end of the market. It would initially seem that gains from the job and housing markets are in fact related and to some extent mutually reinforcing.

While homeowners may have been advantaged overall as a group, there are many striations within this category of housing consumers.

In some situations low-income homeowners have been disadvantaged by choosing to buy rather than rent, especially when their tenure status has become insecure because of unemployment or interest rate increases. Hamnett's research (1999) suggests that higher socio-economic groups who buy more expensive housing make higher absolute gains due, in part, to greater mobility and the frequency of trading up. In his study of homeowners in the south east of England he found that, when measured over the whole housing career, professionals and managers gained almost twice as much in absolute terms as manual groups. When length of time in the housing market is held constant, social class reasserts its importance and is strongly manifest in the levels of capital gains made by comparable cohorts of house buyers (p. 100). It is apparent, therefore, that while economic inequalities created by housing tenure enhance those created through the job market, housing has become an engine of economic differentiation.

What has become most significant, as home ownership rates have grown and house-prices have risen, is that access to owner-occupied housing, normally determined by income and social class, has become increasingly critical to patterns and experiences of wealth accumulation. As Malpass (2006) observes,

> There can be no doubt that, by redistributing the ownership of domestic property from the few to the many, the growth of owner-occupation has enabled a large proportion of the population to acquire valuable capital assets and to accumulate wealth on a scale not previously contemplated. However, within the owner-occupier market there is very wide variation in the amounts of wealth accumulated by owners in different circumstances. And in an era when owner-occupation is not only a main source of wealth accumulation for the majority of people but also a key factor in determining access to credit and local advantage, to be excluded from that market is more disadvantaging today than at any time in the past. (p. 8)

Essentially, assertions that housing has become the basis of significant social inequalities appear valid to the extent that access to owner-occupied property has become more central to the polarization of wealth between classes, as well as exposure to economic risks. Forrest et al. (1990) point out, on one side, that as more and more households become owner-occupiers, greater fragmentation and differentiation amongst owners will occur, while on the other, inequalities between household abilities to procure desired housing within the market fragments social classes along tenure lines. Marginal homeowners have become the most vulnerable group as they make least capital gains if prices go up and are most likely to lose their homes should economic conditions change or couples break up (see Forrest et al., 1999).

Home ownership has indeed reformed and restructured wealth and opportunity inequalities between social groups and has become more central to social identities and socio-economic security. This does not necessarily mean that social divisions between traditional occupational groups that formed the basis of traditional social classes have been undone, but rather that restructuring and re-signification have occurred. This has been mediated for many through the housing market, in which the pattern but not the basis of social inequality has been transformed.

Consumption and identity

Although there is little convincing evidence to support Saunders's suggestion (1990) that capital gains made through home ownership level out social inequalities formed along social class or labour market divisions among homeowners, the impact of apparent property asset growth may still have social significance. Saunders's views on housing and social change are aligned with theories of individualization, which suggest that traditional social identities based on class and ascribed characteristics are losing their significance in shaping the lives of individuals. In his individualization hypothesis, Beck (1992) stated that as educational opportunities expand and geographic and occupational mobility increases, family and class have become less important. Social class loses its subjective relevance and people begin to interpret labour market risks in terms of individual risk and not class risk. In terms of housing, while the resilient relationship between income, social class and capital gains made on housing property undermine Saunders's assertion that society has become more equal through the expansion of home ownership, the individualization of risk, choice and economic gain in the housing market may contribute to the erosion of feelings or perceptions of social class identity. This may subsequently support discourses that assert that individual wealth can be augmented irrespective of social background and occupation.

Another key aspect of Saunders's work was the suggestion of a growing significance of individual housing consumption in processes of self-identity and ontological security in the context of declining solidarities and traditional communities. While the assertion that owner-occupation enhances ontological security more than other tenures is questionable, the consideration of home ownership as identity and lifestyle consumption has become more central to debates on the impact of home ownership.

Following postmodern theories that assert that structures of modern society such as class, family and community are under dissolution, attention has increasingly turned to how individuals create their own individual identity. In the construction of identity all consumption, from clothes to food, to housing, is considered central. This approach marks a move away from the consideration of fixed social groups and fixed meaning attached to commodities (see Chapter 3). The changing significance of consumption in understandings of processes of self-identity and social identification slowly stimulated a shift in thinking about the impact of home ownership and the role housing consumption.

Following the work of Giddens and others it is argued that housing has increasingly become a means to an end rather than an end in itself. The end is personal fulfilment and the task of housing research is to elucidate the links between housing and this overall aim; in this pursuit the concepts of identity and lifestyle are key (Clapham, 2005, p. 1).

New approaches to housing as consumption have stimulated some novel ways to think about housing consumption as the play of identity (see, for example, Miller, 2001). Nevertheless, the ease with which identity consumption theories abandoned traditional social class relations and their failure to pick up on the resilience of social inequalities and practices of subjugation is somewhat disconcerting. In postmodern approaches to consumption, the primary foci are identity related processes while exchange and material use values of commodities are ignored or relegated to a minor role, or are themselves treated as values that cannot escape symbolization (Lodziak, 2002, p. 30). Although much research has focused on the play of identity and signification, some theories of consumption have retained a sense of the persistence of material conditions of social reproduction under capitalism. There is an undeniable significance of consumption in the mediation of power and the maintenance of social relations of production in contemporary societies.

> This means that individuals are now engaged (morally by society, functionally by the social system) first and foremost as consumers rather than producers.... The crucial task of soliciting behaviour functionally indispensable for the capitalist economic system, and at the same time harmless to the capitalist political system, may now be entrusted onto the consumer market and its unquestionable attractions. Reproduction of the capitalist system is therefore achieved through individual freedom (in the form of consumer freedom to be precise). (Bauman, 1992, pp. 49–51)

Indeed, the type of material consumption associated with owner-occupied private property appears tied up with ideologies of choice and individual freedom and may be implicated in serving the interests of capital. For Malpass (2005, 2006), choice has become central to government policy rhetoric and the concern with choice in housing has been at the forefront of an attack on public housing more generally. The state, by focusing on the status of individuals as consumers has arguably shifted the focus of housing provision issues to the market, which has provided a means to rationalize a withdrawal from social housing and collective forms of public provision. The concept of choice in housing also obscures inequalities between renters and homeowners and the uneven benefits that better-off homeowners make through the property market.

Thinking of home ownership consumption as ideological in these terms adds substantial sophistication to the Marxist approaches to home ownership ideology of the 1980s and identity consumption approaches from the 1990s. I shall ultimately argue in the coming chapters that ideologies related to the ascendancy of consumption and markets in social relations are central to understanding the role of home ownership in many advanced industrial societies. In the consideration of the relationship between housing and society I implicate home ownership specifically as a policy, practice and ideology which has played a critical and increasingly important part in relationships between governments, structures of welfare provision and households.

It is difficult from such a short appraisal of considerations of home ownership in consumption, social class and identity to unravel the relationship between housing tenure and social relations. Nevertheless, the analysis has suggested that home ownership and its proliferation may well be critical to emerging constellations of class or classless identities, and emerging relationships between individuals as property owners, and society and the state. This is not to suggest that fundamental relations of subjugation in advanced capitalist societies have been diminished, but rather restructured in line with other social transformations associated with late modernity.

Home ownership and ideology

Housing and ideology

There are multiple definitions of the concept of 'ideology'. In simple terms we can identify two general meanings, one political and one cultural. In terms of the former, Marx and Engels's (1965) understanding concerns systems of ideas that contribute to the constitution and reproduction of the social relations of a particular material existence in terms of relations of production and consumption, the division of labour and the distribution of wealth. The dominant mode of ideology within a society at any particular time thus reflects the contemporary mode of production and the division of labour. In terms of its cultural denotation, ideology has been conceptualized as a system of meanings or worldview. Ideology can thus involve practices such as religion and even manners that can be studied in the context of any particular society (see Geertz, 1973). These two different aspects of ideology can be considered in terms of what ideologies *do* and what they *say*. Alternatively as Goodman and Refsing (1992) put it, 'one can examine ideologies as systems for maintaining social solidarity, providing charters for social order or preventing social disintegration; alternatively one can examine how ideologies are symbolically represented' (p. 9). The former is the task of social and political theory, the latter, of anthropology.

The focus of this book is the political aspects of ideology. The concern is how social discourses and practices function in power relations and reflect and sustain contemporary modes of production and consumption. This section deals with the conceptual aspects of home ownership ideologically. This involves developing the concept of ideology and how it functions. The analysis begins by considering the traditions of Marx and Engels, Gramsci and Althusser. Understanding the role of housing tenure systems in ideological terms has been made difficult by, first, the over-embedding of ideology in economic-structural conditions, and second, the lack of methodological apparatus by which to assess ideological processes. I specifically deal with how the concept of ideology has been applied to home ownership and potential evidence to suggest that tenure has clear ideological outcomes in terms of political 'attitudes'. The empirical investigation of ideology has turned increasingly to the analysis of units of discourse, and the discursive constitution of reality and systems of knowledge by which power is circulated. Discourse and ideology, however, have not been simple to integrate.

Dominant ideology

In the post-war era many social theorists came to emphasize the significance of ideology in explaining the persistence of bourgeois ideals and capitalist socio-economic relations (see Larraine, 1979; Thompson, 1984). An idea of 'dominant ideology' evolved which conceived of a coherent set of values and beliefs expressed across society in such a way as to either constrain consciousness or radical action, or both. This set of dominant ideas does not reveal itself and unequal social relations as false or of an imaginary order. Instead, it necessarily presents itself as essential, objective and universal. Abercrombie et al. (1980) explicitly set out the constellation of ideas constituent of dominant ideology, which includes ideologies of accumulation, managerialism and individualism, which legitimate social inequality. It is not surprising then that home ownership has been implicated in the mediation of these ideologies.

Marx's and Engel's approach to ideology (1965), while sensitive to the role of systems of ideas to the reproduction of social relations, is subject to the primacy of economic structures. Essentially, ideology is a specula image – a *camera obscura* – of what is really there. Ideology operates to obscure object and social reality in a way that supports the interests of the domination of the bourgeoisie and inequitable relations of wage labour and capitalist production. Nevertheless, even though Marx and Engels advance the concept of ideology and elevate its role in constituting and reproducing the social relations of a particular material existence, they provide a poor insight into the social mechanisms by which ideology constitutes material practices.

In explaining how society is infused and held together by ideology, the works of Gramsci and Althusser have been drawn upon in particular. Gramsci (1971) emphasizes how dominant ideology permeates social institutions, acting like some sort of cement in binding society together. At the level of civil society, 'hegemony' is formed around an ideology that becomes central to maintaining the state and capitalist institutions. State power is thus always held in balance with the legitimizing strength of hegemony. Gramsci argues that the dominant hegemony of the ruling class is never complete and is actively maintained through moral and political leadership as well as some direct coercion. In the formation of their subjugation individuals develop a 'dual consciousness': one derived from lived experience and the other by dominant ideology.

Althusser (1984) develops the political conceptualization of the ideological mediation of the individual by capitalism in more psychological terms. First, he asserts that ideology doesn't merely represent reality, it constitutes reality. This is because the relationship between the subject and the object world is itself of an imaginary order. In other words, living 'as if' constituted as a subject. Essentially, a sense of autonomy and free subjectivity is authored under conditions of subjugation by ideological means. Ideological apparatus ensure the social reproduction of the form of subjectivity necessary for the reproduction of state power and relations of production. Althusser also emphasizes how ideology is materially constituted or has a material existence. The representations that make up ideology are inscribed in social practices and experience, and are expressed in objective forms. For example, religious ideology is manifested as beliefs in god, which have a material existence in social practices and are regulated by social institutions.

In the case of home ownership it is possible to identify simple ideological connections between housing systems and residential practices, and Gramsci and Althusser's categories. For example, the practice of owner-occupation is bound together with ideologies of consumption, private ownership and autonomy achieved through market choice, which has a material existence in the owner-occupied home. Various cultural practices surround home ownership, which is supported by legal and financial institutions on one hand, and consumer culture and family practices on the other. Nevertheless, there are problems with these theories of ideology in that they tend to constitute a model of dominant ideology which over-determines ideological forces in social reproduction, overstates the case of top down processes and state manipulation, and considers ideology and hegemony as too coherent and unified (Thompson, 1984).

Indeed, it has been easy to generalize about ideology in the consideration of housing. There has been a tendency for research to focus on government policies and institutional structures when investigating ideological practices rather than the language and structure of everyday life, which is the locus of meaning that sustains relations of domination. For example, Ball (1986) addresses how ideology, politics and economic interests become inexorably woven together in terms of 'structures of housing provision'. In his analysis, institutional relationships between housing agents have determined the political terrain of housing policy with the predomination of provision orientated around owner-occupation resulting in a determined set of social relations, associated with the material process of land development, building production and exchange of land property. In this ideological conceptualization these structures are prior to the ideas and policy responses that they produce. While Ball's analysis is insightful, it neglects the circular, discursive and subjective nature of ideology. As Dodson observes (2007), structures of provision do not simply arise from structural relations between institutions, but find support in broader social and cultural practices.

A large part of the research on home ownership in the housing literature addresses housing policy, dealing with the categories of policy documents as real and given, which ignores their ideologically charged nature and the role of language and discourse in constituting particular objects and subjects, and problems and solutions in the housing field.

While other approaches recognize and address the significance of policy discourses in generating systems of knowledge about housing (for example, Jacobs and Manzi, 1996; Gurney, 1999a,b), there have been difficulties in relating them to practices of hegemony and ideological power (Dodson, 2007). Moreover, the focus on government policy neglects the everyday aspects of ideologies which function at the individual, subjective and inter-subjective levels. Dodson's critique of housing researchers who have previously identified the significance of discourse and ideology is that they have remained decidedly inattentive to how ideology is actually generated and propagated (p. 12).

An ideological critique on home ownership systems and social practices may arguably be better maintained within a more reflexive framework where the interests of capital and the state are embedded with the analysis of policy measures, institutional and political discourses on the provision side, and everyday meanings and practices of home ownership on the consumption side. It is important that conceptions of ideology move away from a simple determinism and towards the study of the complex ways in which meaning is mobilized for the maintenance of relations of domination. Ideology thus requires further unravelling, as do the variety of roles it plays in both social change and social reproduction. A fundamental argument in this book is that home ownership does not fit a simple Marxist ideological model where capitalist states have pursued tenure policies designed to subjugate increasing numbers of the working classes to the logic of mortgage based property ownership. The relationship between housing and society is more multifaceted than that, and has grown in centrality in the structure of social relations along with the advancement of globalization and competitive states, the retrenchment of welfare states and the individuation of risk.

My analysis of home ownership ideology and its influence in changing patterns of social organization is thus two-sided. On one side I consider how consumer based subjectivities are interpolated in material practices, rituals and discourses surrounding home ownership. I address how homeowner ideolog*ies* are structured through the dominant mode of residence or dwelling into practices of everyday life, which is wrapped up in discourses of property and ownership (see Chapter 3). The generation of such subjectivities may be central to processes of hegemonic formation which in turn legitimate the state and market orientated policies. On the other side, I consider the role owner-occupation plays hegemonically in undermining welfare states and public provision, and promoting neo-liberal ideologies that appear central to processes of globalization (Chapter 4). The relationships between housing systems, social structures and political power will also be argued to be divergent leading to different outcomes in different societies (Chapters 5 and 6).

I develop the conceptual approach more explicitly in the third section of the chapter, which addresses issues of discursive, ideological and comparative investigation. First, however, it is necessary to deal with the idea of home ownership ideology and how it has been historically treated in the housing literature. The consideration of home ownership ideology is not new. The debate that has emerged contests what kind of effect home ownership has on the values and behaviour of homeowners.

Home ownership ideology

Home ownership has developed a particular salience in recent decades, specifically in Anglo-Saxon socio-political contexts, as an ideological medium of socio-economic organization. The values and ideas surrounding owner-occupied housing have been acclaimed as the epitome of conservative values and as a 'bulwark against bolshevism' (Forrest, 1983). Indeed, Kemeny (1981) explicitly identifies that home ownership has been politically sponsored to sustain a stabilizing effect in civil society by offering a stake in a 'property owning democracy'. In short, home ownership fosters conservatism and incorporates households into the capitalist system. It has further been argued that home ownership now dominates discourse and thinking concerning normal family life and social participation (Richards, 1990; Gurney, 1999b). It even dominates the policy debate itself, as demonstrated in housing policy discourses on ownership and control (Murie, 1998). Underlying these assertions are a range of assumptions concerning the nature of ideology and the system of values and beliefs surrounding home ownership.

Discussions concerning growing levels of owner-occupation have been dominated by what Gurney (1999b, p. 163) refers to as pull-versus-push explanations. These explanations either emphasize the natural basis of the pull towards owner-occupation or the push of socio-ideological forces into private tenure. In terms of understanding the role of ideology, these approaches can be crudely separated into *neutral* and *critical* ideological conceptions (Thompson, 1984). *Critical* conceptions generally fit into a Marxist framework and present home ownership as ideologically coercive and divisive, portraying homeowners as passive recipients of hegemonic projects. The *neutral* conceptions are loosely associated with pluralist approaches and tend to essentialize the need or desire to own one's own home and thus present homeowners as passive respondents to innate desires.

Nevertheless, on either side of the housing debate 'home ownership ideology' has remained largely under-theorized and empirically under-operationalized (Richards, 1990; Kemeny, 1992; Dodson, 2007). Increasingly, the concept of 'home ownership ideology' appears as one that needs to be challenged, because no developed and coherent theory of home ownership ideology, per se, exists. To consider a single dominant ideology surrounding home ownership implies a strong and direct link between social structure, stability and legitimation. Nevertheless the nebula of ideas and values surrounding this tenure in homeowner societies is complex. For Thompson (1984), the effect of ideology should be considered in terms of complexity and fragmentation as much as social cohesion, and empirical research with homeowners has illustrated that owner-occupiers can demonstrate a range of contradictory responses to the status quo (Winter, 1994). In consideration of the nebula of ideas surrounding home ownership the concept of 'home ownership ideolog*ies*' may better reflect the eclectic nature of housing discourses.

The premise of Marxist approaches to home ownership ideology is largely determinist and focuses on the bourgeois elements of home ownership and private property relations. Home ownership oriented housing policy has been perceived as a conservative strategy which, by providing an artificial system of inducements and subsidies, entices individuals into home purchase, which materially and ethically bind individuals into wage labour, private property and the maintenance of prevailing socio-capital relations. It is argued that these material inducements, from the structuring of both private and public finance systems and government policy in favour of ownership, are reinforced through ideological control. In other words there is an assumption that a co-responding nebula of ideas and values accompanies the material manipulation of housing behaviour. As such, current tenure preferences appear to be the product and not the cause of tenure systems (Kemeny, 1981, p. 63).

Marcuse (1987) asserts that people may naturally prefer shared rather than competitive housing aspirations where individuals help each other in the housing system irrespective of profit. Market based home ownership is not the result of genuine choice but is fostered by government housing policies and commercial interests that materially and ideologically coerce individuals into one form of living arrangement or housing aspiration. As such Marcuse proposes that the, 'typical suburban middle-class home often represents more a commercial, artificial and profit induced, exclusionary picture of conspicuous housing consumption sold to its occupants as the ultimate "dream", than what those occupants would really want if they had a choice' (p. 232).

Marxist approaches have ostensibly resolved the preference for home ownership as 'false consciousness', as evidence of people's enslavement to their own domination. Home ownership thus becomes part of a system of oppression, dividing people from one another, encouraging conformity and inhibiting human capacities. The housing that the individual *believes* they want is separated from the housing they *really* want (Marcuse, 1987). For Boddy, 'The myth of an innate desire for private property functions by projecting onto individuals the characteristics of the particular socio-economic system in which they are located. ... The desire for private property springs not from the individual but from the socio-economic system' (1980, p. 25).

In these terms it seems easy to connect home ownership ideology to the maintenance of capitalist domination and social reproduction. But how relevant or useful is this conceptualization of home ownership ideology? There is a clearly structural and functional over-emphasis in explaining the actions of the state and relationships between social classes. Moreover, there appears a very simple relationship between home ownership and ideology, and any claim to the authenticity of home ownership preferences is immediately dismissed as false.

Arguably, these problems originate in the Marxist conception of ideology itself. The Marxist resistance to the authenticity of home ownership preferences is inevitably grounded in the assumption that, as home ownership can be seen to serve the interests of capital accumulation and bourgeois values, it is inevitably false. A basic implication of this conceptualization of ideology is the inference of critique. To identify certain beliefs as ideological is to disembed them from 'truth' or the 'real'. To characterize a view as ideological is already to criticize it, by separating it from a natural basis and identifying it as the thought of others (Thompson, 1984). From this understanding of ideology and home ownership the authenticity of dwelling preferences are inevitably intangible.

Assuming that ideology is simply received and internalized and this is how social relations are maintained is indeed problematic. Ideologies are not simply 'swallowed' with individuals uncritically submitting to hegemonic values and behaviour. Furthermore, ideology is not simply a form of social cement that binds members of society together through collectively shared beliefs. To understand the impact of ideology we must consider the complexity of how residential and experiential forms interact with systems of ideas. It has been suggested that it is the very diversity of ideologies and lack of consensus that makes ideology significant in the maintenance of social cohesion. Abercrombie et al. (1980) attempt to establish empirically that there is a fundamental lack of ideological consensus in advanced industrialized societies, and that dominant ideology is largely fragmented.

Saunders (1990) provides a broad critique of the development of the ideological analysis of home ownership, suggesting that leftist academics have been too dismissive of empirical research on preferences for owner-occupied tenure. They have considered tenure preferences as the mechanical product of dominant ideologies and manipulated choices. The evidence of a variety of positive perceptions of home ownership across classes, occupational groups and cultures is, however, overwhelming in Anglo-Saxon societies (see also Littlewood, 1986; Holmans, 1987; Ruonavaara, 1988; Rohe et al., 2002). Winter's research (1994) found that preferences for home ownership are not bound up with a bourgeois and passive citizenry. Home ownership can often be a basis for the mobilization of resistance to the state, local authority or capitalist interests. Local groups, identified through their tenure as much as their community identity, may actively resist external intrusions from developers, local authority planners, and so on. However, Winter does overstate his case in that even the most 'radical' of homeowners is unlikely to challenge the principle of private property relations and thus their own interests.

Saunders (1990), among others, identifies a range of advantages of ownership and has demonstrated how strong and complex subjective rationalizations about the relative merits of home ownership can be. Similarly, the fact that in the United Kingdom, home ownership came to dominate immediately after a period of mass building of public housing challenges the assumption that housing desires are state manipulated. Nevertheless, Saunders's assertions are equally problematic as he attempts to ground the pattern of predominant tenure preferences on a 'natural' basis. Emphasis is placed on territorial and possessive tendencies in humans, as well as the greater economic security and potential for ontological security in home ownership. Arguably, it is equally implausible to ignore the significance of home ownership in maintaining hegemonic and politically complicit values, or the role of the state in enhancing the advantages of home ownership. Housing tenure policy has clearly been an arena of political self-interest. For Forrest et al. (1990) many governments have been keen to promote home ownership due, in part, to political motivations to resist civil unrest or where the expansion of owner-occupation is associated with political conservatism. Saunders's position has thus been considered reactive to the growth of home ownership and lifestyles focused on domestic consumption. There is also neglect for diversity in the constitution of households and of gender differentiation within the space of the home (Warde, 1992).

Political attitudes

Following debates on the ideological effects of home ownership, a simple empirical question emerges. Does home ownership cause owner-occupiers to be more politically conservative? As the relationship between ideology and causality is not open to simple testing, a more realistic question for researchers becomes, 'are owner-occupiers more likely to be politically conservative than rental tenants'? The logic of *critical* approaches of home ownership ideology asserts that owner-occupation should propagate more conservative, individualistic and privatistic political ideologies, and invests homeowners with the task of maintaining the stability of private property relations. *Neutral* ideological conceptions commonly see the effect on public and political attitudes more positively, with home ownership enhancing the 'civic virtue' of citizens and subsequently the democratic 'civic community'.

For Kemeny (1981) the ideological importance of tenure derives from the effect it has upon lifestyles to the extent that they become privatized. Home ownership restricts the opportunity and even desires of homeowners to engage in collective action on political and social issues. For Saunders, alternatively, the private home is more of a condition of social participation than the antithesis of it, and homeowners are more often actively engaged in social life than tenants. Saunders (1979) suggests that owner-occupiers acting to defend their property values may not only constitute a highly articulate and effective political group, but also achieve their successes at the expense of both business and class interests (p. 206). In the past thirty years or so, these different theories have been the subject of notable discussion and social investigation.

Research in America has certainly shone a very rosy light on the effects of home ownership on values and behaviour. For Rohe et al. (2002) there are diverse impacts including improved psychological health, greater participation in voluntary associations and political affairs, and even better school results and reduced delinquency among children. Empirical findings, however, may often reflect the ideological context of research, which may assume that positive effects are out there to be found. Certainly, British research has been much gloomier about the 'perils' of home ownership.

DiPasquale and Glaeser (1997) identify numerous correlations between home ownership and measures of civic participation. For example, American owner-occupiers are approximately 10 per cent more likely to know their government representative by name, 9 per cent more likely to know the name of their school board head, 15 per cent more likely to vote in local elections, and 6 per cent more likely to work to solve 'social problems'. Moreover, owner-occupiers are 12 per cent more likely to do gardening and 10 per cent more likely to own a gun! These effects however, appear stronger for those in the top income quartile. In the majority of regressions carried out, tenure had least impact on those at the bottom of income distribution. For example, home ownership only increased the likelihood of voting by 4.3 per cent for the poorest homeowners, while the impact on those with high incomes was 29.1 per cent. Moreover, comparisons with Germany, where home ownership rates are much lower and owner-occupiers move less, suggested that many effects on social attitudes and public participation associated with tenure were influenced more by length of residence. Indeed, many of the measured effects of tenure on attitudes may have more to do with other aspects of dwelling. In the United States renters maintain their residences for an average of 2.5 years, while homeowners stay approximately 13 years (Anily et al., 1999).

A considerable amount of research has focused on how housing tenure produces certain types of voter or generates particular allegiance to one party or another (see Dunleavy, 1979; McAllister, 1984). However, research generally fails to ask how, or what is it about housing tenure that causes such identities and voting patterns. Empirically, relationships have been difficult to demonstrate clearly due to parallel patterns of occupation, class and tenure (Williams, 1989; Lundqvist, 1998). Essentially, data on homeowner activism (see also Cox and McCarthy, 1982; De Leon, 1992; Kingston et al., 1984; Winter, 1994; Field, 1997) remains generally inconsistent and the rationalizations and sociopolitical responses of homeowners are varied. Tenure may be a vehicle for establishing one's political or social identity, but for many, tenure status is not the way they choose to measure themselves, and tenure status is irrelevant to their lives (Bounds, 1989, p. 16).

Pratt (1986, 1987) found that amongst white-collar workers, homeowners have different political attitudes to renters but this is not true amongst blue-collar workers. Blue-collar workers tied to production-based organizations like trade unions are often more concerned with production-based issues rather than consumption based issues such as housing. The process is thus more complex and contextual than the simple conceptual association of home ownership with political conservatism. Self-definition, meaning and social identity are critical concepts in understanding the political impact of housing tenure (1986, p. 378). The rise of home ownership in Western homeowner societies is almost directly paralleled by the decline of production-based collectivism, trade unionism and industry based communities. Home ownership has indeed increased as union support declined suggesting that 'meanings' and 'identities' have been transformed.

Agnew (1981) distinguishes between different home ownership 'interests' and attempts to link them to political activism. His approach addresses how social being and identity are related to housing tenure. He concludes that the interests associated with home ownership, such as personal autonomy (political interests), the realization of social esteem (cultural interests) and the maintenance/enhancement of exchange value (economic interests) are sufficient to require 'community consciousnesses' on the part of homeowners. The result is greater community activism among homeowners compared to renters. Although this approach gives some appreciation to the potential tenure identification may have, it tells us little about processes or meanings involved.

Lundqvist's research (1998) suggests that there is little discernable effect on self-reported political interests, although his data also identified that homeowners are more favourable towards dismantling or privatizing the welfare state, which favours Kemeny's conceptualization of home ownership ideology. Data illustrated that rather than being more 'virtuous citizens', homeowners are more active in public affairs when it is in their own interests, or to the extent that their privileges as property owners are threatened by political decisions. They are a mixed and heterogeneous group who only act in a common way when property rights are directly challenged. Lundqvist's analysis, while illustrative of some outcomes, essentially leaves us with no clearer picture of ideological processes. For Murie (1998), the problem may lie in the causal confusion in conceptions of the relationship between home ownership, political conservatism and the civic virtue of homeowners. This confusion derives from the fact that more affluent, stable and secure households are normally more likely to become homeowners. This association becomes converted into a view that it is home ownership which creates affluent, stable and secure households (p. 84). In other words, the tendency for conservative individuals to become homeowners becomes converted into the view that the tenure produces political conservatism.

The debate on the role and effect of home ownership ideology has been far from conclusive. Essentially, the tools and concepts of analysis are limited in scope. A central problem has been identifying the impact of housing on ideology in social and political processes, and tying it to practices of legitimation and power relations. In order to demonstrate the impacts home ownership may have in each society, this book takes a broad perspective. It seeks to maintain a critical conception and does not simply look to political outcomes among citizens and voters. The approach is more comprehensive and seeks to relate ideological practices at various levels including government policies and discourses as well as individual ideologies at the meaningful level of dwelling and consumption. The hope is to clarify the features of home ownership ideology and divergence between different societies in these terms. Another focus is transformation and the growing significance of home ownership in contemporary social relations.

Social structure, discourse and ideology

Capturing ideology

A central problem in the consideration of ideology is the means by which to capture it and make it accessible for reliable interpretation and analysis. Empirical research in housing has often relied on the analysis of the talk of residents, housing managers and other key agents in order to understand the relationship between structures of power and meaningful expression. To study discourse is to study the actual instances of expression in actual occurrences of everyday communication within which ideological elements are mediated. Characteristic concerns are with linguistic units such as extended sequences of expression, as well as relationships between linguistic and non-linguistic activity (Thompson, 1984).

Nevertheless, making direct connections between institutional structures and units of discourse is more problematic. Methodologically, there has been greater emphasis on form and structure than content in traditional discourse research. Despite the interest in non-linguistic and linguistic behaviour, there has largely been a failure to account for the non-linguistic sphere while there has also been a neglect of the meaningful component of what is said, and its interpretation. Essentially there is a resistance to the exploration of the social relations within which discursive sequences are embedded (see Thompson, 1984; Parker, 1998). Consequently, discursive approaches often end up being descriptive rather than analytical.

Some approaches to ideological analysis have provided a more explicit approach to the complex relationship between discourse and ideology. For example, in Riceour's (1981) Depth Hermeneutics, the first phase of analysis of ideology involves a social analysis that is concerned with the social-historical conditions within which agents act and interact. The second phase may be described as a discourse analysis, involving a study of a sequence of expressions, not only as socially or historically situated occurrence, but also as a linguistic construction that displays an articulated structure. This is complemented by a third phase of analysis described as interpretation. Through interpretation we move on from the structure of discourse to construct a meaning that shows the relationship (service) of this discourse to the maintenance of social relations. Riceour's approach is attractive to the extent that it addresses both structural-contextual and discursive elements. In the housing literature however, it has been widely neglected. Recent approaches in housing research have moved away from a strong conception of ideology and domination, and instead focused on discourse and processes of social construction (Franklin and Clapham, 1997; Jacobs and Manzi 2000; Jacobs et al., 2004). Others have attempted to follow the logic of Foucault's methodology (1970, 1977, 1980) in order to relate institutions and objects to discourses and subjects (Gurney, 1999a,b; Dodson, 2007). In establishing a base for the consideration of ideology these approaches are now considered further as a means to develop a more adequate conception of discourse, power and social structure.

From ideology to discourse

Following the influence of postmodernism and post-structuralism in mainstream social sciences, in the 1990s a number of housing researchers began to readdress housing practices in terms of language, discourse and the construction of meanings which mediate housing provision and dwelling practices. The approach of 'social constructionism' asserts that social reality is constituted by the systems of meaning located in everyday discourses. Within housing studies this has provided some important insights into ideologies surrounding housing practices (see Jacobs et al., 2004). The approach has elevated the sophistication of analysis of ideologies and provided a means to consider ideological practices in terms that can be collected and substantively analysed. The paradigm has, however, also demonstrated a lack of socio-political lustre due to the limited extent that it makes allusions to structural processes (King, 2004; Ronald, 2004; Dodson, 2007).

Historically, research on the housing dimension had primarily followed the principles of empirical positivism which has prescribed the researchers' task as one of discovering objective 'facts' and 'truths', and presenting them in a descriptive format (see Kemeny, 1992; Jacobs and Manzi, 2000; Clapham, 2005). Research on the meanings associated with housing in housing studies has consequently dwelt upon socio-economic characteristics and consumer preferences. The home or house as a concept becomes objectified within this approach, which discursively reifies the very concepts or assumptions it uses in conceptualizing the housing field. For example, the use of the concept of 'housing ladders' leads to conceptual models which fit housing pathways into a structured framework where household moves can only be measured or understood in this way. Furthermore, such categories normally correspond to the language used in government policy discourses that reflect particular conceptions of social 'problems' and issues.

The development of social constructionist approaches marks an attempt to broaden the scope of housing studies by relying upon a different conception of reality from the one advanced by positivism. It essentially rejects claims to objective measures of facts and redefines the scope of social scientific investigation within the limits of social interaction, discourse and representation. There is the assumption that society is the product of the definitions held by people, and such definitions are changed or sustained through interpersonal interaction. Social constructionism in housing research has drawn upon a range of conceptions about the nature of social reality. The Negotiated Order Theory of Berger and Luckmann (1966) is one approach drawn upon to conceptualize the construction of social relations. It asserts that through interactions individuals collectively create, change and sustain group reinforced meanings and understandings that are in turn interpreted as, and believed to be, structural constraints on future actions. These negotiated definitions constitute the basis for social action and the way in which we organize our lives. Other approaches to the socially constituted nature of reality emphasize the importance of signification and meaning (see Derrida, 1998; Lacan, 2002), where power is bound to systems of signification and relationships between signifiers. Social reality thus makes sense by means of how it is represented within a system of signification. Following this approach, the content of housing discourses has become a particular focus of empirical research in recent years in housing studies.

Gurney (1999a) for example, draws specifically on the discourses of owner-occupiers. It is argued that in homeowners' 'talk' can be seen the application of a specific ideology to a particular culture or social circumstance. It takes the form of a myth, a moral tale, analogy or image that is symbolically illustrative of the ideology and is used by homeowners to constitute 'opinions' about homes. The selective and deliberate employment of analogies and metaphors lets them do 'ideological work', with the selection of one metaphor over another enabling the exercise of power or resistance. The analysis also addresses the language of official and unofficial documents, of policy makers, managers and professionals as significant in understanding the construction of tenure discourses (1999b).

Discourse and 'reality'

Essentially, the crude set of assumptions about the role and effect of home ownership implying a largely deterministic relationship between the social conditions of production, ideology and housing tenure, which had dominated approaches to home ownership ideology have been, to a large extent, transcended by social constructionist conceptualizations. Rather than considering housing discourses as aspects of existing social relations and reflections of powerful mechanism of ideological control, social constructionists have focused on how housing policy discourses have constituted a set of realities about housing which subjugate and define the possible relationships between subjects and objects, and how individuals go about creating and communicating the experience of home ownership in specific social contexts.

Despite the insights and enhanced textural applicability of social constructionist approaches, by locating reality at the level of inter-subjectivity, socio-structural forces beyond the realms of discourse become theoretically difficult to incorporate. The analysis of discourses thus often becomes descriptive and relativistic, lacking adequate critique of the world beyond 'talk'. It becomes difficult to consider the existence of an objective reality or extra-linguistic structures and systems (Burr, 1998). Statements about the universality of phenomena are largely rendered meaningless by the scope of discourse, and thus significance at the macro-level of society is negated (Collin, 1997).

Dodson's critique (2007) of the social constructionist paradigm in housing studies specifically concerns failures to move from discourse analysis to ideology. For example, in Jacobs and Manzi's work on policy language (1996) they draw upon Fairclough's (1992, 1995) 'textually orientated discourse analysis' to consider how power can be understood as a network of relations in policy development with regard to homelessness and housing affordability. Dodson argues that Jacobs and Manzi are limited in their sensitivity to ideology by Fairclough's methodology. The suggestion is that the analysis fails to relate the role of the state or government agents in the production of housing discourses due to the inadequacy of connections between state-produced discourses and state practices, particularly in relation to the constitution of subjects and the treatment of these subjects via the practices of housing policy.

> Social constructionists are typically adept at presenting the discursive articulations of the state but poor at demonstrating how these discourses were generated and what the role of the state is in constituting housing reality.... The result is that problems of government, governance and discourse in relation to the practices of the agents, actors and institutions of the state remain ignored or obscure. (2007, p. 19)

Indeed, there are various ways of conceptualizing discourse as a means to make more or less convincing accounts of ideological processes in relation to the state. Dodson makes the case for Foucault's conception of relationships between government institutions and discourses, which tends towards a more circular understanding of discourse and power. The state is not viewed as structural monolith, but becomes itself a discursively constituted site through which social relations of power and discourse pass and circulate (p. 48). Institutions are explained in terms of diagrams or abstract machines. They are a kind of social non-structures that function as an abstract arrangement of social forces, constituted and reproduced through the exchange and flow of discourses and practices of subjectivity. The state is thus no longer seen as an ideological foundation but a discursive apparatus that operates to constitute the reality or truth of empirical categories which make up the world.

Rather than a structured and determinist understanding of power and ideology, Foucault considers power to be subtle and discrete. Power is everywhere in society and is largely unseen as it is exercised in the discourses and daily and intricate routines of modern lives. While power produces domains of objects and rituals of truth, it is never localized here or there and never appropriated as a commodity. Critically, individuals are the vehicles of power, not its point of application (1980, p. 98). For Foucault therefore, language and the construction of truth and knowledge are critical in social relations, as are processes of normalization which imbue discourses with power. The nature of discourse becomes critical to this conception. Discourses establish a set of possible symbolic positions and behaviours for an individual or group of individuals as a subject or subjects. Discourses are thus 'practices that systematically form the objects of which they speak' (Foucault, 1970, p. 49).

Gurney (1999b) proposes a more Foucaultian approach to the social construction and housing discourses. He identifies the process of normalization of home ownership as central to the analysis of housing in contemporary social relations. The argument is that tenure, and in particular the complex situation constituted by the forces and tactics which socially construct home ownership as a majority housing tenure, is imbued with power that normalizes individuals and subjugates them to coercive practices. Essentially, homeowners are both the subject and object of disciplinary power. This power has gone unnoticed as it is regarded as natural or is simply unseen, but the discursive practices by which home ownership has become normalized in housing policy discourses, residential discourses and everyday practices, are significant.

Foucault's approach arguably provides a more convincing means to develop the ideology debate concerning housing discourse, policy and home ownership ideology. Relationships between housing policy and social power can be considered in relation to systems of ideas and the codes by which culture and knowledge are structured. The analysis therefore becomes more concerned with the concept of 'discursive practices' and not simply discourse as a means of examining the significance of home ownership and housing policy.

Another theoretical means by which researchers in housing have sought to deal with the intangibility of the state and social structures in constructionist approaches has been the appropriation of Sociological Realism. In this conception, social reality is comprised of different layers of being with certain layers normally viewed as more fundamental than others. The importance of the realist approach is that it provides an opportunity to consider deeper layers of reality, or processes of domination, underlying surface appearances necessary for a more comprehensive consideration of housing discourses, ideology and social relations.

A draw back identified with this approach is that it presents an ontological dualism. In this conceptualization, the social world is made up of two distinct types of being: societies and agents. This generates a conceptual split and implies that society exists independently from human subjects (Craib, 1992, p. 21). Some sociological realists however, have more convincing explanations of the relationships between social structures and social actors. Bhaskar (1979) asserts an interdependent and dynamic relationship between structure and agency. Unlike natural structures, social structures do not exist independently from the actions they govern, or agents' conceptions (p. 48).

Somerville and Bengsston's argument (2002) is that neither social constructionism nor sociological realism appears to lead to convincing substantive explanations of social relations as we are left with either a linguistic reductionism or an epistemological dualism, respectively.

They maintain that to be able to empirically interpret and explain social interaction between real-life actors and real-life contextual settings we need conceptualizations that allow for determinate empirical variation (2002, p. 5). Sayer (2000) puts forth a conceptualization of a weak social constructionism that merely emphasizes the socially constructed nature of knowledge and institutions, as well as the way that knowledge can bear the marks of its social origins. Somerville and Bengsston argue that an ideal approach can draw upon a weak constructionism and attempt to assert a realist position without being objectivist.

Forming an approach

While there are concerns with the conceptualization of social structures, discourse and power, social constructionism has stimulated considerable debate over the significance of housing discourses and how to consider the production and relative salience of policies and housing practices. Moreover, it has moved ideological appreciation of home ownership well beyond simple Marxist categories. Arguably, Dodson is polemic in his criticisms of social constructionism as conceptions of hierarchies of discourse (for example Fairclough, 1992, 1995) often appear convincing enough to make credible connections to ideology. For Kemeny (2002) there has been a substantial misconception concerning constructionism. It inevitably addresses how institutions and organizations that comprise a society are changed or sustained as a result of interpersonal interaction (p. 140). Constructionism can tell us more about real-life actors in real-life contextual settings as interpersonal interaction results in practical decisions that have significant consequences.

There is neither the scope nor the intention in this chapter to revolutionize housing theory. The aim is rather to constitute a working conception of ideology and the role of housing as a dimension of the social structure. A more practical approach would err towards a form of constructionism in which discourse and human agency are neither under- nor over-socialized. For Granovetter (1985), the notion of embeddedness is a principal concept by which institutions and agents are understood as being located in broader social networks of sociability, approval, status and power. These are neither insignificant and marginal nor dominant and determining, but rather constitute the grounds upon which institutions rest (for example, Governments, markets and so on), and without reference to which, they cannot be properly understood. In terms of ideology it is useful to isolate the concepts of home ownership ideology and homeowner ideolog*ies* (Ronald, 2004) as a means to embed the approach. The former denotes ideological relationships that represent discursive practices of power and legitimation with regard to social production, and the latter, discourses and systems of values related to the consumption of, and dwelling in, owner-occupied housing.

In the course of this book I consider home ownership ideology and homeowner ideologies in relation to three dimensions: socio-historical contexts of housing policy and housing system development; policies and policy related discourses; dwelling and housing consumption practices and discourses. The empirical analysis of these dimensions across two groups of countries identified as homeowner societies provides a framework for the development of understanding of the role of home ownership in different societies, socially and ideologically. The approach I adopt is broadly constructionist, and emphasizes how discursive processes and housing practices, policies and discourses have constituted or transformed housing objects as well as individual subjectivities and social relations. Although discourse and discursive practices are dealt with, greater attention is paid to socio-structural features, and specifically relationships between housing, the state and individual households.

A central focus is the changing significance of home ownership in different societies in relation to the state, markets and families. These transformations are arguably related to shifts in social and economic relations connected to intensified globalization and the subsequent responses of states to market competition, the organization of labour and social security. While I argue that the development of home ownership ideology has followed very different paths in each society and that homeowner ideologies are diverse, more universal aspects are identifiable in terms of types of commodified forms of provision.

Comparison

The final issue that presents itself in setting out the conceptual basis of this book concerns the comparison of societies. Theories of housing have been predominantly based on cases from Western societies and have failed to unpack the culturally loaded aspects of housing systems and theories. Moreover, there has also been a failure in analyses to move beyond the cultural and contextual assumptions of the societies within which they have been conceptualized and developed. Saunders's (1990) explication of home ownership, for example, is ethnocentric, explaining the rise of home ownership in rather normative terms. He states, for example, 'recent reforms in the former Soviet Union seem to precisely have been prompted by the recognition that human motivation is ultimately tied to private ownership and possession of material resources' (p. 77).

Saunders ignores cultural dimensions and fails to either challenge the neo-liberalist assumptions of individualism in Anglo-Saxon conceptions of tenure, or deal critically with the 'desire to own' as socially constructed. Even between English speaking homeowner societies, transitions from rental to owner-occupied or public or market modes of provision and consumption is irregular (see Chapter 5). The model of housing privatization and public housing sell-offs advanced in Britain, for example, does not apply to Australia or New Zealand, where there was never a sustained period of public housing provision (Thorns, 1992).

When societies outside the Western sphere are considered, comparisons of home ownership and housing practices become even more problematic because of differences in culture and social organization. Lee (1999), for example, demonstrates that although Hong Kong is considerably different from Western models of social class and stratification, there has been little concern with this in international comparisons. In Japan too, features of modernity, self-identity and social change fundamentally differ from Western theoretical assumptions. This has not, however, hampered the generalization of ethnocentric social and economic theories (Clammer, 1995). Research on non-occidental societies have, by-and-large, either inappropriately applied universal models across societies, or, have overemphasized uniqueness of socio-cultural contexts. Indeed, many contexts and cases have been shielded from the application of theoretical models by resorting to a veil of culture, or by labelling them 'exceptional', especially when models lose their explanatory power in such contexts (Pickvance, 1999).

The analyses presented in this book not only involve comparison of societies, but also, specifically, of discursive aspects of housing provision and consumption between two groups of the most ostensibly divergent social, economic and cultural systems among industrialized nations. The objective, ultimately, is to identify both divergent and universal aspects of home ownership ideology by making comparisons within and between a group of Anglo-Saxon liberal-capitalist homeowner societies and another group of East Asian productivist-capitalist homeowner societies.

Qualitative housing research has not been well developed in international context (see Elsinga et al., 2007). Consequently, comparative work has not generally been based on an intimate knowledge or phenomenological feel for the societies being compared and has not been integrated with ideological and theoretical aspects (Haworth et al., 2004). Indeed, power relationships and aspects of integration of structure and agency have not been explicit in much of the comparative housing literature. Adopting a broadly social constructionist approach to comparison is very attractive, but necessitates an explicit concern with a number of comparative methodological issues.

The first issue relates to the idea of translation or transfer of concepts. Ruonavaara (1993) has identified considerable incomparability in housing and tenure concepts and measures across societies. Housing studies have often failed to deal with the place boundedness of analyses where housing systems represent the interaction of various specific and located institutions, practices and definitions in a particular place at a particular time. For Harloe and Maartjens (1983), tenure, 'can be seen in each country to be the product of a specific interrelationship of political, economic and ideological factors' (p. 266). Dimensions take social, economic, legal, ideological and political forms. Mandic and Clapham (1996) illustrate this in the case of Slovenia where the social and cultural contexts of tenure are emphasized in understanding and explaining tenure patterns. They argue that the variation within tenures can often be greater than that between tenures. Tenure may only be a meaningful comparative concept to the extent that it clarifies how tenure is conceptualized and constructed in ways that inform housing discourses and decisions in each society.

Another concern is the applicability of theoretical frameworks *across* societies. Theorization and conceptualization is normally based upon sets of assumptions about similarities in social processes, and institutional practices and values in different countries. The persistent logic has been that all societies are on a single path of modernity, which has reinforced the domination of theories of social and economic convergence. The most contemporary form of convergence thinking is the globalization thesis, which sees all countries as being subject to the same universalistic imperatives and largely ignores the influence of culture and indigenous processes. Until the mid-1980s housing approaches often attempted to provide unified theories which suggested a process of evolution among industrialized societies (see Boelhouwer and van der Heijden, 1992). Subsequently, divergent housing studies approaches have proliferated which have concentrated on more comprehensive understandings of housing system formation and highlighted more specific aspects of housing systems in different cultural, social and economic environments (see Lux, 2007).

Sensitivity to different localities and cultures has been highlighted by many authors as a concern in housing research (Dickens, Duncan, Goodwin and Grey, 1985; Forrest and Murie, 1995; Haworth et al., 2004). A large body of the research which has purported itself to be comparative is primarily constituted of a juxtaposition of detailed statistics based descriptions of different societies, where each national writer applies his or her national perspective to his or her own country, or more imperialistically, to other countries (see Kemeny and Lowe, 1998; Oxley, 2001; Somerville and Bengsston, 2002). The effect has been both the underestimation of potential divergence between societies and the neglect of culture, value systems and ideologies as significant dimensions of society and social change. However, cultures and ideologies affect more than just surface practices and rituals, and indeed mediate social and economic processes.

A central problem in comparison has been the underdevelopment of comparative frameworks by which non-quantifiable elements can be identified and compared. This book adopts the view following Oxley (2001), that research with an international dimension becomes 'comparative' where there is some systematic comparison using a common theoretical approach. The approach in this book may not be as quantitative as studies that compare transferable measures of social variables, due to the substantive topic. However, by retaining a strong reflexivity to interpretations of the logic of social organization in 'other' societies and by maintaining a consistent theoretical approach to ideological practices, the objective is to develop a middle-range theory of home ownership ideology across societies.

The societies I compare include Britain, the United States and Australia, in one category, as types of Anglo-Saxon homeowner society (Chapter 5), and Japan, Hong Kong and Singapore as East Asian types (Chapter 6). I set out key social changes, housing policy shifts and government discourses in each of these societies to identify particular housing system pathways based on ideologies of owner-occupation. I ultimately address the complexities of convergence and divergence within and between the two groups of homeowner societies (Chapter 7), and while asserting diversity in housing system development around the discourses and logic of owner-occupation, specify two general patterns of home ownership ideology.

Conclusions

This chapter has considered conceptualizations of housing and ideology in addressing the embeddedness of home ownership in social relations. There has been a focus throughout on unravelling the concept of ideology and how it should be applied in the study of housing and society in order to clarify conceptual assumptions applied in this book. In Marxist approaches to housing and ideology, a strong and explicit relationship has been asserted concerning the socially conservative effects of home ownership. Owner-occupation has figured strongly in political rhetoric as a 'bulwark to bolshevism', and subsequently analysts have taken this phrase at face value to mean that home ownership has an anti-revolutionary influence on the working classes. This approach has dwelt upon the significance of relations of production in maintaining traditional social structures and inequities, and has seen the growth of home ownership as a politically sponsored project that has only enhanced existing social disparities, rather than as fundamental to the changing structure of social relations.

In recent decades however, qualitative changes in society and shifts in patterns of inequality and social identity have arguably led to changes in the social and ideological significance of home ownership provision and consumption. While it is difficult to maintain a strong determinist idea of dominant ideology, it appears that housing markets and housing consumption, along with the sets of meanings, identities and ideologies associated with them, are becoming more deeply and complexly integrated with socio-economic and socio-political relations. The theories and methodologies applied to discourses have developed rapidly in the last decades in sophistication, sensitivity and reflexivity. However, in the conceptualization of relationships between meaning and discourses, and social structure, ideological power relations have not been as well developed. Moreover, little attention has been paid to divergence in these dimensions between societies. The analysis set out in the rest of this book seeks to develop understanding of the characteristics of, and differences between, housing systems, discourses and ideological practices in a range of societies where home ownership dominates how governments and individuals think about housing. In identifying divergence in housing relations the hope is also to shed light on convergence.

3
Homeowner Ideologies

Introduction

Historically, policies and physical standards have dominated thinking on housing issues, reducing the housing dimension to units of accommodation and measures of habitability. However, meanings, values and ideological formations guide how individuals use this space and relate from within to the outside world (Arias, 1993). In understanding the role and impact of home ownership therefore, it is necessary to address effects at the subjective and inter-subjective level, where material practices and discourses related to owner-occupation are considered to have particular outcomes on individuals (or 'housing consumers' as they have been increasingly constituted) and social relations.

This chapter addresses home ownership at the level of individual meanings, discourses and homeowner ideologies. I draw from a variety of research developed in the English speaking homeowner societies that dominate the literature on modern home ownership. The consideration of homeowner ideologies constitutes the basis for the appreciation of home ownership ideology. Essentially, I try to move away from a simple consideration of home ownership as a socially conservative or bourgeois ideology within 'property owning democracies' to a more dynamic and discursive consideration of home ownership and neo-liberal ideologies in late modernity as embedded features and mechanisms of restructuring of relationships between the state, the market and individuals. In Anglo-Saxon homeowner societies the re-signification of the home as a privately consumed commodity has arguably redrawn the role of housing and has impacted much broader sets of economic and political relations that have transformed residents into 'investor subjects'.

This chapter begins by examining meanings and discourses associated with owner-occupied housing in Anglo-Saxon societies in which the qualities of 'home' have become intrinsically bound up with those of tenure. While I identify some central themes in meanings and discourses, I also challenge the assumption that the values surrounding home ownership have become homogenized, and further identify a gap in explaining how meanings attached to home ownership support a unified hegemony. The second section moves from ideologies to the ideological, dealing with how privatism and individualism have been associated with home ownership and how owner-occupation restructures relations in these terms between private and public spheres. I then address the role of housing in processes of consumption and how theories of consumption align with meanings and discourses on home ownership. In the final part of the chapter a more discursive notion of power and ideology is developed. With this approach the emphasis shifts from the hegemony and ideologies of individualism associated with home ownership, to processes of individualization and normalization in the summoning of neo-liberalized property consumers and investor subjects.

Housing discourses and ideologies

Meanings of home and tenure

Empirical research on meanings related to homes and houses has largely been phenomenological or has tended to neglect the social dimensions of housing (Somerville, 1997). However, meanings are a useful starting point in understanding the impact of housing and tenure at a subjective and discursive level. For Després (1991) there tends to be a set of core categories of meaning associated with the home: as the centre of family life; a place of retreat; safety and relaxation; freedom and independence; self-expression and social status; a place of privacy, continuity and permanence; a financial asset, and a support for work and leisure activities (pp. 227–228). In this section I deal with the relationship between the meanings of home and tenure as has been examined in the post-war period in Anglo-Saxon societies. This provides the basis for developing a more ideologically integrated understanding of these meanings and values and their broader social, cultural and political significance.

The difference between the housing unit and the home conceptually demonstrates the significance of housing subjectively and socially. For Dovey (1985), although a house is an object and part of the environment, the home is best conceived as a kind of relationship between people and their environment (p. 33). Furthermore, home and family are two closely related concepts that are often intertwined into one picture of a normative lifestyle. Oakley (1976) suggests that if society has grown more 'family orientated', the family itself has identified more and more squarely with its physical location, the home, to the extent that 'home' and 'family' can be seen as virtually interchangeable terms (p. 65). Thus, in one sense, home is the heart of the family, a backstage area for social roles and performances, and a place to relax and 'be yourself' (Goffman, 1959; Allen and Crow, 1989). Conversely, the house represents the public face of the family and self, and its presentation in terms of cleanliness, tidiness, taste and style (Lawrence, 1987; Madigan and Munro, 1996).

Gurney (1996) asked a number of English homeowners about the meanings associated with their homes. Emotional discourses of family, intimacy and love were the most significant rationalizations drawn upon in making sense of this relationship. Along with emotional factors connected to family relationships were aspects of privacy, relaxation, comfort, safety, autonomy, personalization, creativity and display. The home was also sometimes a millstone or burden, a scene of violence, abuse or emotional trauma. What was also important to respondents was tenure, where ownership related to pride and a sense of achievement, as well as financial benefits.

What appears significant about the meaning of home in contemporary homeowner societies is that not only has the 'home' become integrated with the understanding and expression of the self, the family and the private sphere, it has also become appropriated by those who *own* a house or apartment. The meaning of a 'home of one's own' has changed over the twentieth century and in many societies no longer means living in a self-contained dwelling but rather being an owner-occupier (Allen and Crow, 1989). Tenure has thus been integrated strongly with meanings and idealized images of the house and home.

Tenures are social and legal institutions that are socially constructed and vary over time and between countries and cultures. Tenure defines social relationships, rights of ownership and the use of housing, and can mirror relationships in society at large. Gurney's research (1996, 1999a,b) demonstrates that in England, home ownership is considered the 'natural' basis of residing in a home and that homeowner's discourses are strongly prejudiced in these terms, with renters, particularly in public rental housing, occupying qualitatively different types of dwelling. Clapham (2005) identifies that renting is often relegated to a minority status, confined to those who do not share the dream of ownership or cannot aspire to that level (p. 146). The effect of the normalization of home ownership as the 'natural' tenure in society undermines the meanings attached to rented homes by appropriating the concept of home as exclusively the condition of owner-occupation. Renting and owning have arguably come to represent mutually defining, oppositional concepts and there is convincing evidence that, in homeowner societies, tenure is strongly differentiated and has a substantial impact on the meaning and perceived stability and quality of a home and its occupants (see also Kemeny, 1981; Forrest et al., 1990; Richards, 1990; Saunders, 1990; Murie, 1998; Ronald, 2006).

Another aspect of the growth of home ownership has been the meaningful transformation of homes into housing 'properties'. Rose (1980) and King (1996) strongly emphasize the marketization and monetization of housing through the promotion and growth of home ownership. The polarization of tenure between owning and renting also appears related to the process of transformation from dwelling to property where family life and security, privacy and permanence, independence and status have been bound together with the economic qualities of housing as an investment and asset.

So far I have considered the meaning of home and home ownership in general terms, but have identified how the family, privacy and intimacy have been bound up with the private sphere of the home, and, moreover, how the home in societies where home ownership is considered the normal or natural tenure, has been semantically hijacked and bound up with a single tenure, owner-occupation. A premise of my analysis is that home ownership is not 'natural', but a constructed set of social relations and legal norms, and I shall demonstrate in following chapters that there is little evidence to suggest that home ownership is indigenous or natural to any modern society or culture. A development in many modern societies has been the integration of owner-occupied tenure with specific meanings related to privacy, autonomy, family, control, status, security, lifestyle and identity. These meanings may be considered as a key set of value markers that are demonstrated across many homeowner societies and are central to a process of appropriation and normalization of the meaning of home.

Social status

Initial considerations of housing and its effect on social status focused on social class stratification. Young and Wilmot (1957) identified how housing can peg its occupants to a particular status associated with a social class position. 'A house is one bearer of status in any society, it most certainly is in a country where a semi-detached suburban house with a garden has become the signal mark of the middle-classes' (p. 155). Seeley too (1956) found that one's home played a central role in confirming status and helping in upward mobility. However, the salience of housing as a signifier of status across classes is difficult to clarify and we should also be wary of differences between generations, genders and ethnic groups. Furthermore, status judgements are often associated with class judgements, and individuals in discourse are often resistant to acknowledging such attitudes or relations. Adams (1984) emphasizes that in the United States, where an established class structure is more visibly lacking, other markers are introduced to maintain social order and to communicate its meanings, which may thus elevate the significance of tenure and housing (p. 520). Housing inevitably becomes, implicitly or explicitly, a judgement criterion of the social standing of the household within.

Class and status are key elements in understanding both the cultural meaning of the home and relationships to structures of social stratification, social judgement and identification. Class has been linked in theoretical terms with shared life chances, relations to production and levels of relative power within the market (Saunders, 1990). Status, alternatively, is expressed by lifestyle and status groups conserve 'conventions' and 'styles of life' in order to create a closure of status and identity (Gerth et al., 1991). Since the 1960s research has increasingly suggested that the working classes have become more like the middle classes in seeing their homes as symbols of acquired status (see Rubin, 1976; Thorns, 1976; Holme, 1985). At the same time, it has been argued that collective identities and class solidarities have been eroded making housing status more salient in terms of status groups. The role of housing has arguably expanded as a marker of difference and identification vis-à-vis other social identities and as a means of expressing the relative importance of the household in the social pecking order where the house is the most visible marker of individual taste and family wealth.

Housing tenure is not a visible element of housing status. Nevertheless, types of housing and neighbourhood, especially in homeowner societies, are strongly associated with either owner-occupiers or renters, to which residents can be very sensitive, or even 'prejudiced' (see Gurney, 1999a). Perin's research (1977) identified that entry into home ownership is indicative of a mutually agreeable relationship between the individual and the bank, which demonstrates a level of perceived stability and permanence on the part of the owner-occupier (p. 74). Becoming a homeowner, however, is associated with a broader range of ideal advantages.

Rowlands and Gurney (2001) discovered home ownership to be a status 'package' that even children aspire towards. Essentially, home ownership is perceived as a symbol of success, and can thus be considered central in creating inequalities based upon the advantages owner-occupiers have, where the physical structure of the dwelling becomes a frame or a container of the trappings of status.

Winter (1994) found that Australian homeowners expressed status meanings in relation to owner-occupiers as the ones who have 'made it'. They have climbed the ladder of social expectation and bought their 'quarter-acre block'. By the same process renters are heavily stigmatized. He thus argues that this status or stigmatization is a lived experience rather than just an end point of inequality or social distinction, the packaging of this social distinction being 'lifestyle' (p. 121). Jager (1986) has suggested that the privately owned home has become an important stage for promoting fashion and new urban lifestyles. The elaboration of consumption techniques is increasingly centred in the private residential and cultural domains, rather than the public or occupational spheres (p. 86). Home ownership has thus come to signify a consumer identity and a standard of personal autonomy, which can also be considered a marker of status.

Security and economic advantages

Arguably, in societies dominated by owner-occupier housing markets, the most salient aspects of public and individual discourses (particularly in light of cyclical house-price booms) has been the augmented significance of privately owned housing as an asset, as a property in a market and its general monetization as a commodity. In Winter's interviews (1994), meaningful associations between owning property and specific economic advantages were fundamental to discussions on home ownership. Meanings such as 'making money via sweat equity', 'saving money via forced savings' and the 'devaluation of mortgage payments by inflation' dominated the discourses of owner-occupiers. Homeowners strongly attributed financial security to ownership and predominantly perceived the home in terms of investment. This financial security, was interpreted as security for later life, and was also seen to extend beyond their owner's own lives to their children's. Moreover, financial security was understood to directly flow from the fact of rising property values.

Homeowners have increasingly applied investment discourses to describe their homes, indicating that owners view their tenure form as a rational economic choice with a likelihood of realizing monetary gains.

Numerous studies have demonstrated that, especially in Anglo-Saxon homeowner societies, housing through home ownership has come to represent a means of building an asset, nurturing an investment and making capital gains (see Sternlieb and Hughes, 1982; Madge and Brown, 1981; Saunders, 1990; Forrest and Murie, 1995; Searle and Smith, 2006). The indication has been that most people buy property as they view it as a reliable store of wealth. The possibility for financial gain has been bound tightly to home ownership within the specific context of building equity in conditions of house-price inflation. In societies where house-price increases have not been so radical and home ownership does not dominate the housing system, the economic salience of housing may not be so explicit. Nevertheless, there is evidence that housing remains central to discourses on financial security across Western societies. In Germany, for example, where home ownership is a minority tenure, housing purchase still represents financial security in later life, or a 'pension in stone' (Elsinga et al., 2007).

Home ownership as a road to accumulating or securing wealth must also be understood in terms of other significant social dimensions such as employment and welfare systems. Doling and Horsewood (2003) have strongly linked the levels of home ownership with direct effects on labour markets and employment participation where unemployment, re-employment, retirement and pension strategies are strongly influenced by ties to property, property equity, redundant housing costs and rental incomes. Housing equity is normally regarded as a source of financial security during periods of unemployment, although, in real terms, home ownership is often a central mediator of risk, especially for marginal and low income households (Ford et al., 2001). Housing assets that accrue have been increasingly seen as liquefiable, which has been enhanced by the diversification of equity release products (Smith, 2006).

Richards's study (1990) emphasizes *security* in explaining the economic meanings attached to home ownership in Australia. Three aspects of security were identified in this research. First, the economic advantages of ownership were often couched by homeowners in terms of the economic disadvantages and lack of control of renting. Second, 'security for the future' concerned 'family futures', where ownership was the basis of unity and stability and related to meanings of settling down, foundation and permanence. Third, 'building up' of both family and finances was an important aspect of the security of the home. Views about the development of family life were intertwined with financial concerns such as mortgages. In other terms security was associated with haven, privacy, exclusion, relaxation and self-expression, and it was absent in discussions of other tenures. Similar findings concerning the centrality of security in discourses of home ownership have been illustrated in a number of societies (see Elsinga et al., 2007; Ronald, 2008) and may indicate that the significance of investment discourses vis-à-vis security discourses may shift in context of housing systems and markets. Nonetheless, in homeowner societies the meaning of security attached to housing appears bound up with family pathways, economic security and associated exclusively with owner-occupation.

In terms of economic values renting is usually the inverse process of owning. The 'wasted rent argument' can be considered a key discourse in homeowner societies. Expressions like 'dead money' and 'money down the drain' are so common place in home-owners' accounts of reasons to buy housing that their metaphorical status is often obscured (Richards, 1990, p. 120). Gurney (1999a), however, considers the power of these statements as critical to creating prejudice. Indeed, money has an anthropomorphic quality as there is an assertion that a tenant, by paying rent, is somehow responsible for its death. 'The powerful negative image of bank notes being eliminated or murdered by the tenant is the antithesis of the positive images of 'husbandry' and 'stewardship' associated with home-owners' (p. 1715).

There is indeed, a range of evidence to suggest that housing property purchase is considered the primary investment strategy of a majority of households, and has eroded the development of broader investment portfolios which spread financial risks (see Smith, 2006). Munro and Leather (2000) found that investment motives are expressed most clearly by homeowners in relation to preserving the value of what owners already have because of the anticipation of an inevitable sale in the future or because they hope to pass down the property to their family (p. 519). However, there is evidence to suggest that many see housing investment in terms of gambling where housing gains are experienced more like winning the lottery than accumulating interest on savings. Owner-occupiers even use gambling metaphors to account for purchasing activities (Bondi et al., 2000). The process of house-price inflation also tends to feed itself in context of such volatile circumstances, where those who might have rented enter the market as early as possible in order to insure against the risk of further price increases (Banks et al., 2004).

In the early 1990s, housing market decline in Britain began to disproportionately affect younger cohorts of homeowners, with growing numbers of households finding themselves in negative equity (where the value of a property is lower than the debt owed on it). However, among this group the economic advantages and security of home ownership were strongly engrained despite contradictory experiences. Forrest et al. (1999) found that the desire to get a foot on the first rung of the home ownership ladder, and negative associations with private rented sector were the most common motivators identified by households in negative equity for house purchase. As well as economic motivations, respondents expressed fear of being 'left behind' by the market suggesting that investment discourses reflected fear of financial losses made by renting rather than hope of money to be made by speculating. There was a strong belief that a mortgage is buying something in a way that rental payments are not. Even in negative equity a debt was being reduced and at the end of the day there would be something to show for it (p. 99). Despite experiences of negative equity, home ownership remained associated with security, investment and social status and was far preferable to renting.

Housing as investment property in Britain assumed significance following house-price booms in the 1970s and 1980s and an exceptional period of public housing sell-off in the 1980s. British homeowners' accounts, however, reveal the persistence of home ownership as a household economic strategy despite any real or perceived capital losses. The resurgence in the housing market and the expansion of home ownership (to 70 per cent by 2005), with the average debt required to finance home purchase doubling between 1992 and 2002, demonstrate how quickly the risks of housing investment are negated or overridden when prices begin to escalate again, or at least how embedded the perceived advantages of owning housing property are.

The data suggest that in the Anglo-Saxon homeowner societies tenure is strongly linked to security and economic rationality. These links have been consistent even where the security and economic prudence of home ownership has been fundamentally challenged by market conditions. Key in the embedding of security and economic rationality with owner-occupation has been the concomitant association of insecurity and economic irrationality with rental tenures, as well as the endurance of economic discourses concerning mythical and real house-price inflation.

Control and autonomy

Control has also been demonstrated to be crucial within the nexus of meanings contemporary homeowners attach to their residency. One interpretation of control, identified in Winter's Australian sample (1994), was the ability to carry out physical changes to the house and garden. Control gained from ownership also included control over other people who may want to enter your property. Most significantly, for both owners and renters, control was simply synonymous with home ownership. For Richards's interviewees (1990) control had two meanings, a positive one epitomized by the key phrase 'you can make it yours', and a negative one captured in the phrase 'no one can put you out'. There was also a connection with control and the connotation of 'home as haven'. Statements in this case concerned the peaceful aspects of privacy. Rather they evoke privacy to be yourself and privacy from others. They offer themes about adulthood, independence, control and individuality (p. 125).

Control is often connected to feelings of autonomy, and homeowners in Britain have talked about the sense of independence and autonomy which ownership confers: the freedom from control and surveillance by a landlord and the ability to personalize the property according to one's tastes. Saunders (1990) found autonomy, security and control to be highly salient in the reasons given for a first house purchase. The 'desire to own', 'security', 'autonomy' and 'independence' were ranked highly by homeowners, as were the advantages of 'you can do what you like' and the 'security of tenure' (pp. 85–87). In Madigan's study (1988) homeowners normally favoured home ownership for reasons of 'choice, mobility, freedom and autonomy' (p. 38). The freedom to decorate and make changes to the structure and appearance of the home has also been stressed in studies across Western societies and strongly associated with the self and individual expression.

In the United States, there is a similar pattern of meanings and the control of the homeowner has been historically embedded with the principles of freedom, autonomy and individuality. Rosow (1948) identified early on a strong association between owning and designations of the house as a source of personal autonomy that emphasized 'the feeling of ownership and independence' through the potential to 'fix it up to suit self'. For Rakoff (1977), the house, and particularly the owner-occupied house, represents a powerful symbol of order, continuity, physical safety, and a sense of place and physical belonging. Even renters in his study agreed over the significance of autonomy, security, control and status that could be expressed through owner-occupation. Control, freedom and autonomy, while having differentiated aspects based on control of space and freedom from external authorities such as landlords, thus appear central features of discourses on owner-occupation as well as the ideal advantages homeowners enjoy within Anglo-Saxon societies.

Homogeneity and heterogeneity of meanings

So far the focus has been on common discourses about home ownership. However, this belies more diverse patterns of meaning and discourse between owners. For example, evidence has suggested that while men are more likely to see home in terms of status and achievement, women perceive home as an emotional refuge, haven or source of protection (Seeley, 1956; Rainwater, 1966). Also, it has been shown that women care more about the home and derive more satisfaction from it (Mason, 1989). The demarcation of social and cultural spheres identifying women with the home (homeliness) and the men with the world (worldliness) is argued to originate in a tradition of domesticity dating back to the nineteenth century (Elshtain, 1981; Siltanen and Stanworth, 1984; Coontz, 1988). For Rapoport (1981) there is a cross-cultural dimension to this difference with women being more intimately linked to the dwelling in terms of their self-identity.

In Richards's study (1990), perspectives on 'security' represented a central gender difference. While men focused on the financial security home ownership gave them, women focused on security in terms of more general stability. For women and men security referred to necessary steps on the ladder to family life, but these steps were constructed differently. For men it was more likely to mean 'getting established', 'starting out', 'setting up' as an independent marital unit. For women it was usually a necessary condition for having children. Women seemed to imagine longer paths through life stages and considered families with needs rather than autonomous couples. Home ownership as a step in life preceded the step towards having children. Richards's key assertion is that home ownership may affect women differently from men. 'Privacy means autonomy and togetherness and it involves work for women, not only as administrators for homes and managers of family status, but also in jobs fitted into the corners of proper paths through family stages' (p. 139).

Indeed there are diverse differences between homeowners and how they relate to their homes. Based on his field research, Gurney (1996) sets out a typology of five different types. The first are *Lexic owners* who have a strong ideological attachment to home ownership. The second are *Pragmatic owners* who focus on practical benefits when justifying their tenure choice (accessing good schools, financial benefits, and so on), but do not celebrate self-actualization aspects of ownership practices (such as personalization and renovation activities). The third group is made up of *Petty tycoons* for whom ownership is a financial investment and who keep an eye on market movements. The fourth group is comprised of *Extrinsic owners*, who see ownership as an achievement and a demonstration of individual success. This group is most likely to take pride in home-improvement activities. The final group consists of *Conflictual owners*, for whom there is no clear view on ownership as it is often a source of conflict between household members. Knight (2002) provides a parallel typology of renters. In most cases renters defined their tenure choice in terms of the owner-occupied alternative. What these typologies illustrate is the diversity of meanings and satisfactions individuals draw upon in accounting for their housing situation.

Life cycle, class, location and length of residence are also factors in the consideration of variation in the meanings attached to home ownership. In terms of lifecycle Saunders (1990) suggests that in the daily round of living in a house, as opposed to the special occasion of moving into or out of it, it is the 'use value' rather than the 'exchange value', which is likely to be of greatest concern (p. 88), while Cox (1982) proposes that with length of residence the memory of the investor role fades and the house as a provider of use values rather than as a repository of exchange values becomes more salient (p. 121). Deverson and Lindsay (1975) found contrasting attitudes towards house ownership between younger, lower-middle-class, heavily mortgaged interviewees living in the 'newer' suburban areas and the older, established upper-middle-class ones living in older areas, with the latter being much more positive about their homes as investments. The heterogeneity of meanings within and between cohorts, social groups and across societies implies some necessary caution when generalizing about the meanings and experiences of homeowners and home ownership cultures.

Meaning, discourse and ideology

Although there are some significant connections between discourses, housing practices and social processes, the ideological relationship is not transparent. Moving between meanings and structures of social relations has been fundamentally challenging. This has been compounded by methodologies for capturing meanings, which have historically been categorical rather than discourse based. While coded studies that attempt to quantify the meanings of home have consistently demonstrated the predominance of two main themes – it is natural to own, and it is necessary for family life – meanings are ambiguous making it difficult to assert ideological constructions. Richards (1990) is cautious about asserting home ownership as an ideology in itself as the reasons subjects give for owning are often quite muddled. Rakoff (1977) also identified that while investment is normally an obvious value, behind it are tangled meanings concerning family life, social status, security and control. He argued that the house is a dominant symbol of a variety of conflicting life experiences: personal success and family happiness, mobility and permanence, privacy and social involvement, personal control and escape (p. 86). Approaches to relationships between subjective assertions of individual homeowners and ideological processes thus require development.

Gurney (1999a) is very critical of approaches that essentialize the relationship between discursive positions and the actions of individuals. Like Richards, Gurney problematizes the process of 'capturing ideology', and argues that the traditional way data has been collected, which categorizes responses, does not permit an assessment of home ownership ideology amongst the people who respond to such surveys. Alternatively, he focuses on the salience of the active construction of subjective accounts of housing experience in understanding what ideological impact home ownership may have. 'There is clearly a big difference between reporting or reflecting upon tenure preference data and understanding the processes by which these preferences are constructed and articulated' (p. 1708).

What is significant ideologically about the discourses expressed is an ostensible homogenization of meanings and positions above a contradictory layer of division and diversity. There appears to be a normalizing commitment to the ideology in itself. Richards (1990) found the homogeneity of aspirations towards home ownership to constitute an ideal concerning both tenure and lifestyle. In her fieldwork, among groups of unequal status was an acceptance and tolerance of those with the same 'dream'. Arguably, this reveals the power of common goals of home and family to unify or to veil disunity. For residents, the purchase of a house was a preoccupation and, moreover, the common link felt with other residents (p. 115). Respondents expected that non-owners were potential owners, although 'renters' were suspect, transient and usually perceived as different.

Richards's argument is that home and family are bound together ideologically as the 'proper paths' to life and constitute a normalizing ideal of the private world. There is a hegemonic commitment to a normative form of residency incorporating marriage and children on one side, and progression towards an ideal form of dwelling on the other. Richards thus contextualizes meanings expressed concerning the home, the family and 'proper paths' in relation to an integrated ideological realm. For example, in terms of the family, the home is a pathway to autonomy. Independence is a recurring aspect of owner-occupation and in many cases, it was seen by respondents as central to the transition into adulthood. The private world within the house described by subjects was one where adults were free to make families in self-sufficiency. 'Those threads interweave so tightly that it is grammatically impossible to pull them out: family is in the same sentence, the same phrase, as investment, control, security' (p. 128). Perin (1977) has shown that in America also, home ownership is viewed as a mechanism for placing people on the proper 'ladder of life'. 'The family and good citizenship that home ownership is believed to instil are equally idealized and, thereby equated' (p. 47).

The literature addressing the meanings of home ownership is not particularly integrated, but illustrates a constellation of values and discourses which mediate housing choices and dwelling practices. The dominating themes of discourses relate to status, security, investment, autonomy, control and family life, but are strongly intertwined with each other. Analyses have failed to demonstrate effectively the differences between different types of homeowners in terms of local differences as well as differences between those on the margins and those better-off homeowners who have experienced greatest advantages.

The data considered here has drawn primarily from British, US and Australian contexts, which I implied, at the beginning of the book, forms a particular model of 'Anglo-Saxon' homeowner society. Clearly this is a problematic assertion as the pattern and contextual differences between housing, social development and home ownership in these societies is quite diverse, as shall be demonstrated in later chapters. Indeed, home ownership became the majority tenure in Australia and the United States long before the United Kingdom, and it was not until 1971 that British owner-occupation rates breached 50 per cent. Furthermore, home ownership rates until the 1990s in Britain and the United States were not substantially higher than the rates in countries like France that are not so strongly associated with the tenure. Nevertheless, what is important is that in recent decades these countries have begun to follow a more unified pattern of housing consumption centred on a 'culture', or 'cultures', of owner-occupation reflecting strong tenure prejudices and related to features of deregulated market practices and neo-liberal ideologies.

The core of meanings considered so far tell us more about discourse and the specific role home ownership has played in *some* societies rather than about the 'nature' of home ownership. Indeed, Richards (1990) proposes that the dream of home ownership and 'proper paths' to life does not necessarily reveal it as natural and universal. The growing demand for privately owned housing may merely indicate the absence of perceived alternatives and that ideologies which present home ownership as 'an innate desire' hide the failure or reluctance of governments to create viable rental alternatives (p. 102). In many European countries where rental housing is of good quality and more accessible, the family and the private realm can be established in very different forms of housing and tenure.

The following sections deal with meanings and discourses more explicitly as homeowner ideologies in terms of the ideological. It begins by addressing the prime association of ideologies of individualism and privatism with the interests of legitimation and social reproduction in Western capitalist societies. The ideological focus on 'individualism' and 'privatism' in Marxist theory has a strong hegemonic notion of power and their service to socio-economic interests. More recent approaches to individualism and 'individualisation' have placed individualistic discourses more centrally in conceptions of social relations in late modernity, although the interests of power have been poorly integrated. I attempt to develop ideological understandings of homeowner discourses in which the focus of ideological critique becomes the normalization of tenure practices and the constitution of homeowners as investor subjects. Such an approach is more integrative of different levels of discourse, allowing for the interaction of government discourses, individual discourses and practices of self-regulation, constituting a more dynamic conception of power relationships in this sphere. Essentially, in the consideration of homeowner ideologies, the development is from a hegemonic conception of home ownership ideology to a more discursive one.

Privatism and individualism

Ideologies of privatism and individualism

Central to considerations of home ownership ideology has been the association of the tenure with privatistic and individualistic ideologies, and privat*ism* and individual*ism* (for example, Kemeny, 1992). Although the socially conservative aspects of attitudes related to owning your own home are difficult to connect directly (particularly in the case of voting and political attitudes), practices and values of privatism and individualism are more immediately implicated in relations between private and public spheres. Home ownership has been seen as a force that has enhanced privatism and more individualistic predispositions, while undermining collective identities and associations. This has been considered a historic process and linked to the erosion of communities and collective solidarities in late modernity.

There has thus been a conceptual convolution of the ideology of privatism with patterns of home-centredness, political withdrawal and compliance. The privatistic characteristics of home ownership have consequently been seen as socio-ideological. My analysis, however, also stresses subjective and motivational understandings which make privatism, as a discursive ideological process rather than a hegemonic process, more adaptable to more diverse social contexts. Indeed, it attempts to trace the growth of home ownership beyond Anglophone countries that have not been so clearly connected to individualistic ideologies and the erosion of collectivistic associations. The objective is to untangle the individualistic elements in the understanding of privatism and develop a more effective understanding of home ownership and individualization.

Theories of privatism in Anglo-Saxon societies emphasize the growth of individualism and retreat from collective participation to the private sphere of the home. It is argued that the separation of home and work that accompanied industrialization promoted privatized living and, consequently, the demarcation of privatized space from public space, between the house and the outside world (Daunton, 1983; Williams, 1987), with the desire for privacy gradually becoming a status symbol. The physical idea of privacy of the nineteenth-century bourgeois middle-class home was grounded in the system of room divisions, walls, gates and hedges (Davidoff and Hall, 1987), and has been argued to be the cultural origin of more contemporary structures of privacy and privatism. For Chaney (1993) privatism was part of the modern rationalization of space and there was a concern for reformers, in the process of urbanization, with the lack of physical boundaries. Distinct physical spaces were not reserved for certain activities and heterogeneous mixing was seen as destabilizing and cause for disorder. Nineteenth-century reforms sought to distinguish social spaces, such as the home, as the terrain of the single family, and work, recreation and care of the sick as activities belonging elsewhere.

The struggle to establish a clear division between the external world of work and community, and the internal, private space of the family was crucial for nineteenth-century middle-class families in attempting to establish status identities and respectability. In the twentieth century, the values of privatism and privacy became even more strongly entrenched in discourses on the home. In the meanings examined in this chapter, the potential for privacy and self-determined activities are recurrent in discourses on the qualities and advantages of owner-occupied tenure in particular. The connection between home ownership and privatism took on greater socio-political salience in the post-war period as growing rates of home ownership, increasing affluence and reduced working hours generated a conspicuous interest across social classes in the domestic sphere. While values and activities associated with the house, garden and family were argued to promote a more 'home-centred' spirit, owning a single-family house also became a conspicuous form of affluence for those on middle incomes with middle-class aspirations (Goldthorpe et al., 1969).

Privatization and hegemony

It became increasingly apparent that the preoccupation with privacy was not just a bourgeois ideology but had a broader socio-ideological salience. The privatization of social life was associated with the 'privatisation thesis', which stressed the comprehensive withdrawal from public life into the home driven by a sense of powerlessness in the spheres of work, politics and civil society. In the case of homeowners, the issue was whether or not people had retreated to a sphere of autonomy and control that would restore to them a sense of identity, attachment and belonging (Franklin, 1986). From this understanding home ownership developed a political salience in understanding the currents of capitalist modernity where growing numbers of owner-occupiers across social classes were seen as withdrawing to the private realm and disengaging with political activity and the public sphere. While my analysis is wary of arguments that assert a golden era of pre-modern collectivism, to which modern privatism is contrasted, the concept of privatism as a material and ideological force is compelling, and a common theme in understandings of the qualities attached to home ownership.

The privatistic qualities of home ownership have seemingly influenced political conceptions. Governments have arguably seen home ownership privatism in terms that influenced tenure discourses and policy strategies. In Britain, for example, the Thatcher government sought to privatize housing more comprehensively (along with other public services and utilities), through the mass sell-off of public rental housing. This was assumed to enhance the privatistic and self-reliant traits of households, erode class-based and collective solidarities, and bolster a spirit of individualism (see King, 1996, 2001). Housing policies ostensibly constituted a means to reorientate individuals around individualistic ideologies and privatistic social worlds. For Kemeny (1992), re-moralization around privatism and individualism has led homeowners to favour private solutions and self-reliance over collective or public solutions. The implication has been that the privatism generated by home ownership contributes to the building of hegemony around individualistic values that support the interest of capital and the political right (see Chapter 2).

Nevertheless, it is difficult to generalize about home ownership and privatism across societies and over time. The normalization of home ownership policy across political parties in Britain since the 1990s arguably marks a shift in perceptions of the political left about home ownership privatism as a facilitator of social participation. In Australia, trade-union groups have fought for greater access to home ownership for the working class (Troy, 2000) and have not seen homeowner privatism as a contradiction to collective political interests. Indeed, there is an argument that home ownership is more conducive to social participation, with owner-occupiers more often engaged in community issues than renters (Saunders, 1990; Winter, 1994; Rohe et al., 2002).

The strong association between home ownership, privatism and hegemony has thus been rather simplistic. Social stability and political power has not simply relied on intensified privatism and the growing orientation of discourses around an individualistic hegemony. Arguably, the privatistic influence of home ownership and homeowner discourses is deeper and has much more impact on the life-world. It is useful therefore, to develop the concept of privatism and its relationship to experiences of tenure.

Privatism

There has largely been an under-theorization of privatism in housing studies, which has tended to overemphasize the ideology of individualism in homeowner privatism. The ideologically centred approach adopted has essentially reduced privatism to ideologies of individualism which underestimates the significance of human agency to the extent that it assumes actions are ruled by beliefs (for example, Papadakis and Taylor-Gooby, 1987). Habermas (1973) considers privatism in terms of a 'needs-based syndrome of motivation', rather than an ideology, where the reproduction of structures of domination has been achieved primarily through the social system's ability to meet necessary and existential needs 'organized' in syndromes of privatistic motivation. This pattern of motivation is referred to by Habermas as 'family-vocational privatism', and is complemented by 'civic privatism'. The former consists of a family orientation with interests in consumption and leisure, along with career orientation suitable to status consumption, and the latter reflects the self-seeking interest in the operation of the political system (p. 75).

What Habermas describes as 'family-vocational privatism', which is similar to what Williams (1983) recognizes as 'mobile privatism', can be considered in terms of a category of 'self-seeking privatism' (Lodziak, 1996), which is pursued by those for whom capitalism 'pays off' in terms of status, financial rewards and so on, or by a larger group in society during periods of full employment and increasing affluence. Identity based on membership in the community, it is thus argued, has been replaced by privatistic pleasures and identities. Those engaged in self-seeking privatism are not merely publicly apathetic but are also often hostile to political activities that threaten to destabilize the status quo or challenge the freedom of private consumption. It is this aspect of privatism which is recognized by Kemeny (1981, 1992) and Franklin (1986) in relation to home ownership.

Lodziak (1986, 1996) refers to another aspect of privatism as 'self-maintaining privatism' where withdrawal to the private sphere and preoccupation with consumption and self-identity is promoted by unemployment, monotonous working routines, loss of community and experiences of powerlessness and meaninglessness in everyday life, rather than the rewards of status and growing affluence. This new privatism has proliferated in late modernity and can be seen in the preoccupation with consumerism and identity, where individuals are 'preoccupied with self needs'. This form of privatism is motivated by socio-psychological shifts or what Lasch (1984) considers a 'defensive contraction of the self'.

Privatism and individualism are difficult phenomena to unpack and the introduction of a social-motivational analysis complicates simpler ideological models applied to home ownership privatism. Habermas's concept of privatism is not limited to homeowner societies, but can be seen as more manifest and embedded in these cases where privatism is explicitly tied up with tenure discourses, with tenure thus standing out as a central cross-societal variable. While privatism and individualism appear entwined with Anglo-Saxon homeowner societies, which have, characteristically, more neo-liberal structures of governance, in other contexts where home ownership has recently expanded, which includes more socio-democratic North European societies and 'Confucian' East Asian ones, the integration is not so apparent and household privatism seems a more salient link than individualism. To this extent, Kemeny's model (1992) of individualistic homeowner societies and collectivistic rental ones is perhaps slightly over-embedded ideologically in terms of an individual-collective axis (see Chapter 4).

It is arguably more effective to consider the effects of home ownership on individuals in terms of individualization rather than individualistic ideologies, as the experience of the tenure has not augmented a political ethos *opposed* to the collective, but instead placed greater stress on the self and the potential functions and satisfactions of privatism and the private sphere, which may have similar but not identical effects. The growth of demand for owner-occupied housing in homeowner societies is understood more dynamically in these terms: not just as an outcome of government hegemony, but also as an effect of shifts in social conditions and relations between the self and social structures.

Consumption and individualization

Housing as consumption

Many recent social theory approaches have linked the individualism and privatism associated with owner-occupied housing practices and discourses with the growing salience of self-identity and individualization in commodity consumption. The play of identities in the consumption of goods and the role of individuals as consumers, as highlighted in the previous chapter, have been argued to mediate contemporary forms of social relations under capitalism (see Bauman, 1992). Growing levels of privatism and individualism from this perspective are seen to reflect the break-up of traditional class affiliations and collective structures and underplay the social and ideologically manipulative effects of home ownership orientated policies in neo-liberal social regimes.

Although the consumption of status and consumer goods is an aspect of Habermas's consideration of shifts towards privatism, many approaches to consumption neglect its role in power relationships, social reproduction and the maintenance of legitimacy of the state. Early theories of consumption elevated the significance of consumption vis-à-vis production in the structure of social inequalities, whereas later approaches dwell upon consumption as a cultural act, or as dreams, images and pleasures (for example, Featherstone, 1991). In perspectives on what can be referred to as 'symbolic consumption', the meanings and ideologies of homeowners concerning housing consumption are considered in terms of self-identity and structures of social and symbolic exchange, rather than ideological frameworks and embedded power relations.

The analysis now picks up on the consumption and social construction debates identified in the previous chapter in order to develop them in the understanding of homeowner ideolog*ies*. I first consider the assertion that consumption is primarily symbolic and reflects the growing individualization of society where class analyses are increasingly redundant. Second I address the re-signification of housing within symbolic networks of identity and lifestyle consumption. My argument inevitably emphasizes the transformation of housing as an exchange commodity rather than symbolic consumption, which maintains the significance of power relations in ideological analysis.

From social class to individualization

In some approaches to consumption a social class basis has been maintained. Bourdieu (1984) considers consumption in terms of how more powerful and wealthy social classes distinguish themselves from the lower classes, where, in the case of housing for example, the expression of taste in, and differentiated capacities for, consumption of types of housing goods and neighbourhoods, can be seen as part of the symbolic power structure of society. Levels of cultural and economic capital determine the ability of individuals to consume goods, which act as markers of social class.

Alternative approaches have asserted that the growing significance of lifestyle and consumption reflect the decline of traditional structures of class, community and the family, where the construction of individual identity and the redistributions of risks from institutions to individuals through individual consumption choices in various markets have become more central in social processes. A growing emphasis on 'freedom' and the power of the individual as a creator of their own identity via consumption choices, are thus argued to reflect increasing pressures on the individual and self-identities where ontological security and more traditional identities are in decline (see Giddens, 1990; Featherstone, 1991; Beck, 1992; Campbell, 1995; Miller, 2001). It is a freedom orientated towards self-realization and pleasure, where individuals are willing to sacrifice some of their security for these goals. Freedom and pleasures are facilitated by the market, which is organized around sustaining high levels of unsatisfied needs and the generation of desires for new experiences and emotions. While this approach supersedes class with consumption, it is not necessarily a more equal society as the ability to consume is central to one's place in society (Bauman, 1997).

For Beck (1992, 2000) individualization is central to the fundamental social changes that have been seen as the basis of the decline in traditional social structures and affiliations and the augmented emphasis on the self. Individualization is a multifaceted process which underscores transformations in personal relationships, family structure, education and employment (1992, p. 127), where more open practices of personal choice and reflexivity take precedence. Labour-market-deregulation, globalization and flexibilization have caused many people to become susceptible to the unsettling forces of mobility, competition and risk (Giddens, 1990; Beck, 1992). Spatial and temporal transitions have had a transformative effect on cultural experience, 'chopping up' the structure of family and community life.

For Giddens (1990) contemporary social conditions increasingly force individuals to focus on lifestyles and long-term strategies in relation to available resources. Self-image and self-reflexivity become brittle and vulnerable to a sense of failure, which can impact the self deeply as well as erode or enhance life chances. It also involves making decisions and lifestyle choices which impact the life chances of others and which can exacerbate social divisions. The self becomes bound up with an ongoing project immersed in the process of making lifestyle choices and life-planning decisions in which one's self-identity is linked to a biographical narrative about one's life.

Individualization as described by Beck and Giddens has been linked to the increasing pressure on individuals to enter home ownership (Ford, Burrows and Nettleton, 2001). Home ownership, buoyed by perceptions of rapid house-price inflation, is increasingly seen as a means to mitigate risks in the face of the economic effects of global fluctuations, growing employment, casualization and insecurity in work and the decline of formal and support networks of families and communities. At the same time the private realm of the home offers an ontological haven, a means to reify self-identity through decorative and commodity based lifestyle consumption, and mediates social and identificative practices related to biographical narratives. Privatism and individualization, in this context appear to have a very different meaning or significance compared to the socio-ideological one described previously, which emphasized the manipulative promotion of privatism and individualism by the state. When individualization is related to consumption in postmodern terms, focus is drawn more substantially onto the symbolic and ontological pleasures and satisfactions of home ownership in explaining its recent expansion and augmented popularity.

Housing consumption and individualization

Rapoport (1981) emphasizes the role of housing in the communication of identities. In Western homeowner societies, communication of identities is based on differentiation, achieved through the selection of housing goods and the manipulation of semi-fixed feature elements.

Consequently, personalization is stressed in housing and identity processes. Rapoport accounts for the importance of this personalization in terms of the 'product', where the changeability of semi-fixed features can be highly distinctive and can communicate a complex message of identity, and the 'process', where the feedback from the environment which responds to the active effort of the individual (that is, a sense of control over the environment), is perceived as competence and hence positive self-identity. Research on the meaning of housing and home have increasingly emphasized individual identity where the concept of self-identity and self-esteem are seen as linked and the house becomes a symbol of the self (see Clapham, 2005). Indeed, in recent decades the significance of the home has been elevated in terms of a centre for self-identity, lifestyle and cultural life, which in themselves have been seen as increasingly important in late modernity.

Giddens (1984) emphasizes the home as the prime locale for the creation and sustenance of 'ontological security' and self-identity, which is increasingly important because of the social changes described above. Feelings or emotions may be expressed through changes to the physical fabric of the house with the internal appearance of the house often seen as a form of identity and self-expression (Clapham, 2005). For Allen and Crow (1989) the significance of the project of creating an appropriate environment in which domestic life can take place has grown to the point at which it stands alongside paid work and bringing up a family as a major life-interest (p. 10). Concern for the appearance of the personal space of the home and decorating styles have been elevated to the extent that they constitute a 'reflection' of personality and the projection of a public image. For Csikszentmihalyi and Rochberg-Halton (1981) possessions and their display not only add to the personalization of space but constitute an 'ecology of signs' that reflects as well as shapes the 'self' (p. 17). Craik (1989) further points out that decorative styles and interior design tend to reflect an idealized image of family life and have replaced household management as the focus of domestic ideology (p. 59).

There is a growing literature that demonstrates the emergent significance of housing in identity formation and that the augmentation of privatistic practices, which have been normalized within owner-occupied tenure, can be integrated with the understanding of the home and home-improvement consumption as an expanding base of meaning and identity. However, approaches to identity consumption are arguably unbalanced to the extent that they marginalize the significance of everyday use and more material meanings. Many approaches overly aestheticize everyday life and largely ignore mundane use values, at one level, and the manipulative role of ideology at another, thus reducing the world to the symbolic and social life to lifestyle.

> the consumer society confronts people with dream images which speak to desires, and aestheticize and de-realise reality. ... The aestheticisation of everyday life can refer to the project of turning life into a work of art ... the heroic concern with the achievement of originality and superiority in dress, demeanour, personal habits and even furnishings – what we now call lifestyle. (Featherstone, 1992, p. 270)

For Baudrillard the transition to post-Fordist or postmodern society has resulted in a society that is dominated and organized by a system of signs. Material commodities have a sign value generated semiotically within the system of signs. Exchange value and use value are no longer relevant, therefore, in consumption. Identities are essentially the product of the signs that we consume (Baudrillard, 1994, 1998). Following the logic of this argument, the consumption of goods, even those goods that might count as basic necessities, is argued to embody cultural meanings and symbolic values, and the preferences of individual consumers become the reflections of symbolic values rather than use values. In their treatment of identity, symbolic theories of consumption thus ignore the many other sources of self-identity other than commodities: they ignore identity needs, they re-define identity as image and style with 'little reference to economic power' (Lodziak, 2002, p. 5). Symbolic consumption, moreover, in its estimation of social fragmentation and the decline of structures of modern society – class, collectivity and the family – dematerializes society and undermines the sustained relevance of such structures to most people.

Although housing research has demonstrated the symbolic role of home ownership consumption on the one hand, it has also identified the resilience of use meanings and traditional family and class structures on the other. Gram-Hanssen and Bech-Danielsen's research with Danish homeowners (2004) found identity processes in household decorative practices to be conspicuous and explicit, but also found substantial variation between households structured within class terms and grounded in ordinary consumption.

> It is obvious that the more economically fundamental decisions, such as what house to buy, still reflected a deep-rooted class-power structure, whereas the interior design is much more easily changed and thus suitable to a more playful attitude to identity. ... However, the empirical

study also shows that too strong a focus on the communicative aspects of house and interior decoration fails to understand that some families may have a more use orientated approach to their house, also described as ordinary consumption. (p. 23)

For many householders in this study, family-owned decorative items held sentimental meanings rather than communicative ones. Presentation of the house in terms of tidiness was often more important than the communication of lifestyle identities through decoration and display of the home, especially for women from lower-income classes. Following Merleau-Ponty (1969), Gram-Hanssen and Bech-Danielsen point out that while many families tell stories of conscious identity-creating through interior design, humans *directly* relate to the material world, which means something to them regardless of power structures and symbolism related to material objects. Housing practices were most importantly symbols of family building, which seems to belong to the modern structures of society with the family as a core institution. It may, however, also be viewed as a past modern struggle to sustain a family that is under constant pressure of dissolution that could result in the loneliness of an individualized society. In this way they claim to have shown that both modern and past modern structures influence housing consumption (p. 22).

The idea that modern structures of society such as class, collectivism and the family have broken down leading to greater individualization and stress on communicative aspects of consumption has come under sustained criticism. Although individualized experience and identity formation in Western cultures is more demanding and discrete than it was in the 'golden age' of Fordism, definitions and measures are vague and processes amorphous. There are thus difficulties in calibrating the extent and effects of individualization and, moreover, the import of individualized experiences in relation to collective experiences remains largely untapped. Mythen (2005) argues that we need to be sensitive to social and cultural continuity as much as change as writers like Beck overlook the cohesiveness of social structures. To argue that class and the nuclear family are losing relative cohesion as primary agents of socialization is one thing. It is quite another to suggest that these structures are being replaced (p. 144). An important aspect of home ownership consumption, although it has been marked as either vehicle or barometer of individualization, is that it is still primarily bound up with discourses of the family, and links individuals to families and spaces and places of belonging. Moreover, the logic of class and structures of inequality, as mediated by, for example, access to housing, demonstrates remarkable continuity.

From symbolic consumption to commodification

In principle, the focus on meaning in symbolic consumption is consistent with a concern with ideology in that cultures and ideologies are both organized sets of meanings that are normally supportive of the interests of particular groups. However, rather than explore the obvious power of capital in shaping meaning, culture and ideology, symbolic theories of consumption approach ideologies as discourses or texts materialized in all consumer products, with little reference to economic context and power interests. Nevertheless, if we consider the process by which housing has been commodified, which is most evident in homeowner societies, what is most apparent is the augmented significance of housing as an asset and investment. While the case of housing does demonstrate the increasing force of lifestyle consumption, the growing salience of private housing as property within a market, or as an economic commodity, has been most central to housing discourses (as illustrated earlier in the chapter), which is also bound up within an integrated nexus of meanings related to security, autonomy, husbandry, adulthood, family and status. The analysis of consumption in terms of commodification illustrates more directly the significance of economic context and power relations.

Housing may potentially be considered de-commodified to the extent that it can be consumed and produced according to criteria unrelated to market considerations. However, housing in homeowner societies has increasingly been orientated towards systems that wholly commodify homes in market terms. Indeed, advanced capitalist economies have developed in terms of commodification processes where objects become tradable and commensurable to the market. In order for market systems to function they must commodify goods, services or attributes that people value. Increasingly, pressure to compete and accumulate drives a continuous search for profitability and expansion of markets with consequent continued growth of commodity relations and increasing penetration into all aspects of social life (see Giddens, 1981; Sternberg, 2000).

Hamilton (1999) suggests that transition to market economy relations embody a commodification process that alters perceptions and consciousness of the value functions of spatial elements, with exchange values increasingly replacing previous principles of utility value. Furthermore, Forrest and Williams (1984) identify how de-commodified forms have been eroded and commodified relations have been reorganized more generally in the housing sector in homeowner societies, leading to intensification in commodification processes in both production and consumption. The increasing significance of housing as an exchange commodity has, moreover, been argued to be at the centre of behaviours which have resulted in the booms and busts of housing markets (Maclennan et al., 1997; Munro et al., 1998).

Indeed, the commodification of housing appears the most fundamental element of housing consumption. While home ownership mediates identity practices and has a fundamental use value, there is also an integrated realm of security, investment and status values bound up with owner-occupied tenure, which remains of central importance to homeowners. Considered in terms of ideology, homeowner ideologies can thus be integrated with market relations and the interests of states which seek to increasingly commodify social relations and welfare services. For King (1996, 2006) the most significant aspects of transformation in policy towards mass home ownership are the effects of re-signification of the home as property where dwelling is transformed from a practice to an object. What are important in consumption and the meaning of housing, therefore, are socio-ideological outcomes that can be linked to broader shifts in ideological systems towards the preeminence of markets, self-reliance and citizenship rights based on property ownership, which form the basis of neo-liberal power regimes.

Normalization and subjugation

Normalization

In this chapter I have examined homeowner ideologies as meanings and discourses, hegemonic features and aspects of commodification and individualization. In this ideological integration of homeowner ideologies the aim is to move from more hegemonic theories of power to a more discursive one. The operation of power in discourse, however, is often illusive. The consideration of discursive ideological approaches to housing consumption adds considerable insight. I address this further now by analysing the forces and tactics which socially construct home ownership as a majority housing tenure. I consider housing and tenure discourses as imbued with power that normalizes individuals and subjugates them to coercive practices. I also deal with how changing housing relations have constituted individuals, or residents, as investor subjects, which has implications for the restructuring of risks and responsibilities between individuals and the state. The basic understanding is that discourses are 'practices that systematically form the objects of which they speak' (Foucault, 1970, p. 49). Discourses thus establish a set of possible symbolic positions and behaviours for an individual or group of individuals as a subject or subjects.

Gurney emphasizes the power of normalizing discourses and how they have become embedded in the meanings, values and social practices surrounding owner-occupied tenure. In Gurney's analysis (1999a,b) of government housing policy discourse, as well as individual meanings of home ownership, he focuses on a particular set of discourses and practices that have come to constitute home ownership as a 'natural' tenure. This process of 'normalization' of one tenure as natural may be seen as coercive with homeowners themselves becoming both the subject and object of a disciplinary power. His research highlights three elements to this discourse. Each of these elements contributes to a system of knowledge and a code of cultural practices that constitute the play of power that subjugates and 'disciplines' individuals.

The first of these elements is 'homelessness', by which Gurney means that the idea of 'home' has been appropriated by homeowners. As suggested at the start of the chapter, home is a central and evocative concept in the discursive production of housing and housing relations. In homeowner societies the term 'home' has come to denote the differences between the dwellings of householders in owner-occupation and those in rented accommodation (see Allen and Crow, 1989; Clapham, 2005). The disciplinary power of this discourse enables normalizing judgements to be made about homeowners and tenants. This judgement underpins expectations of housing and the householder and creates a form of homelessness for those outside the tenure, asserting that the 'home' exists in a much more meaningful way for those in owner-occupation.

The tenure analogies applied by homeowners provide a means to understand this process at the everyday level. A common vocabulary concerning tenure can be discerned in housing discourses and ideologically tied to contemporary versions of the phenomenon of owner-occupation. Owner-occupation is like, 'owning a book rather than borrowing it', 'buying a car rather than hiring it' and 'buying a television rather than renting it' (Gurney, 1999a, p. 1714). Such analogies highlight the common-sense responsibilities of stewardship and husbandry which have accompanied the post-war growth of home ownership. Such discourses may have been particularly significant in post-war Britain where home ownership has competed with public rental housing as the majority tenure. Wilmot and Young (1971) recognized the emergent significance of such analogies in housing practices nearly forty years ago. 'The new husbandman of England is back in a new form, as horticulturist rather than agriculturist, as a builder rather than cattleman, as improver, not of a strip of arable land but the semi-detached family estate at 33 Ellesmere Road' (p. 33).

A second normalizing discourse associates pride, self-esteem, responsibility and citizenship with owner-occupied housing, or what Gurney defines as 'being good citizens'. The effect of home ownership in polarizing groups of individuals based on their tenure has been consistently highlighted as an aspect of contemporary housing relations and discourse. Public rental tenants have been consistently portrayed as a feckless class who practice an inferior form of citizenship (King, 1996; Murie, 1998; Gurney, 1999a). The discursive expectations constructed in discourses represent homeowners as superior types of parents, better caretakers and good citizens. Gurney suggests that as a normalizing discourse, home ownership facilitates a judgemental discourse by which those outside of the 'normal' tenure category are inferior and abnormal. It is possible to consider in discourses concerning tenure and housing, that public rental housing itself has become a metaphor for a feckless class of people in societies where it has been a residualized tenure. Gurney (1999a) suggests that the discourses on public housing at a variety of levels have constituted council housing as a metaphor for a particular social class of scroungers located within a mythical realm of 'the estate'. Arguably, council tenants represent an out-group that feature in moral tales and moral panics.

The positioning of good, prudent and worthy owner-occupiers against bad, prodigal and feckless tenants constitutes a morally laden mirror image of housing tenure, and can be argued to be powerful in the process of informing tenure meanings, preferences and social practices. More recent research in the United States demonstrates that the normalization of tenants and tenures has become even more embedded (see Shlay, 2006). The discourse has become overwhelming and is practiced in the concepts of housing research itself.

Another element of normalizing discourse relates to the construction of private tenure as 'being natural'. De Neufville and Barton (1987) have argued that there is an emotive force that has helped to build up home ownership, which is aligned with moral tales about a homeland for which one must fight. A frequent juxtaposition of home and heart are embodied in discourses about home ownership and bind tenure with a concept of a natural and instinctual predisposition. Gurney (1999b) argues that the association of the natural with home ownership means that any rejection of what home stands for can be constructed as unnatural (p. 178). Malpass (2006) has also identified how governments have increasingly constituted home ownership as the ideal, and while policy discourse has utilized the concept of 'choice', the 'natural choice' for a household has been to leave rental housing as soon as possible and become a homeowner.

These normalizing discourses are clearly powerful and are central to understanding the impact of home ownership. Instead of considering structurally determined relationships between social institutions and homogenization of values in processes of hegemony, the significance of normalization and discourses themselves can be appraised. The exercise of the power of tenure discourses is not top down but ubiquitous. Homeowners are neither being duped by the powers that be, nor satisfying a deeply seated desire by buying into the housing market. Individuals can be excluded, marginalized and subjugated on the basis of their adherence to the cultural norms established through tenure and housing discourses. It is precisely because home ownership is 'normal' and seen as natural that the process of social judgement and social inequality is practiced through tenure. The gradual expansion and normalization of home ownership and subsequent embedding of meanings of tenure during recent decades thus illustrate an emerging relationship between power and tenure within homeowner societies. While the state may identify self-interests in housing policy manipulation, assumptions about the benefits reflect the social embeddedness of meanings and ideologies.

In traditional ideological approaches, home ownership has been considered a stabilizing force and a means to resist collectivist social tendencies (see Chapter 2). Critiques have emphasized home ownership as ideologically conservative in that it supports the commitment to private property and, as such, research has focused on housing tenure and political opinions. However, homeowner discourses effectively highlight a particular pattern that substantially complicates the ideological role of home ownership. Richards (1990) identifies that while there is some dis-consensus and confusion concerning the meanings attached to home and tenure, what is significant is the overwhelming commitment to home ownership as a proper path to normal family life. The norms about housing and tenure are bound up with a series of norms and ideologies about citizenship and society. Indeed these norms are embedded in the owner-occupied house and the image of the 'good' household inside it. Gurney, more incisively, identifies tenure-normalizing discourses. The power of discourses in prescribing proper ways to acquire a life within a dwelling, subjugate individuals to the logic of this discourse inside home ownership, and marginalize those outside of it.

Another way to consider the power of home ownership discourses is the way they have polarized advantages and disadvantages between tenures in homeowner societies. Discourses and meanings of security, economic rationality, autonomy and control, along with the idea of 'home' itself, have been arguably appropriated by homeowners in various social contexts, while the inverse of these meanings have been associated with tenants and rental tenures. It is not only state discourses that constitute one form of tenure and resident as inferior or superior, but also those individuals that occupy these tenures. Arguably, this constitutes a process of 'tenure polarisation' in thinking and discourse. The flow of power is discursive, with residents of different sorts becoming both the subject and object of a disciplinary power. The state's role is central, but it too is mediated, and its role in housing provision constituted, by normalizing discourses.

Economic subjects

Harmes (2001) has identified how the development of financial 'technologies' has contributed to the expansion of a 'mass investment culture' of global finance. Such technologies have been most strongly experienced in neo-liberal societies where home ownership is prevalent. Although some writers have emphasized the roles of stocks, pension plans and mutual funds in the globalization of markets (see Clark, 2000; Engelen, 2003), owner-occupied housing consumption, in terms of finance and markets, has become a central feature of financial technologies and arguably plays an equal or greater role in the proliferation of investment culture (see Smith et al., 2006; Langley, 2007). What is also important is that financial technologies have an impact in the construction or constitution of individuals as economic subjects.

Langley (2006) has suggested that an individualization of risk is underway, characterized by the summoning up of the responsible individual as an 'entrepreneurial investor subject'. More collective technologies for managing potential risks have been sidelined in favour of the promotion of individual investment to 'calculate, bear and embrace risk as opportunity or reward' (p. 919). The shift towards home ownership investment has been the most conspicuous and arguably successful technology in the transformation of individuals into 'investor subjects'. Such subjects experience greater individualization and increasingly relate to the world in terms of markets and calculations of risk and opportunity. At the same time, more collective dispositions for dealing with security and risk have been eroded by the commodification of mechanisms.

Langley argues that the prevailing neo-liberal form of capitalist government respects the formal freedom and autonomy of subjects, and in part exercises control within and through those autonomous actions by promoting the self-disciplinary discourses and technologies deemed necessary for a successful and autonomous life. For Peters (2001) this responsibilization of self requires 'new forms of prudentialism (a privatized actuarialism) where risk management is forced back onto individuals and satisfied through the market' (p. 91).

Essentially, Peters and Langley are talking about the promotion and expansion of investment practices as mechanisms by which subjectivity is moulded around a particular image of an autonomous self. Such a self is realized through investment and financial product consumption practices which involve taking risks. However, risks are in this case seen as opportunities and the exercise of the free self. Consequently, investment discourses and practices appear to be 'technologies of the self' and are engaged in willingly as part of our evolving as free subjects. Inevitably, such practices serve the interests of the neo-liberal state which relies for its continuation on, not only the growth and perpetuation of markets, but also the construction of individuals as market subjects.

Clark and Whiteside (2003) suggest that the conjuring of the investor subject through financial products and pension plans has not been successful to the extent that the state has failed to create the trust and confidence necessary for collective participation in many forms of individualized investment (p. 18). What has been more attractive to individuals as conditions of risk have become more immanent and investment finance more available, is housing property investment. Demand for housing property has grown rapidly (see Chapter 1), and across homeowner societies (and beyond) housing constitutes the largest debt, asset and single investment for the majority of households. It has also been shown that home ownership constitutes a primary alternative to pensions as a plan for later life and old age. It represents, for many, a personal provident fund against individual, social and economic vicissitudes (see Castles, 1998; Doling and Horsewood, 2003; Kemeny, 2005).

Knorr-Cetina and Breugger (2000) address how market professionals come to relate to markets as 'objects of attachment'. Markets work because people relate and define their actions in terms of markets as objects with their own sets of characteristics. Smith, Munro and Christie (2006) have identified similar processes among housing professionals, who shift any accountability for their actions in the market to the market itself. Their study found that markets were discursively constituted as external to people, with an actancy of their own. They insist that the market sets conditions to which individuals can only respond or adapt. Individuals thus come to relate to markets as objects with specific qualities and invested with a life of their own. They get heated and active, become strong or stubborn; they can cool down and even be aggressive or frightened. Inevitably they 'move on' and the only 'rational' response for any individual is to follow them. Significantly, individuals who submit to market imperatives subject themselves to its often arbitrary logic.

Arguably, housing has become a primary, if not *the* primary means of situating individuals in a market and thus as an investor subject. Housing discourses, of course, comprise a range of meanings beyond just investment (such as, family and use values), and investment discourses are more evident in some societies than others. Nevertheless, other housing discourses may also be significant. For Martin (2002), in the financialization of the subject, it is not just investment that appears significant to the achievement of successful and autonomous life, but rather a number of financial practices and subject positions that are called up in order to secure, advance and express individual freedom. The polarization of meanings of home in homeowner societies considered in this chapter essentially reflects such discourses (related to autonomy, control, security, self-determined family life, and so on) and can be strongly implicated in the construction of a particular type of subjectivity which serves a discursive process of subjugation to changing relationships between governments, policy, markets and individuals.

The consideration of homeowner ideologies in these terms suggests that ideological processes are not just hegemonic, and involve a complexity of normalizing practices and discourses that establish a set of possible symbolic positions and behaviours for individuals as subjects. The transformation of housing objects from dwellings to property investments and objects of consumption also appears particularly salient in understanding dynamic ideological relations between housing, individuals and society. In subsequent chapters, the government and socio-political sides of this discursive process are considered in the constitution of an ideology of home ownership, where discourses of choice, opportunity and the market are more central. Homeowner ideologies are thus considered in terms of the changing role of housing in homeowner societies, where housing has been specifically implicated in transformations in relations between the state, markets and families, and where the state has increasingly sought to transfer risks onto individuals.

Conclusion

An exploration of homeowner ideologies and meanings attached to owner-occupation reveals the growing influence of the home and tenure status in symbolic relations. Research in Anglo-Saxon, homeowner societies has illustrated patterns of values related to status, economic rationality, security, autonomy, control, adulthood and good citizenship, which have been bound up with owner-occupied tenures. Discourses have arguably normalized and polarized the meanings of home and differentiated the perceived viability of different tenures, with renting becoming symbolically undermined. While there is little evidence of any 'natural' superiority of this tenure system, the discursive construction of home ownership as natural is in part self-fulfilling where it contributes to over-demand and the acceleration of property prices, and the status erosion of renters and rental communities. Inevitably, tenure has been manipulated leading to transformations in experiences, meanings and expectations that have enhanced individualization, elevated the market function of housing and eroded collective structures and identities. Such transformations favour neo-liberal social developments and thus appear to constitute an ideological power relation.

An assumption in housing debates has been that home ownership has socially conservative effects on the values of residents, which is a rather simplistic analysis. Homeowner's ideologies can only be crudely linked to political values. More important is how households relate to their homes, which forms the basis of discourses and subjectivities related to ideologically discursive social relations. Postmodern foci on consumption and identification processes have also failed to capture the politically divisive nature of the expansion of owner-occupation, although they do demonstrate the nature of individualization, commodification and identification in relation to consumption and changing socio-psychological pressures in post-Fordist socio-economic conditions. My argument is that home ownership in many societies commodifies social relations, materially and ideologically, which serves the interests of economic neo-liberalization and has been important to the restructuring of welfare systems and the distribution of welfare responsibilities and risks between individuals and the state. It is also an important element of social divergence between groups of advanced industrialized societies.

The research in the societies examined so far is dominated by a particular socio-cultural perspective on tenure and housing and, arguably, tells us most about the commonalities among socio-economically similar Anglophone societies. A central problem in assessing the ideological constitution or significance of values attached to home ownership is how to understand their construction in specific societies and locate them within a coherent framework of social relations. Many meanings associated with the home may vary individually, over time and between contexts. It is important therefore to address more concertedly the significance of diverse social structures, ideologies and housing systems in societies dominated by owner-occupied housing. What international housing comparisons have lacked is a cross-cultural axis by which to identify the conceptual and contextual bubbles within which home ownership and ideology is understood.

4
Housing, Globalization and Welfare States

Introduction

Housing, and specifically home ownership, has gained in importance in the economic structures of a growing number of industrialized societies and has begun to play an increasing role in the structure of emerging welfare systems. This chapter sets out to explore the growing centrality of home ownership in relationships between welfare and social change. In recent decades, increasing pressure has been put on nation states to reduce welfare spending and liberalize markets in order to keep up with the competitive demands of global capitalism. This has been related to socio-economic changes associated with intensified globalization, where greater integration of international markets and communication networks has amplified the socio-economic effects of capitalism. While theories of globalization have tended to support the notion of convergence in social organization among similarly advanced societies, theories of welfare states focus on how the organization of welfare leads to different patterns of socio-economic development. A particular feature in some societies, and a growing feature in others, has been a shift towards owner-occupied housing policies and practices as a means to restructure the organization of welfare.

It is not coincidental that owner-occupation has expanded as the dominant housing tenure across societies at the same time as the legitimacy and viability of public provision has come under increasing pressure. Many governments have sought to shift responsibilities for welfare back onto individuals by encouraging personal saving, investment and asset accumulation. Housing purchase has thus become increasingly seen as a vehicle for, and container of, household asset accumulation with which to protect households against increased risk in the labour market in a context of declining public welfare support. The aim of this chapter is to illustrate changing roles of home ownership in Western societies, specifically where owner-occupied housing has become more central to social organization as well as individual mediation of risks. Its ideological salience has also advanced. Home ownership no longer simply concerns the promotion of politically conservative ideologies, but is part of a neo-liberal restructuring of ideological relations around subjective positions in markets. This restructuring is fundamental to the changing organization of relations between the state, markets and families. This restructuring, however, is not even across industrialized societies.

The first section of the chapter sets out a debate concerning divergent relationships between societies and welfare systems. The purpose is to develop understanding of the relationship between housing systems and welfare regimes in patterns of social divergence. Housing systems have largely been considered the 'wobbly pillar' of welfare states (Torgersen, 1987), although, increasingly, research has tried to identify a relationship between housing policy, tenure systems and the development of welfare. The ideological and hegemonic basis of divergence between welfare systems is also addressed, along with how housing tenure has interacted with different welfare structures in different groups of societies. This analysis provides a basis for understanding the changing role of home ownership in homeowner societies where housing has become more central to welfare structures. The second section of the chapter addresses the differentiated impacts of global forces and the restructuring of social relations around more fragmented and insecure employment and welfare structures. It has been suggested that in many societies, households have increasingly relied on the augmentation of housing assets to build wealth and hedge against unemployment insecurity, unexpected welfare needs and potential pension shortfalls (Groves et al., 2007). The third section of the chapter attempts to demonstrate the function of home ownership in the advancement of the logic of neo-liberalism and the restructuring of government obligations, citizen rights and expectations.

Housing systems and welfare regimes

Welfare regimes

For Habermas (1973) the development of welfare states was a necessary step in many capitalist societies for alleviating the negative consequences of unrestricted competition of private capital. The state has thus often replaced market mechanisms in order to help the realization of private capital. While eroding principles of the market, public welfare goods and services even out some extreme social imbalances and thus help maintain public support for governments as well as stabilize social conditions necessary for capitalist production. How welfare states develop in each country has, however, been uneven. Wilensky (1975) proposes that the welfare state will be most developed, and welfare-state ideologies most powerful, where a centralized government is able to mobilize, and must respond to a large, strongly organized working class with only modest rates of social mobility (p. 68). Conversely, public welfare provision is likely to be least developed where the interests and ideologies of capital dominate. How housing systems and policies fit into welfare-state development, however, has proved analytically and theoretically problematic. My first concern in this chapter is thus how housing can be integrated into the examination of how different capitalist welfare regimes develop.

Esping-Andersen's (1990, 1999) analyses of different forms of welfare capitalism proposes that the advancement of welfare states in each society is related to the constitution of different models of post-war capitalist regime. Three factors are argued to be of prime importance in determining which policy regime will emerge: class mobilization, class-political coalition structures, and the historical legacy of regime institutionalization. In his original model, societies are grouped into three worlds, each with 'qualitatively different welfare-state logics' (1990, p. 5). These welfare 'regimes' generate 'systems' that can be described as de-commodified (social democratic), conservative (corporatist) or residual (liberal). Essentially, regimes are understood to be the result of inter-class alliances and power conflict resolutions in each society leading to social and institutional processes, and discernable and divergent structures of relations between the state, economy, legal organization and institutional structures, which are systematically interwoven.

In terms of understanding power relations 'labour movement theory' is central to Esping-Andersen, with differences between societies shaped by how labour unions and parties have been more or less successful in shaping government policies. Social democratic welfare regimes are dominated by working-class movements establishing alliances with other groups and classes while keeping conservative forces divided or isolated. A typical example is Sweden where collective interests have been supported and social welfare programmes developed more comprehensively. Corporatist welfare regimes are effectively deadlocked power systems in which no interest can dominate with each party negotiating its own welfare sub-system from corporatist political horse trading. Germany is more typical of this case. Liberal regimes emerge in systems dominated by capitalist interests who oppose a divided working class. It is the reverse of a social democratic regime as conservative forces hold the middle as well as right-wing ground. The United States is considered a key example, where there is generally an assertion of market interests over collective ones in social provision.

Three further criteria are used to distinguish worlds of welfare: the quality of social rights, social stratification, and the relationship among state, market and family (1990, p. 29). Focus on the latter has led to the assertion that there are also South European and East Asian regime types (see Esping-Andersen, 1999; Holliday, 2000; Allen et al., 2004). In the Southern European regime the family plays a very important role in providing welfare of different kinds, and is integrated within broad kinship networks among extended family members. Castles and Ferrara (1996) identify the key features of a South European system, with Spain and Italy as typical cases.

> the Southern European family tends to operate as a clearing house for the pooling of social and material resources and for the redistribution among its members according to need: most notably those needs which arise at critical junctures of the life cycle (housing, employment, childminding, income), not infrequently as a consequence of defective public policies. (p. 181)

By considering the sources of welfare provision in more dynamic terms greater subtlety is added to the concept of welfare systems. While the family is often the main provider of welfare goods, the market also provides a means by which welfare goods can be bought. The state is thus only one of many service providers (see Rose and Shiritori, 1986). The relationships between welfare services, sources and providers is indeed complex, and housing itself, although often neglected from analysis of welfare systems is central to these relations between household, market and state. Housing is not just a form of welfare good in itself in terms of shelter and so on, but also forms the basis of how the household or family procure, use and share other welfare goods. It acts as a store of welfare resources that can be exchanged for other goods and also carried across generations. Housing also situates the household in a market where people compete for and trade housing goods, and establishes more or less dependent relationships with the state for the satisfaction of welfare needs. Home ownership may thus be more important in welfare relations in some societies more than others, especially where families or markets are primary sources of welfare provision rather than the state. Conversely, owner-occupation may make some households more dependent on the state for tenure subsidies and taxes, but may also de-commodify relations with labour markets where housing costs are minimal and housing equity adequate to support withdrawal or early retirement (Doling and Horsewood, 2003).

Welfare systems in economically developed East Asian societies have also been identified within a common welfare regime type. For Holliday (2000), among the East Asian Tigers social policy is strictly subordinate to the overriding policy objective of economic growth. Everything else flows from this: minimal social rights with extensions linked to productive activity, reinforcement of the position of the productive elements in society, and state–market–family relationships directed towards growth (p. 708). I argue later in this book, and elsewhere (Ronald, 2007a), that housing is also central to the welfare mix and regime orientation in East Asian contexts. Many governments have sought to intervene in the housing system and promote forms of home ownership as a means to orientate households towards family self-provision practices and legitimate state strategies orientated towards rapid economic growth at the expense of public welfare provision.

The cases of Australia and New Zealand have also demonstrated specific regime features. Although the orientation of the welfare system appears liberal (a weak welfare state), the corporatist balance has historically been strongly influenced by union based collectivism. Castles (1985) argues that labour movements in these societies adopted a different political approach from those in Europe, which has not been based on expanding the social wage (in terms of social security, welfare benefits, and so on). Workers have alternatively turned to a high private wage strategy or 'wage earner's welfare state'. This kind of 'workfare' approach is different from other societies considered welfare-state 'laggards' due to the existence of a statutory wage regulation system combined with low marginal tax rates, which has generally provided a national level of needs-fulfilment below which the vast majority of wage-earners could not fall (p. 103). This approach suggests that the measure of social wages is unsatisfactory for understanding the degree of welfare in a society. It also questions the assumed class, power bases of welfare systems, where an organized, mobilized working class is assumed to demand higher social wages. Home ownership has also played a more central role in this system. As the number of working-class homeowners has grown, the benefits of high wages have been increasingly transferred into housing properties, which have subsequently augmented in value to constitute a residual of household wealth and an asset base for household security. In this context communist trade unions have long been proponents of working-class home ownership (Troy, 2000).

Although housing is a key welfare resource, it has largely been missing from the mainstream welfare regime debate. Wilensky (1975) excludes housing from his analysis as there are fundamental measurement problems in assessing the dimension of housing in relation to the state (p. 7). For Harloe (1995) the barriers to the de-commodification of housing are greater than for other forms of welfare. As so much is provided through the market, it largely exerts an exogenous influence on welfare systems. For Kemeny (1992), however, the housing dimension provides a particular insight into processes of divergence between social regimes as it is so deeply embedded in social structure and so difficult to disentangle from other forms of welfare. Moreover, Kemeny states, 'Housing, because of its central importance to the nature of the social structure and its pivotal role in state welfare provision, provides a crucial link between the welfare state and the social structure' (p. 111).

Housing and welfare

So far I have explored patterns of social development and divergence within capitalist societies along lines of welfare systems and the political regimes behind them. While the housing dimension has been largely absent from debates, housing systems are influential in patterns of social change, not only because they structure the dependency of providers and users on welfare, but also because of the way housing tenure impacts the social structure and orientates ideologies and social relations. Greater consideration of the role housing and home ownership may thus advance welfare regime approaches in the understanding of welfare system pathways and hegemonic power relations. My objective here is to develop appreciation of the role of home ownership that elevates its significance in patterns of social divergence and processes of globalization, the effects being socio-economic, socio-structural and ideological.

The concept of de-commodification of services based on social rights, in which people are allowed to meet living standards independent of pure market forces, is critical to Esping-Andersen's understanding of welfare states. Esping-Andersen operationalized the concept of de-commodification in order to establish at what level different welfare systems enabled people to maintain their livelihood without reliance on the market. However, Groves et al. (2007), among others, argue that such measures aren't enough to provide an adequate base by which to compare different welfare systems as social security systems are designed to complement and integrate with other related measures. Critically, housing was not taken into consideration in Esping-Andersen's de-commodification scale, but plays a crucial role in mediating forms and levels of welfare provision among the family, the state and the market. For example, non-profit housing contributes substantially to the framework of state welfare and services in some societies, whereas home ownership grounds welfare more firmly with the family and the market in others. Arguably, the absence of housing and tenure in welfare models has led to substantial underdevelopment in the understanding of the nature of regimes.

Kemeny not only introduces housing as a key element in understanding welfare regimes, he also adopts an alternative approach to Esping-Andersen regarding ideological power relations and social structure. In his model of housing and society, Kemeny (1992) draws a distinction between private and collective forms of social structure. Societies with highly developed welfare states have more collectivized social structures reflecting a more collectivist hegemony. Poorly developed or residualized welfare states tend to be characterized by privatized social structures reflecting individualist and privatist hegemonies. Kemeny proposes that the long-term viability of the welfare state varies in relation to the degree of collectivism or privatism contained in the ideology underlying the social structure. In understanding this relationship housing plays a key role. Essentially, ideologies leaning towards either collectivism or privatism are thought to have a substantial effect on housing policies and the organization of tenure, with privatistic societies being dominated by private home ownership and collectivistic ones more orientated towards social housing and particularly social renting. Home ownership in line with ideology thus has a considerable effect on social structures which become orientated towards privatistic policies and welfare frameworks.

The effects of home ownership on welfare have a material and ideological basis. The material effects are determined by how home ownership restructures or redistributes wealth over the lifecycle from the young to the old, with the 'front-end loading' of debt (Kemeny, 1981, 1992). Housing costs are heaviest in the early years (mortgage burdens on first-time buyers can consume more than a third of household income) but diminish as the household ages, becoming minimal after the mortgage is paid off. Elderly households can thus survive on a smaller pension, as housing costs are minimal, and use their housing property assets as a reservoir of capital to cover the costs of extra welfare needs and possibly care. In societies where renting dominates housing costs vary much less over the lifecycle and households rely more on welfare and pension systems. For Kemeny then, there is an expected effect on welfare in homeowner societies. The pressures put on a household to pay for private housing are thought to engender a strong resistance to public expenditure that necessitates the high taxes needed to fund quality universal welfare provision and provide for those who haven't paid high housing costs to cover themselves in later life. Homeowners are thus thought to be more orientated towards individualized self-reliance and resistant to indiscriminate forms of welfare.

In the early 1980s, Kemeny thus predicted that countries where privatist ideologies prevail, rates of home ownership should be higher and relative levels of public spending should be lower than in countries where collectivist ideologies dominate. This was tested by looking at correlations between home ownership rates and welfare spending in a small number of countries, but was reinforced by later studies that tended to confirm the relationship (see Schmidt, 1989; Castles and Ferrera, 1996; Castles, 1998; Doling and Horsewood, 2003). Other outcomes have also been demonstrated in terms of quality of housing and characteristics of tenants across rental sector types (Hoekstra, 2005). Following Kemeny's understanding of relationships among welfare, society and the organization of housing, the role of tenure has thus been strongly implicated in processes of social divergence.

The analysis of housing, welfare and social divergence also lead to the identification of two forms of rental systems in industrialized societies: dualist and unitary (Kemeny, 1995). In dualist societies the non-profit housing sector tends to be 'residualised' and does not compete directly with the mainstream housing market. Such societies normally feature mass home ownership. This model can be aligned with privatistic, economically liberal societies which seek to provide some minimal safety-net while maintaining the integrity of market relations in the mainstream housing sector. Unitary societies have 'integrated' housing systems where state subsidized and not-for-profit housing compete directly with the private housing sector. In this way the government is able to maintain control of the housing market and distribute housing on a more universally equitable basis. This is considered characteristic of collectivist, social democratic as well as some corporatist societies, normally featuring a developed social rental housing sector. In Kemeny's estimations, dualist societies will have less developed welfare systems and unitary societies well-developed ones, with housing systems as determining factors.

Kemeny's theoretical approach to divergence between capitalist societies embeds the ideology of privatism and home ownership more directly with social structures and hegemonies. Esping-Andersen's approach to power is neo-Gramscian, based on the formation of coalitions where ideological elements are important in the struggle between the left and the right to achieve a hegemonic position. Within this theorization hegemonies are formed through the struggle for leadership, which may take different forms and be more or less comprehensive. Most central in Esping-Andersen's approach to power and hegemony, therefore, are labour movements and corporate coalitions. Kemeny's approach to hegemony focuses, however, on dominant ideologies and modes of discourse in understanding differences between social and welfare trajectories.

Abercrombie et al. (1980, 1986), identified a break down in ideology as a unified and dominant force, instead asserting dominant 'modes of discourse' as critical, not in creating or sustaining an economy or social structure, but in giving it a certain shape by constituting the economic subject in a particular way. Following this approach, Kemeny (1992) addresses the relationship between ideology and hegemony in supporting the social structures that constitute the basis of welfare regimes in terms of modes and multiple discourses in power relations, rather than the relative force and fragmentation of the political left and the political right. Divergence between societies is thus better understood in terms of the establishment of a dominant ideology and associated modes of discourse. These discourses frame and delimit the major social, cultural and political debates within a society, and act as guidelines for the social constructions of institutions. On this basis, Kemeny identifies a process of divergence between societies where either individual or collective based modes of discourse are possible, and modes of discourse can provide the means for the emergence of different kinds of social structure (pp. 86–89).

While Kemeny's model of ideology appears hegemonic, it embeds ideological processes more strongly in the lifeworld, where the organization of residence and tenure enhances or reinforces privatistic or collectivist modes of discourse and practice, and constitutes a basis from which privatistic or collectivist hegemonies and social organization emerge. Variation in the orientation of housing and household provision towards family, market or state thus plays a significant role in the formation of hegemonies which drive welfare regimes. This is not to say housing and tenure are the most important factors or are simple dimensions, but that they play influential roles. Home ownership plays an evident role, for example, in discourses of individualism, autonomy, self-reliance and consumption aligned to the ideologies of liberal welfare regimes. In terms of the formation of a political hegemony therefore, power is reliant on the ability to establish modes of discourse where ideologies attached to residential organization play a significant part. This is an important departure from 'labour movement' approaches to welfare regimes. Indeed, for Kemeny, the tenure dimension may have multiple effects on social structures and hegemonic practices in the way it organizes living and social space.

> It profoundly affects, for example, the balance between public and private space (for example, parks and gardens), between public and private modes of transport and between domestic and wage labour female roles. This suggests that the single difference between societies of the predominance of one dwelling type over another can have such profound consequences for the social organisation of everyday life that this fact alone could possibly constitute the basis for understanding divergence between industrial societies. (p. 124)

Kemeny's approach to ideology (2005) has recently taken another turn as he has begun to entertain the idea that changes in welfare systems may affect approaches to owner-occupation in corporatist and social democratic societies where home ownership may increasingly be seen as a good investment against potential pension and welfare shortfalls in old age. This turns the original approach to ideology, where privatistic ideologies and modes of discourse lead to particular sets of housing tenure and welfare relations, on its head.

Kemeny's consideration of social structure, hegemony, welfare regimes and tenure patterns elevates the role of housing and ideology in the understanding of divergence in welfare systems and policy regimes. Divergence between societies can be understood in terms of regimes which generate systems, but the hegemonies which form the basis of welfare regimes are maintained in more complex and dynamic ways, where housing tenure and housing relations, along with other practices and discourses, have as much of a role as labour movements and corporate relations. Indeed, we can consider housing along with other modes of discourse in the development of different kinds of subjectivity and social practices which bear on different types of social structure.

Housing tenure and welfare regime divergence

While Kemeny's approach to housing tenure, welfare and ideology and Esping-Andersen's welfare regimes do not align, much has been made about the relationship between welfare regimes and housing systems. It is easiest to draw a line between Esping-Andersen's liberal regime and Kemeny's dualist societies dominated by home ownership. The main elements of classic liberal ideology: individual freedom, individual property rights and individual responsibility, lead to the assumption that in a liberal regime private home ownership will be the preferred form of housing tenure (see Lipset, 1991; Barlow and Duncan, 1994; Kurz and Blossfeld, 2004). Free markets lie at the core of economic liberal principles that assert that markets should operate without restriction in order for both economy and society to flourish. Indeed, we do see high levels of home ownership (between 65 and 70 percent) and strongly reinforced policy mechanisms which support market relations in the provision of housing in countries like Britain, the United States and Australia, identified as liberal regimes. Nevertheless, housing markets in liberal economies are not truly free as they are regulated as social institutions by rules such as private property, which are enforced by the state. Indeed the state intervenes substantially in the owner-occupied market by regulating supply and price of land or subsidizing housing costs via tax relief, and so on (Barlow and Duncan, 1994). The main point, however, is that there is considerable alignment in terms of home ownership and privatistic modes of discourse, and liberal regimes.

In social democratic regimes we should generally expect little private ownership as central to collectivist ideology is the belief that housing costs should be re-distributed in order to guarantee good housing conditions for all households. Essentially, housing should be de-commodified so that labour market position becomes less important for attaining a decent housing standard (Kurz and Blossfeld, 2004, p. 10). Nevertheless, de-commodified housing provision can be achieved, in theory, through private home ownership so long as it is subsidized on the basis of equity. Moreover, as land and house-prices are highly regulated in social democratic societies, we should expect home ownership to be accessible to all social classes. There is an assumption within collectivist ideologies however, that home ownership erodes the solidarity of labour movements. Consequently, social democratic parties in Europe have historically favoured rental or cooperative housing over private ownership (Häusermann and Seibel, 1996).

It is most difficult to make predictions concerning welfare and housing systems in corporatist regimes and owner-occupation rates vary from 42 per cent in Germany to 54 per cent in France to 70 per cent in Belgium. One of the features of this regime type is that neither individualistic nor collectivistic hegemonies achieve dominance. However, we may expect more state involvement in public and private renting than we would in a liberal regime (Kurz and Blossfeld, 2004).

The analysis of housing across Western societies illustrates a number of inconsistencies in the relationships between regimes and housing systems. Kemeny (1992) suggests that there is not a simple one-to-one relationship between welfare regimes and housing tenure, which vary considerably in terms of degrees of collectivism and de-commodification. Housing is an unusual element in the welfare mix because of the way it straddles the state and the market, and because vested market interests are more prominent (Torgersen, 1987). While housing has been under-represented in the comparative analysis of welfare systems because it fails to fit neatly, it is arguably the way that housing intersects both markets and welfare, and the structure of collectivism and privatism, which make it more central.

Kemeny (2006) attempts to identify how Esping-Andersen's regime typology can be modified with reference to features of housing markets and power systems. Kemeny's critique points to a mis-categorization of some corporatist regimes as social democratic. This point is based on the use of 'labour movement theory' in contrast to 'corporatist theory'. Within corporatist theories of power, societies such as Norway, Sweden, Denmark and Finland rank very highly as corporatist regimes (see Lijphart and Krepaz, 1991), which are categorized as social democratic within Esping-Andersen's approach. For Kemeny it is more appropriate to subdivide the corporatist group to include social democratic societies, with the stalemate among the blocks of state, labour and capital being considered in more dynamic terms. The balance of power between the blocks can result in numerous forms of compromise, one of which can be a 'labour-led corporatism', which fits Esping-Andersen's category of social democratic where workers have a relatively strong position, another can be 'capital-led corporatism'. The difference between corporate societies becomes move variable in terms of the direction of the power balance and how strongly it leans (p. 8).

The difference between regimes based on tenure thus becomes more consistent. Corporate and social democratic regimes demonstrate variations in the structure of integrated rental housing systems, where the owner-occupied sector may vary in size and influence depending on the relative influence of capital or labour within the corporate compromise. This approach may explain high levels of home ownership in countries like Norway, often considered social democratic, with owner-occupation rates around 80 per cent. Home ownership may represent, in societies with broad subsidies and easy access to owner-occupation, a 'strong' approach to housing welfare. The tenure balance within social democratic and corporatist societies may thus be more influenced by the balance of ideologies and housing system pathways than by the level of commitment to welfare states.

The consideration of welfare regimes and housing systems so far has aimed to illustrate connectivity between them transnationally. The point is not to reduce understanding of advanced industrialized societies into camps of either privatistic, economically liberal homeowner societies on one hand, or more collectivistic, social democratic, rental orientated societies on another. Indeed, some corporatist and social democratic countries (for example, Belgium and Norway) have very high rates of owner-occupation, while many liberal, home ownership orientated societies (like Britain and Ireland) have in the past had strong rental sectors and more social approaches to housing subsidy. Rather, the point is to embed housing in the analysis of welfare systems and the structure of different social systems. There is considerable path dependency, and cultural, geographic and historic diversity in housing systems and how they relate to power structures and welfare states. I am attempting to situate home ownership better in the understanding of differences between societies. A specific concern is thesystematic differences between societies orientated towards home ownership generated by discursive ideological processes and the features of welfare mixes.

Competitive states and asset-based welfare

Globalization and competitive states

Following the logic of globalization debates, societies are increasingly synchronizing in line with the expanding, deepening and speeding up of interregional flows of capital and information, representing a fundamental transformation in the scale of human organization. The implication for welfare states and housing systems is that globalization will lead to greater alignment among nation states. There are, however, broad variations in how different countries have interacted with global forces and trends. What appears to be more universal is that economic changes and discourses of globalization have pushed welfare states into a new stage of transition. Nation states have begun to renegotiate approaches to welfare provision along with shifts in the balance of political forces in favour of capital (see Coates, 2001; Cerny and Evans, 2004). The main effects have been increasing pressure for states to be competitive, which has been understood to require reduced public provision and increased privatization of services. For Peck and Tickell (2002) such moves characterize a neo-liberalization of governance and 'roll-back' of the welfare state.

In this section I address the changing international context of welfare regimes and nation states and the implications for housing systems. International forces of capital have put increasing pressure on employment systems and welfare states, which has exacerbated individual exposure to economic risks. Home ownership has arguably become more prominent in this context as a way for governments to shift responsibilities for household well-being onto households. At the same time, households may have sought to invest in housing as a means to build an economic safety-net in the form of an owner-occupied property asset.

Welfare states evolved in the early post-war era when centralized institutions enabled governments to act with some degree of autonomy and enforce a local level of control over markets via levies, taxes, and so on. National governments also had the ability to redistribute market advantages and disadvantages among regions, groups and individuals. Such freedom was central to the development of separate welfare states and practices, and allowed many social democratic governments to redistribute substantial resources based on principles of social equality. However, in the 1960s a period of de-territorialization of financial institutions and markets was initiated. Running parallel with the globalization of financial capital was a globalization of manufacturing capital. This meant greater standardization of products offering greater economies of scale alongside a new international division of labour with semi-skilled manufacturing increasingly moving to the developing world (Levett, 1983).

Since the 1970s the sovereignty and potency of nation states is argued to have been undermined by these new patterns of global economic interconnectedness and supranational organizational relations, with the autonomy of national governments increasingly limited by the complex displacement of powers upward, downward and outward (Jessop, 1996, p. 178). Globalization debates have thus considered the end of 'national capitalisms', which demonstrate characteristic welfare systems and national policies, and have alternatively emphasized the power of financial and economic forces to reshape and relocate boundaries and relationships among countries, cultures and communities.

The perceived impact has been that capitalists have become more active in regime shopping and social dumping, while national governments have had to increasingly deal with the demands of the global system rather than manage their own economies. With capital, technologies and skills being attracted to low tax systems with poor labour rights, the drive to maintain economic competitiveness and submission to the logic of globalization is characteristic of new state ideologies and approaches to socio-economic development. While this has led, in many societies, to residualization and commodification of welfare systems, the deregulation and casualization of labour markets has also undermined the security of employment. There has consequently been an increasing focus on household self-reliance and market based forms of provision. These changes mark a shift in risk from states and institutions, which were once compelled to provide substantial social safety-nets, to individuals (see Beck, 1992; Weiss, 1998; Cerny and Evans, 2004).

There have, of course, been variations in responses to global pressures and differences in the degree to which countries have sought to manage international competition by deregulating employment markets and welfare systems. Indeed, many commentators are sceptical of deterministic, convergence based globalization approaches, arguing that nation states have significant choices (White, 1996; Weiss, 1998; Hay, 2005). States, it is suggested, have often used globalization as an excuse for their own failures or as a convincing cover story for policies they want to promote anyway, and in doing so, may in fact be guiding globalization (Waters, 1995).

In developed countries where the impact of the logic of globalization appears most substantial – normally assumed to be liberal regimes – a key social feature has been the embeddedness of neo-liberal ideology and a globalization discourse endowed with meanings of a consumerist free market world (Steger, 2003). Neo-liberalism has prevailed as a policy imperative as many governments have followed its directives in forming their relationship with the globalization of capital and markets. Furthermore, through deregulation of financial markets, governments have mediated the penetration of agencies into areas in which they previously had no foothold (Helleiner, 1995).

Globalization discourses have been directly associated with developments in housing policies in liberal regimes. For Clapham (2006) policy has been subjected, first, to the logic that the government is limited in its manoeuvrability because of global forces, and second, the need to retain the confidence of investors and capital flows by keeping both tight control over public spending and limits on taxation at the top end of incomes. The effect has been substantial reductions in state spending on housing and deregulation of private housing markets. In the United Kingdom, a focus of housing policy has been sustaining the flexibility of labour markets, thought to increase the productivity of labour and the ability of industry to respond to changing demands. Measures taken involve supply side support measures and withdrawal of selective regional assistance. For Clapham, complicity across political parties with discourses of globalization has, 'shaped housing policy through the creation of a new agenda of housing needs whilst also placing constraints on the ability of government to meet them. The response of successive governments to the challenges posed by the discourse has been to answer the neo-liberal discourses with a neo-liberal housing policy' (p. 62).

A number of writers have emphasized the relationship between globalization and transformations in housing, welfare and work with the growth of a 'risk society' (Beck, 1992) where risks are increasingly transferred from institutions to individuals (Ford, Burrows and Nettleton, 2001; Doling and Ford, 2003). Household security is argued to have been aggravated by the retreat of collective provision and the individualization of responsibilities. Home ownership appears to have become more central to relationships between forces of globalization, the state and the individual as the deregulation and marketization of housing has led increasing numbers of households into owner-occupation. This has made residents more dependent on the housing market and vulnerable to economic fluctuations in the maintenance of economic security. The risks of social and economic changes – and responsibilities for calculating and coping with them – are thus increasingly landed on the individual rather than the state.

Housing is not the only or primary feature of risk redistribution and globalization of economic relations. Indeed, employment structures are more central to debates, and the security of income is itself fundamental to home ownership and household security and welfare. However, for Ford et al., (2001) a direct relationship between housing, globalization and risk, where owner-occupiers are strongly affected by international shifts in interest rates and the availability of credit and so on, is identifiable through housing markets (p. 8). A secondary relationship between home ownership and risk is also notable in that home ownership fits into a nexus of uncertainties generated across social and economic life. A consequence of the restructuring of labour market opportunities and welfare provision has been the shift in the long-standing, mutually reinforcing relationships among home ownership, employment and welfare. All three of these features had securer foundations under the Fordist mode of production, where the security of employment was enhanced by welfare safety-nets, which provided the basis for regular incomes necessary for mortgage repayment and the stability of households. Experiences of owner-occupation have become increasingly erratic and unpredictable with loan repayment failures and repossessions becoming characteristic in Western homeowner societies (see Ford et al., 2001; Doling and Ford, 2003).

Despite the intensification of risk and economic insecurity, the role of home ownership has been perceptually enhanced by changes in employment and welfare, where owner-occupied homes, which function in most cases as the main reserve of household assets, are central to household strategies for social security in case of unemployment and retirement. Ironically, home ownership may have become less stable and more risky due to the same changes in welfare and employment which have destabilized the income basis of mortgage repayment. A significant outcome is the re-situating of housing in life-plans and economic strategies. Doling and Horsewood (2003) consider how the position of homeowners vis-à-vis individual economic strategies have been restructured, where housing assets accumulated over the lifetime facilitate early retirement or provide some financial insurance against unemployment and the increasing casualization of work contracts.

While housing policy frameworks appear to have realigned across a range of industrialized societies towards home ownership, systems of owner-occupied housing have also helped maintain the distinctiveness of policy regimes and welfare approaches. Lending patterns and mortgage systems have remained notably parochial in the face of international flows of finance (Doling and Ford, 2003; Stephens, 2003), and governments have actively intervened in markets in different ways to ensure their development. In some countries, like the Netherlands, the growth of owner-occupation has been supported by state backed guarantees on mortgages and tax subsidies for homeowners. Housing systems in other countries like Britain have been characterized by the intensified development of mortgage products and the privatization of social housing. Contextual differences, differentiated labour market trends and the diverse nature of social security frameworks also contribute to a pattern of diversity in welfare development and social outcomes (see Elsinga et al., 2007).

The changing relationship between home ownership and welfare systems in response to intensified globalization has thus been uneven. What has been most consistent across societies is the role home ownership has played in the reorientation and justification of deregulation and marketization where states have increasingly shifted towards market ideologies. I shall argue that the privatization of housing services and commodities has effectively been a means in many countries to commodify welfare more broadly. At one level, the growth of owner-occupation rates has proved effective in promoting neo-liberal ideologies, where homeowner households are increasingly orientated towards markets and expectations of capital augmentation of housing assets. At another level, it has undermined expectations of universal citizenship rights to welfare goods and services, where individuals are instead reliant on market provision and increasingly resistant to higher taxes and public spending. Socio-ideologically, home ownership has thus provided the basis for the further residualization of welfare provision, as well as the centralization of markets in social and subjective relations. Home ownership has in this way become an important means by which neo-liberal ideologies have restructured relationships among households, markets and the state.

The asset-based welfare regime

In economically liberal, Western homeowner societies, such as Britain and the United States, the idea of an 'asset-based' welfare system has become increasingly central to debates on the restructuring of welfare systems. Sherraden (1991, 2003) points to changes in welfare policy in some developed economies as a shift away from a welfare state to a social investment state, where the role of government is to build up individual capacity. Such state approaches emphasize choice and opportunity, individual accountability and the superiority of the market in welfare provision. They are reliant on the investment of individual households in properties and financial products which increase in value over time, and thus provide a base from which to procure welfare services from the market. The proliferation of individual owner-occupied housing assets is a central target of asset-based welfare systems and fundamental to strategies that reorientate welfare systems in these terms. Considering that more than two-thirds of European and North American households are now homeowners and that house-prices have boomed over the last decade, it has been asserted that governments will turn more and more to individually held property assets in reorientating their economic strategies and welfare systems in conditions of intensified global competition. Groves, Murie and Watson (2007) have argued that Western welfare states are essentially modernizing in response to the changing pressures on welfare systems. They identify shifts in state approaches to housing property and welfare provision in which policy measures increasingly seek to encourage people to fend for themselves in old age through acquiring property and building up wealth through the buying and selling of houses (p. 190).

A particular factor in the shift towards asset-based welfare is what has been referred to as the pensions 'time-bomb'. This is based on two developing features of advanced industrial societies. The first is demographic. The nature of social ageing has become particularly exaggerated as post-war baby boomers head towards retirement. Moreover, age distribution over the whole population will become increasingly and more comprehensively top-heavy in the following decades. The median age of the European population was 37.7 in 2000 and is expected to be 49.9 by 2050, while in the United States it is estimated that the population aged over 65 will increase from 37 million to 75 million by 2035 and to 95 million in 2075 (see UN, 2005). Social ageing is having a critical effect on the economic balance of societies as the working population shrinks and the population dependant on pension incomes increases.

The second feature is determined by the failure in some societies to develop adequate welfare and pension systems to cope with socio-economic and demographic changes. In Britain, for example, since the 1980s governments have encouraged private pensions in response to poor expectations concerning the sustainability, or desirability, of the national pension system. More recently, the Pensions Commission Report (2004) suggested that it is unlikely that the present pension system combined with the state one will solve the problem of inadequate pension savings. Of the 28 million working population, around 13 million were found not to be making contributions adequate to provide for a financially secure retirement. Moreover, while state pensions have not been adequately increased, private pension schemes have not proved effective as hoped. Other factors that have exacerbated the pension situation are the erosion of employment stability and the casualization of work contracts, which have undermined the constancy of incomes and thereby pensions contributions.

Housing investment is not the only means households have hedged or been encouraged to hedge against inadequate financial security in retirement. Pension strategies based on individual rather than professionally managed investments in securities, bonds, shares and so on, have also been central to the promotion of asset-based welfare self-reliance. Nevertheless, while most forms of saving and investment (as well as borrowing) have expanded rapidly in the past decade, house purchase has arguably been central. Governments have been explicit about their commitment to supporting household investment, home ownership and housing markets as a means of restructuring growth, security and citizenship (see Chapter 5). Groves et al. (2007) thus argue that a critical realignment in the welfare state towards housing and assets is underway. While this realignment is not evident universally, a model is being established in liberal home ownership orientated regimes, which may influence housing policy in welfare strategies in a broader group of societies coming from more varied regime alignments. This feature may be enhanced by the sophistication in housing finance and investment products underway in high pressure housing markets, which are increasingly intersecting across societies through international finance networks (see CML, 2005).

The functions of the welfare state are increasingly expected by both states, who recognize the significance of property wealth held by older generations, and individuals, who have decreasing expectations of state welfare services, to be met by the market. Governments well appreciate that a likely response by many homeowners to the pension situation is to look to equity release from their properties. In liberal homeowner societies the nature of equity release products has become highly sophisticated along with deregulation and heightened competition in the financial sector (see Smith, 2006), which has made the wealth tied up in property appear more tangible. Homeowners moving into long-term care are increasingly expected to fund their care from equity held in their home. For Groves et al., (2007) this marks a substantial shift in the overall logic of welfare regimes and citizenship rights, with the state less concerned with the uniformity of provision or its outcome, but still committed to welfare needs being met by encouraging people to take care of their own needs.

> The citizen, rather than being guaranteed a range of social benefits as a right of citizenship, is being reminded that they could afford to purchase these services through the market by drawing upon the wealth that they have accumulated through home ownership. (p. 193)

This does not necessarily constitute withdrawal from welfare policy as the state continues to play a role through providing a new raft of policies which seek to enhance saving and investment in housing and the expansion of the tenure across income groups. The state no longer aims to provide many welfare services directly or in de-commodified forms, but still seeks to assist households and individuals.

The enhancement of individual asset development essentially extends beyond housing but involves integrated measures to support individual asset building. The idea is that financial assets provide routes into other forms of asset accumulation (Regan, 2001). A central policy tool in the United States has been the Individual Development Account. This savings account for low-income households, with matched contributions from public funds, can be used for investments in education, home-purchase and business start-ups (see McKay, 2001). Asset building policies in Britain include the Saving Gateway (a matched savings plan) for low-income households and the Child Trust Fund for new born children (involving a lump sum payment from the government which can be cashed in at 18). Direct subsidized home ownership programmes are also significant and include, for example, the American Dream Down-payment programme in the United States, equity stake schemes like HomeBuy in the United Kingdom, and the First Home-owner's Grant in Australia. Another aspect of policy is market deregulation as a means of supporting the growth and stability of assets. In Britain, Australia and the United States, for example, comprehensive state approaches centred on improving accessibility and efficiency of housing property markets have been clearly marked out in recent years, and benefits have been enhanced by a range of tax-breaks and mortgage incentives (Chapter 5).

The emerging state approach to building up wealth reflects a changing ethos in how governments support individuals over the life-course, with expectations that individuals will increasingly save for their own needs via state 'supported' investment vehicles. In the longer term, the ability to save money in early life to support education costs, followed by the building up of assets through home ownership to provide for retirement, are likely to become more central to lifecycles and the distribution of life-chances. This fundamentally constitutes a reworking of responsibility and risk from the state to individuals in the logic of welfare and security.

Asset-based egalitarianism

It has been argued that the growth of equity held in the form of home ownership has caught the eye of government departments looking for ways to exploit the wealth individuals hold (for example, Somerville, 2005). However, for writers like Sherraden (2003) an asset-based approach does not exploit wealth or negate responsibilities for welfare, but signifies that the way such responsibilities should be discharged should be market based, with housing more entrenched in the way welfare is facilitated. Home ownership becomes multifaceted, constituting a means of shelter, a central dimension of intergenerational transfers, and the basis of other welfare services where wealth is released from property to cover needs. Groves et al. (2007) thus suggest that housing is going from being the wobbly pillar to being the cornerstone of the welfare state.

Sherraden (1991, 2003) proposes that a shift to asset-based welfare is far reaching. He argues that traditional welfare-state services and benefits have perpetuated welfare dependency, whereas an asset-based system could free up and enable individuals to make substantive and life-changing decisions (for example, setting up small business or undertaking training). In such ways individuals gain by becoming self-reliant, tax payers gain through reductions in the need for continued state benefit payments and the economy gains though additional participation in the labour force.

A major criticism of asset-based welfare has been the tendency for property ownership to enhance self-interest and individualism. Some approaches to asset-based welfare however, stress the potential to develop egalitarian goals. The central argument is that egalitarian objectives can be pursued through greater distribution of assets which can promote independence and autonomy (Paxton, 2001; White, 2001). Asset-based welfare involves taking the welfare state beyond traditional notions of a safety-net and poverty prevention, to facilitate a wider dispersal of economic and political power. The key to policy is the balance of personal autonomy with reciprocity and involves strengthening the relationship between the individual and the state. It can thus become a mechanism for civic renewal, reflecting citizen's demands for greater choice and autonomy in their interactions with the state.

Despite these positive appraisals, it is easy to be cynical. The shift towards asset-based welfare coherently follows the logic of global neoliberalization. States face a number of choices in terms of how to deal with ageing populations and pension pressures. Reliance on property ownership and the housing wealth of older generations is more opportunistic than ideal. Asset or property-based welfare essentially constitutes a means by which the reactive (rather than reflexive) responses of governments to global markets are translated into the restructuring and reorientation of welfare systems. It provides a means to re-commodify a whole set of established and de-commodified welfare services under the discursive umbrella of providing the most effective means for serving social needs and public well-being.

The shift from reliance on public goods to market goods is essentially grounded on an ideology of superiority of individual freedom, on one side, and 'choice' and the efficiency of the market on the other. Nevertheless, as Malpass (2006) points out, market mechanisms generally promote inequality rather than ameliorating it. Markets give most choice to those with greatest purchasing power, and least to poorest. He identifies that, 'markets tend to sort consumers and patterns of consumption so that the richest people not only have the most choice but also the best of what is available. The converse is also true...and the poor get the least choice and the worst of whatever is available' (p. 112). Moreover, within markets, risks tend to accumulate most amongst the poor and marginalized. This is clearly evident in housing markets during periods of economic decline or crisis, as it is the poorest or most marginal homeowners who become most likely to fall behind in their mortgage repayments or to have their property repossessed (Hamnett, 1999).

For Clapham (2006) neo-liberalization of welfare approaches in housing and social policy, which reflect discourses of globalization, have exacerbated social problems and inequalities. For example, shifts in housing policy towards market deregulation and privatization are argued to enhance the hazards of poverty. The nature of poverty as an experience that touches a wide range of individuals, but is often passed through, can be referred to as 'new poverty' (Leisering and Walker, 1998). Conceptualizing poverty like this illustrates that poverty is not just confined to members of the lower classes but reaches into the middle classes, if only as a temporary experience. British household panel survey data shows, between 1991 and 2000, that although only 2 per cent of households were below the threshold of 60 per cent of median income over this period, 49 per cent were below for at least one year. The point is that increased exposure and dependence on housing markets for welfare and economic security inevitably makes a great number of households more vulnerable to poverty over considerable periods of their housing career. Recent fluctuations in interest rates in Britain and the United States have brought this issue into focus with a sharp rise in mortgage repayment failures and repossessions, especially among the most vulnerable sector of homeowners in the sub-prime sector.

Convergence and asset-based welfare

There have been a number of issues raised concerning growing convergence of societies around an asset-based model. First, links have been made between asset-based welfare in Western homeowner societies and family based welfare systems in industrially developed East Asia, where housing assets are fundamental to household security in a context of underdeveloped public services and goods. Second, many North European countries with developed not-for-profit housing sectors have privatized or deregulated social housing while improving access or subsidy for owner-occupation. Groves et al. thus suggest a growing convergence around the asset-based model (pp. 198–199).

For Kemeny (2005), in collectivist or social democratic regimes, services for the elderly have been cut back substantially and needs testing has become more stringent (enough to effectively exclude or deter large groups of applicants), which may influence the choices of younger, more affluent households who may increasingly see owner-occupation as a means of self-protection for old age.

> As welfare cutbacks undermine confidence in the ability of society to take care of its elderly in a humane and caring manner, this may force increasing numbers of renters – especially among younger, middle-income households – to look for ways to minimize the looming threat of poverty and deprivation in old age.... Societies with currently well developed welfare systems and also possessing integrated rental markets may therefore begin to witness a shift to home ownership. And this could happen quite irrespective of the competitiveness, size and attractiveness of the integrated rental market. (p. 66)

The comparison between Anglo-Saxon homeowner societies and East Asian societies has some foundation. Indeed, East Asian welfare regimes strongly reflect the principles of the 'workfare state' (Walker and Wong, 2005), and states have looked to support family self-reliance built on access to owner-occupied housing and market augmented property equity. However, there are critical differences in terms of the context and structure of welfare services across this region where providing access to owner-occupied housing, support of the construction sector and economic growth are more embedded with the legitimacy of governments and hegemonic power bases (Ronald, 2007a). The expansion of East Asian home ownership has not followed a neo-liberal ethos of property-based citizenship. Home ownership policy has been forged out of necessity rather than principles of public welfare. Recent trends in social policy in some East Asian societies in fact demonstrate movement towards building up welfare states by establishing more equitable social safety-nets based on de-commodified benefits (Goodman and White, 1998). Indeed, welfare spending and welfare rights have increased dramatically since the late 1990s, arguably as a result of greater democratization and an abrupt realization of vulnerability to economic globalization following the 1997 Asian Currency Crisis (Peng and Wong, 2004).

The claim that North European socio-democratic or corporatist welfare regimes are moving in line with a British asset-based model is most questionable. Boelhouwer and van der Heijden (2005) argue that while the philosophy of the 'enabling state' was developed, whereby people were expected to take action based on empowerment and political rights, which had subsequent effects on housing policies, they are not convinced that the Netherlands, among others, will follow a route into dependency on household property assets.

> In our opinion, there is no direct causal relationship whereby the reduction in (public, government administered) pensions will necessarily lead to an increase in home ownership as an 'alternative' form of retirement saving. After all, there are also countless insurance-based investment products, which can serve to 'top-up' the state pension provided by the government. Moreover it must be asked whether home ownership provides a good alternative to such insurance based products. (p. 78)

Indeed, there is little hard evidence of international welfare system convergence, and even in homeowner societies, 'asset-based welfare' means more as a framework for understanding policy discourses than a precise system type. While Clapham (2006) acknowledges convergent global trends around neo-liberal discourses in housing policy, which undermine the logic of strong welfare systems, he also recognizes the potential for societies to deal with globalization in social democratic terms. This involves offsetting risk, reinforcing social solidarity and enhancing control.

Nevertheless, the assertion that asset-orientated home ownership approaches have grown in influence is more convincing in liberal welfare regimes, and more universal increases in owner-occupation rates and house-prices do suggest that home ownership may be becoming more salient to individual welfare strategies outside of this regime type. Moreover, the capacity for housing tenure differences to widen inequalities in wealth and access to market based services has also advanced. What is more important for the current consideration is that neo-liberal ideologies of market relations are expanding along with the privatization and commodification of housing, which has been influenced by global economic changes (and government responses to them), the contraction of welfare provision, and the ageing of societies. Furthermore, growing levels of home ownership and the apparent gains made by homeowners (seen as better able to provide for their own needs through their property assets), undermine collective welfare-state hegemonies and promote individualized and commodified subjectivities, and privatistic discourses concerning welfare objects and how they are most effectively provided.

Home ownership and the neo-liberalization of welfare

Markets, choice and risk

While convergence around a property or asset-based welfare model is difficult to demonstrate, what is clearer is that home ownership has become more central to both welfare systems and individual strategies for providing welfare. This restructuring is critical. My point is that the impact of tenure relations in homeowner societies is much more profound than what previous conceptualizations of the ideology of home ownership, focused on conservatism and political attitudes, have accounted for. Kemeny (1981, 1992) identified the significance of the expansion of home ownership in the promotion of privatism and its impact in establishing modes of discourse which serve particular ideological constellations. My assertion is that the greater emphasis on home ownership forms part of a pattern of restructuring of both ideological relationships between the state and individual welfare responsibilities and, at another level, symbolic relationships among individuals, welfare goods and markets. Consequently, the growth of home ownership is tied up with changing relationships between states and individuals, which are linked to socioeconomic and ideological transformations.

The restructuring of relationships between the state and individuals in terms of welfare relations in societies moving towards an asset-based system has been rhetorically understood in terms of the 'opportunity society' in which individual choice and freedom should form the basis to the organization of welfare. The ideological basis of this approach, which claims that due to growing affluence and technological change in large scale industrialized societies welfare needs can be met in the private market, goes back to earlier neo-liberal debates in the 1950s and 1960s (for example, Freidman, 1962). However, it is arguably recent changes in housing policy leading to the expansion of owner-occupation and the growth of housing assets, that have allowed discourses and the logic of 'opportunity' and 'choice' to take greater hold, which have shifted the onus from direct state provision of welfare to the indirect facilitation of access to welfare goods and services within a market where welfare 'consumers' have 'freedom' to exercise 'sovereignty'.

Essentially, the establishment of mass home ownership and the augmentation of owner-occupier household asset holdings have enhanced the potential for governments to pursue welfare residualization and the competitive orientation of national economies towards global capitalism. Whereas the contraction of welfare safety-nets and greater orientation to global markets has proven to intensify risk and individual vulnerability, access to home ownership and the equity that can be built up within it has been perceived as a hedge against such insecurities. The function of owner-occupied housing is thus transformed where its relative salience as an exchangeable market good becomes increasingly prioritized over use value, especially when housing property also constitutes a substantial, tangible asset from which to draw other goods and services from the market. In this context, access to housing and the freedom to choose from the market is considered necessary for the actualization of security. Whether or not owner-occupied homes can effectively provide insurance against the risks of economic conditions is highly questionable, and they may even constitute greater exposure to risk.

What is also significant is the restructuring or social reconstruction of responsibility and accountability around the individual for security and well-being. This is increasingly carried out in a context where risk is conceptualized not as a danger but as a calculable feature of contemporary existence that can be embraced as an opportunity or reward. What is constructed as security, opportunity and choice, therefore, is essentially risk. By heightening the significance of housing as an investment-good in a progressively asset-orientated system, individuals become increasingly committed to their stake in the market based system. By relating to welfare needs and their satisfaction in terms of goods and markets, rather than public services and collective provision, the relationships of individuals to the state are increasingly realigned in terms of the market. Essentially, we are talking about the restructuring of economic subjectivity around markets which has ideological and political salience.

For Langley (2006) the governmentality of markets and risk has conjured up an investor subject. An individualization of responsibility and risk is achieved through the practices of contemporary neo-liberal governments that constitute individuals as financial subjects. Such subjects, seeking freedom from insecurity (specifically in retirement), may perceive their self-interests to be served through the risks of financial market investment (p. 921). There is a strong conception of the exercise of power in such an account, but not one that relies on public institutions to manufacture collective expectations or constrain individual freedoms. Rather, as I considered in the previous chapter, it is the ability of the state through the heightening of subjective sensitivity to markets and the individual negotiation of risk, that power is exercised discursively.

Critically for Langley, there has been a displacement in government technology for the calculation of risk from *insurance* to *investment* (p. 924). This displacement marks a transformation in welfare security relations from a more secure basis in liberal states to a more destabilized condition under neo-liberal governance. Insurance and investment are similar in that they calculate and engage with risk. They both conjure up uncertain futures as well as sets of calculable, measurable and manageable risks. However, there are fundamental qualitative differences, specifically in how they present risk. 'Insurance' practices were historically developed to protect the individual from loss or hardship. These practices involved risks constructed through expert probability calculations that could be managed, pooled and spread across the population (see Ewald, 1991). This is in contrast to 'investment' as a form of engagement with risk. 'Investment' practices involve endeavours and speculations in financial markets where risk appears as an incentive or opportunity to be calculated and grasped. Baker and Simon (2002) describe this move as 'embracing risk'. It marks a 'historic shift of investment risk from broad pools (the classic structure of risk being spread through insurance) to individual (middle-class) consumers and employees in return for the possibility of greater return' (p. 4).

Miller's contention (1998) is that there is a political interest in reconstituting the world in terms of markets and economic relations. A 'virtual reality' is created that drives economic expectations, which is made possible because economic models have accrued so much power that they can set the terms of reference. Markets are constituted in terms associated with a particular neo-liberal version of capitalism. The focus of policy and social organization becomes the facilitation of economic models of how markets function, even when this requires greater intervention on behalf of the state. This regulation is primarily concerned with making markets work in ways that conform to particular economic expectations of competitive individualism and economic efficiency. For

Smith et al. (2006), 'it is the kind of regulation that sets markets up as (potentially) autonomous mechanisms which work best when freed of interference: thus politics formats the economy to a template of essentials and fundamentals (p. 88).

Malpass (2006) points out that housing and home ownership have largely constituted the avant-garde of the choice agenda and form part of the logical basis of the 'opportunity society' and asset-based welfare approach. The concept of choice was central to British Conservative governments of the 1980s and 1990s, and also became pivotal to Labour policy under Blair. Inevitably, choice, based on market choice, is presented as a superior way to secure housing and generates bias against non-market based tenures and against alternative ways of offering choice (p. 113). Indeed, the concept of choice is biased in housing towards a particular type of choice: to move from rented to owner-occupied housing. In the case of those who have moved out of social rental housing or have exercised their 'right-to-buy' as sitting tenants, there are not the same rights to sell houses back to local authorities or get back into social renting. Malpass suggests therefore, that housing policy in recent decades has really seen the reduction of choice as privatization of public housing constitutes an irreversible reduction of viable possible housing options for most households to market based ones.

While discourses have restructured orientations towards market provision of services by the state, and consumption choices by individuals, they have also restructured relations between individuals and collective consumption more comprehensively. Malpass (2006) suggests that as choices are made by individuals or households, the process of choosing encourages decisions that reflect personal and private needs over more collective ones. In policy terms, providing choices for individuals is often prioritized over collective choice and the general good. Another way in which market choices undermine collective provision is the way in which they differentiate goods from each other. For Bauman (1998), markets rely on the cult of difference in that consumers are driven to make choices between goods based on their difference from each other. 'Goods acquire their lustre and attractiveness in the course of being chosen' (p. 58). This contrasts starkly with the nature of welfare goods that relate to the sameness of human needs and human rights.

In terms of the ideological impact of home ownership and the role of housing systems in welfare regimes, the analysis I have put forward suggests a deep ideological inter-relationship between globalization, welfare and housing. When considering how globalization is restructuring relations between the states and welfare provision, the structure of relations between individuals and markets become more central. The housing market fundamentally draw subjects into investment and exchange relationships through their homes and serves to focus the realization of household well-being and security through a market lens. The shift from liberal to neo-liberal thus involves a deep engagement with technologies of self that render the social domain economic (see Martin, 2002). Whereas 'liberal' governments sought to promote and regulate markets, 'neo-liberal' governments seek to 'stimulate, promote and shape' subjects who further their own security and freedom through 'the market in general and through the financial markets in particular' (Langley, 2006, p. 922). Home ownership and housing markets have become technologies of individualization of investor subjects in neo-liberal states by which governments make it easier to withdraw collective forms of provision and sideline their responsibilities for social protection and individual security.

Clearly the market and investment salience of owner-occupied housing as well as the contextual security provided by welfare states varies substantially from society to society. It is therefore not my assertion that home ownership and neo-liberal individualization will become dominant features in housing systems and welfare regimes in all societies via the practices of globalization. Indeed, the forthcoming empirical analysis of home ownership in different societies identifies the substantial effects of social context and localized features. The point is that housing is strongly embedded in neo-liberalizing social process and, therefore, housing systems and policy regimes may constitute a significant variable in how each society interacts socially, economically and ideologically with forces of globalization. In one sense, the growth of home ownership across different welfare regimes suggests that the commodification of housing is expanding and that the foundations for convergence around an asset-based welfare system, based on a more neo-liberal regime logic, are advancing. In another sense, owner-occupation will develop along very different pathways in line with different housing, policy, welfare, socio-economic and cultural contexts in each society, and will thus have highly variegated manifestations and relative impacts.

Re-commodification and citizenship rights

While the de-commodified provision of goods and services outside of market conditions has traditionally served the interests of collectivistic ideologies and social democratic hegemonies, changes in housing consumption practices and the welfare salience of property assets in welfare systems has arguably undermined de-commodified practices and supported the expansion of commodified relations more generally. This has inevitably enhanced individualization, and strengthened market discourses and the hegemony of capital, while eroding the principles of universal citizenship rights. Home ownership policy can consequently be implicated more effectively in the conceptualization of dimensions of commodification and de-commodification in each society, which have historically been central to models of welfare states, but which have traditionally excluded housing as a welfare feature.

Contemporary capitalist economies have developed in terms of commodification processes where objects become tradable or commensurable to the market. In order for market systems to function it must commodify these goods, services or attributes that people value (see Sternberg, 2000). Critically, commodification involves transformations in perceptions, meanings and relations. I have already addressed in the previous chapter the impact of the transformation of housing from dwelling to property in homeowner societies, where housing has become monetized or 'propertized' and increasingly represents investment and identity consumption. Here I argue that the commodification of housing has implications for commodification of objects, goods and relations more generally and in particular for the provision and use of welfare goods.

Welfare states, while supporting the interests of capital in the long term (Habermas, 1973) challenge the logic of the market and social relations under the capitalist mode of production. Ultimately, public services and social goods provided by welfare states, which base allocation on citizen's rights rather than performance in the economy, have numerous de-commodifying effects (see Dunleavy, 1979; Offe, 1984; Sherraden, 2003). First, the demands for services and goods have the tendency to keep expanding, eventually stretching beyond the state's capabilities. Second, individual dependency on labour or consumer markets is diminished, thus increasing levels of freedom from capitalism. Subsequently, social and public services have been accused of weakening people's work ethic and incentives to take risks in the private market, therefore undermining the effectiveness of markets. Third, state intervention is argued to undermine the ideology of 'possessive individualism', as social outcomes come to be seen as the result of political measures rather than of individual management of property and resources. Fourth, potential to withhold political support for the ruling government, if demands for goods and services are not met, constitutes the expansion of the rights of citizens. As such the exercise of electoral power becomes more divisive, as it is in the interests of many citizens to elect the party that is most able to maintain high levels of state provision.

However, as has been argued, pressures placed on the competitive strength of national economies by global market forces have undermined the hegemonic basis of de-commodification and collective forms of provision. Governments have increasingly sought to re-commodify the exchange of services and goods. Many states have thus sought to become 'commodifying agents' rather than 'de-commodifying agents' with the dividing line between public and private being eroded (Cerny, 1990). The asset-based welfare state represents a fundamental shift towards greater commodification in welfare relations and, as I have asserted, home ownership lies at the heart of this shift. The privatization of housing arguably performs a central role in the balance between commodified and de-commodified forms. As housing forms the basis for other forms of welfare and social exchange, home ownership plays an important role in restructuring de-commodified elements more broadly, relating individual provision to markets and commodities.

The privatization of housing may thus provide a basis for privatization of other kinds of goods and services to the extent that it promotes or structures subjective conditions open to the re-commodification of services and the dismantling of sectors of the welfare state. Home ownership will normally represent the biggest individual household risk, stake or investment. Once market features become the focus of housing processes and the investor subject becomes the focus of discourse, perceptions of other goods and services also lose de-commodified salience. The perceived growth in housing wealth of owner-occupiers has thus formed the major discursive framework for planning and dealing with events like unemployment, retirement or even relationship breakdown. As Kemeny (1992) identifies, owner-occupier households become increasingly orientated towards private spheres and self-reliant solutions to individual and family needs, and support for more collective solutions to the (re)distribution of goods wanes.

King (1996) also suggests that ownership of housing property has been critical to the re-moralization of individuals. It is argued to promote responsible and independent action through, first, enhancing individual self-reliance and second, exercising individual freedom through markets. Governments have also played a role in extending these principles to broader aspects of political rhetoric and social policy. Citizenship defined in terms of private property links individual citizens to the collective through the actions of the individuals themselves, rather than through the state acting on behalf of the collective. Gamble (1988) identifies that 'a central goal has been to discredit the social democratic concept of universal citizenship rights, guaranteed and enforced through public agencies and to replace it with a concept of citizenship rights achieved through property ownership and participation in markets' (p. 16).

Changes in subjective conditions and discourses arguably provide the basis for a more comprehensive hegemonic shift towards the support of markets and private consumption. As dependency on state provision is not evenly distributed, as many can and will (increasingly) pay for services such as education, healthcare and housing themselves, there exists a dual mode of consumption. The power of the state can be strengthened by playing each group of consumers, who have interests in either private or public provision, against the other (Dunleavy, 1979). By promoting home ownership, the number of people orientated towards private provision is augmented and states are freer to make broader and bolder steps towards less equitable and more market based means of social provision. The market commodification of housing is thus far more consequential than contemporary theories of welfare regimes have accounted for.

Conclusion

While the consideration of ideology has been uneven in this chapter, there has been an assertion that discourses and ideological processes surrounding owner-occupied housing have, in recent years, taken on greater significance in the organization of capitalism around welfare systems. The ideological relationship between tenure and systems of legitimation and power have become more evident within the advancing milieu of asset- or choice-based welfare regimes where owner-occupation and the restructuring of social and economic subjectivities around housing goods and markets have become central to the ability of the state to deregulate and marketize welfare provision and undermine collective support for de-commodified services.

The work of Kemeny has done much to establish the embeddedness of housing systems in the understanding of welfare systems, as well as the significance of the spatial and ideological effects of tenure in the development of individualistic, home ownership orientated societies, on one side, and collectivist rental orientated ones on the other. Housing does not fit neatly into welfare regime theories like that of Esping-Andersen, but does provide a point of departure for a better understanding of welfare states. Moreover, the role of ideology is more developed to the extent that structures of privatism and 'modes of discourse' contribute substantially to hegemonic practices and political balances. Nevertheless, recent developments in Kemeny's approach have thrown somewhat of a spanner into the theoretical workings of home ownership and ideology. While a negative relationship has been demonstrated between home ownership levels and public welfare spending, the direction of causality has been reconsidered (Castles, 1998; Kemeny, 2005). Critically, the ideological relationship between tenure and social structure has been undone. The correlation between tenure and welfare spending may be explained by the effects that constrained welfare provision may have on housing strategies as much as by the ideological effects of home ownership.

Kemeny (2005) has suggested that in societies with higher welfare spending, lower home ownership rates and attractive, integrated rental housing markets, welfare restructuring and the declining viability of pension programmes may lead many households, especially younger and better-off ones, to reconsider housing strategies, expanding the owner-occupied sector. This may vary to the extent that home ownership offers a reserve of wealth that can be transferred into cash when needed and minimal housing costs once the mortgage has been repaid. The implications are that as welfare resources become increasingly tight, home ownership may expand across societies traditionally associated with more collectivistic socio-political frameworks and equitable and well-developed social rental housing systems.

Ostensibly housing systems develop along highly differentiated paths defined by localized features and socio-hegemonic and historic contexts. Subsequently, social democratic societies may choose alternative solutions to growing pension and care costs than risky housing privatization strategies (Boelhouwer and van der Heijden, 2005; Somerville, 2005). However, it is likely that home ownership will continue to promulgate market discourses and investor subjectivities, and that it will undermine the collective bases of welfare-state hegemonies in societies where homeowner markets accelerate and concerns over pension provision increase.

What the embedding of home ownership in processes of globalization and dynamics of welfare states, in the terms I have attempted, does illustrate, at least, is the centrality of tenure in hegemonic power relationships which form vectors in the logic and development of capitalist societies. Furthermore, it has developed appreciation for the ideological outcomes of mass owner-occupation, which are more than socially conservative and more fundamental to how individuals relate to market objects and welfare contexts. The power relationship between ideology and welfare regimes is diverse in that while globalization and neo-liberal discourses may influence state agendas, there are practical and subjective changes at another ideological level, in how housing is procured, used and exchanged, with individuals increasingly and self-consciously subjugating themselves to socially constructed market objects and commodified relations.

In patterns of globalization, owner-occupied housing appears to be playing a growing role in mediating constellations of convergence and divergence. In the emergence of asset-based welfare systems and the international expansion of markets, home ownership appears to function strongly in emerging hegemonic and discursive relations in neo-liberal societies. While it has been suggested that a convergence around such a model is advancing (Groves et al., 2007), there is only *some* indication, in the form of growing demand for owned-occupied property and deregulation of social rental housing, that *some* social democratic and corporatist regimes *may* realign. Convergence has been emphasized more effectively in terms of the newly industrialized societies of East Asia that demonstrate an orientation towards property-based welfare systems. However, my analysis of the role of housing in homeowner societies stresses many elements of social divergence. I specifically identify in the following chapters different pathways in the establishment of home ownership as a dominant tenure among ostensibly similar Anglo-Saxon homeowner societies. Although there are some key similarities between Eastern and Western homeowner societies, owner-occupation is related to divergent structures of hegemonic power, distinct types of welfare regime and diverse orientations towards privatism, individualization and neo-liberal ideology.

5
Anglo-Saxon Homeowner Societies

Introduction

The relative size of owner-occupied housing sectors varies substantially among Western industrialized societies and has often been associated with levels of economic growth and affluence. However, national wealth is a very poor indicator of social propensities towards home ownership (Schmidt, 1989) and the proportion of owner-occupiers in a given society tells us relatively little about the function of home ownership within a housing or social system. Moreover, while the debate on home ownership has a rather undifferentiated concept of housing tenure, significant differences exist in the organization or experience of home ownership regarding ways of becoming an owner-occupier, its timing, housing quality, associated rights and advantages, and social and spatial characteristics of areas where households settle (Harloe and Maartjens, 1983; Ruonavaara, 1993). The concept of 'homeowner society' applied so far in this book concerns a particular model based on experiences in the economically liberal, English speaking countries. In these countries there appears to be some consistency in state approaches to the promotion of home ownership, on one side, and a cultural ideal of home ownership consumption on the other, with the tenure achieving an iconic status.

Saunders's (1990) assertion of a 'nation of homeowners' specifically identified England as consistent with a model of home ownership which has been more or less equally applied to the rest of the United Kingdom, Australia and the United States as well as Canada, New Zealand and Ireland (see Winter, 1994; Perkins and Thorns, 2003; Norris and Redmond, 2007). Even within this group there is substantial diversity in the history, distribution and organization of housing which led to the domination of home ownership in housing policy, sector size and preferences. The concept of ideology in its cultural sense is thus problematic, and the moniker of 'Anglo-Saxon homeowner society' is better understood in socio-political rather than cultural-traditional terms. Indeed we should be resistant to the idea that home ownership has a special or natural place in these cultures and societies (or more so than any other) as home ownership in most cases developed from private rental based housing systems and sometimes alongside strong social rental sectors. What is more unifying among this group of societies is a model of owner-occupation characterized by liberal-economic ideologies and market mechanisms.

This chapter seeks to provide an empirical base for understanding the development of housing systems in Anglo-Saxon homeowner societies. While policy structures and housing systems are critically diverse, sets of expectations and relationships among the state, the market and the individual in the provision and consumption of housing are more comparable. The analysis focuses on the development of policy measures, government discourses and socio-ideological frameworks which have structured the contemporary orientation towards home ownership in these societies.

The substantive analysis focuses on three specific cases: Britain, the United States and Australia. These are arguably the most iconic Anglo-Saxon nations of homeowners and also provide a diverse sample of systems and contexts. While housing tenure research in these societies dominates the international literature, there is also a palpable fascination with home ownership in their indigenous academic and public discourses. Although these countries are connected by the English language and colonial history, what is more important is that these societies have been linked in discourses with a 'natural' predisposition towards owner-occupied housing. All three societies currently have owner-occupancy rates around 68 to 70 per cent and there has been recent commitment across regimes to expand home ownership to even more households. The first three sections of the chapter deal with each societal case in turn. A comparison of differences between ranges of homeowner societies is developed in Chapter 7, in which a more consistent model of Anglo-Saxon market-based home ownership is advanced in relation to other modes in other groups of societies.

A British nation of homeowners

An Englishman's home...

The twentieth century saw the development of new systems of tenure and housing provision across most economically developed societies, with a shift away from systems of private landlordism and towards systems of social renting and private home ownership. Although Britain is strongly associated with strong preferences for home ownership, there has been substantial competition in the long term with social renting as a dominant tenure system. An Englishman's home may be his castle, but any implicit association of this figurative castle with home ownership is a relatively recent development and largely achieved through the ideological triumph of the tenure which has reinforced the advantages it offers over other tenure systems it has displaced. Murie (1998) argues that British home ownership grew due to developing housing and political crises, which, over time, were translated into a deeply rooted ideological commitment to home ownership as a superior form of tenure (p. 79). Kemeny (1981, 1986), more radically argues that home ownership has been engineered through government sponsorship as a preferred form of tenure.

Britain (although there is considerable regional variation), provides an exemplary case from which to identify empirically the process by which home ownership has been constructed as traditional and natural, and politically linked with conservatism, social stability and a particular form of citizenship. While there is an intuitive association between political conservatism and private tenure there has been no strong link between political parties and tenure policy. Conservative governments have, historically, administered periods of growth in public rental housing (in both post-war periods) and Labour governments have not resisted periods of growth in private home ownership. Indeed they have come to embrace home ownership policy as a total policy.

A number of links are made between political discourses and social conditions which have facilitated and constrained the development of housing policies and tenure practices. My contention, as explored in other sections of this book, is that the ideological impact of home ownership is, in the long run, farther reaching and embedded with discursive processes which seek to commodify social relations by reconstituting housing objects and individual subjects in terms of markets. This is arguably bound up with socio-economic and political-subjective changes associated with late modernity and the ascension of the logic of neo-liberalism.

The birth of the homeowner society

At the beginning of the twentieth century the rate of return that could be generated from privately renting out property was sufficient to make it a good economic proposition, and as such – following the logic of economic discourses – it had become the most prominent form of tenure across Britain. In 1914, almost nine out of ten households rented their homes from private landlords and one in ten was an owner-occupier. For the Edwardian middle classes there was a plentiful supply of good quality rental housing and thus little need to take on the level of indebtedness associated with individual house purchase. For low- income groups also renting was the norm although slum dwellings were abundant. Options open to lower-income groups were further constrained by a limited borrowing infrastructure.

However, conditions began to change as the inadequacies of the housing situation became more socially and politically salient. Pooley (1993) suggests that the force behind housing legislation at the beginning of the century was the build-up of discontent about working-class, urban housing conditions. Indeed, the organization of the emergent Labour Party was strongly rooted in campaigns to improve housing. There was also a significant decline in investment in private rental tenure in line with pressure on landlords to meet public health and planning standards, as well the higher levels of return available from other sectors. The introduction of rent controls in 1915 also exacerbated the problems of investment for landlords. Murie (1998) argues that housing at this time was reaching a point of crisis. Private renting was decreasingly viable economically and also failing to meet the housing standards of an increasingly agitated working class.

Political and civil unrest became increasingly and more explicitly associated with poor housing conditions after the First World War. Within political consciousness, concern over the material inadequacy of private rental housing and the political unpopularity of private landlords grew. The coalition government was forced to make some considerable concessions. Initiatives made in housing policy at this time marked the first direct government involvement in the mass provision of housing for working-class people. Both public renting and home ownership were developed as the alternative to private landlords. On the public rental housing side, 1919 saw the introduction of The Housing, Town Planning Act which potentially promised local authorities support from the state in providing new housing for rent. The proposals made to expand municipal housing were bold, but much of the programme was downsized and availability of adequate affordable rental housing remained a problem. Merrett (1979) argues that the draining away of working-class protest in the early 1920s allowed the Treasury to slash the programme (p. 40).

The Housing Act of 1923 further eroded subsidies available to local authority rental housing. It instead made producer subsidies and house purchase finance more central in policy. Local authority mortgage loans accelerated during the 1920s and the majority of dwellings produced were built for sale (Merrett, 1982). Although the government had developed potential to expand public rental housing, a number of factors led to the movement of government subsidy out of municipal rental housing and into expanding the owner-occupied sector.

For the Conservatives public renting housing was perceived as a dangerous alternative. State housing was not likely to be a 'bulwark against bolshevism' as there was a danger that it would encourage the growth of demands for collective and state action (Forrest et al., 1990). Certain attributes of home ownership stood out symbolically. Not only did it appear a means to oppose political unrest, it also implied a different form of civil participation superior to renting associated with the responsibilities, obligations and opportunities that accompanied it. Murie (1998) argues that although many had initially been reluctant, housing modernizers of the 1920s began to articulate the merits of home ownership and associate these with 'individual rights' and 'enhanced citizenship' (p. 82). Murie further suggests that the observation that stable and secure households become homeowners when the quality of service provided in that sector is greater than elsewhere was thus converted into the view that home ownership creates affluent stable and secure households (p. 84).

The main obstacle to expanding home ownership was the inability of the working classes to obtain credit. The state needed to make potential buyers more competitive than private landlords. A system of building societies and other institutions organized around self-help housing had long been established in Britain, but was not equipped to support the mass expansion of home ownership. After the Great War these institutions were developed to form a broader and more universal system of housing property finance, along with a municipal housing loan system (see Boddy, 1980; Boleat and Coles, 1987). In the 1920s and 1930s increasing numbers of middle-class and affluent working-class households could afford to buy, and there was considerable reliance on housing built by speculative builders and finance packages provided for lower-income households. Private housing production increased rapidly, peaking at 275,299 units in 1935. This rate was almost double that of a decade earlier (HMSO, 1939). By 1938 private rental housing had declined to 58 per cent of stock and owner-occupied housing had

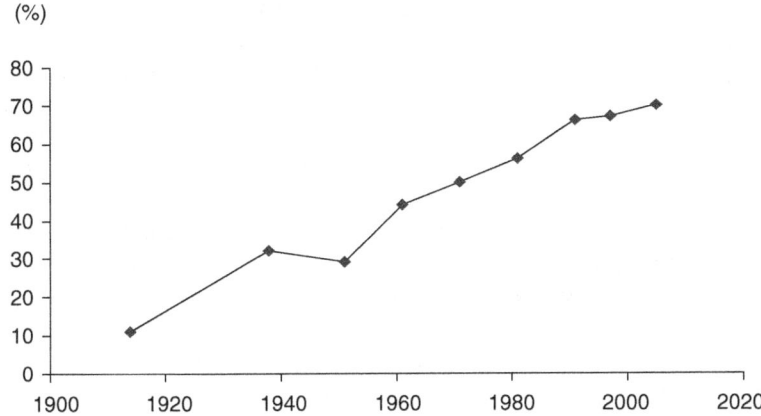

Figure 5.1 UK home ownership rates 1914–2005
Sources: DCLG, 2006.

increased to 32 per cent (see Figure 5.1). Nevertheless, the stock of municipal social rental housing had also increased to 10 per cent.

Post-war home ownership

The immediate post-war period was characterized by massive housing shortages (there had also been a relative cessation of building during the war years with as few as 8,100 dwellings a year being built by 1944) accompanied by a resurgent working class who mobilized behind proposals for a fairer 'welfare state' as identified in the Beverage report of 1942. For Titmuss (1958) the legacy of the Second World War was the creation of a feeling of mass participation and the need for greater social equality. What was also critical was that the consensus and coalition forming between political parties of previous decades had come to an end, marked by a sharp hegemonic shift in favour of a more managed (Keynesian) economy and tax funded, public services that would care for citizens from the 'cradle to the grave'.

Attlee's Labour government established in 1945 called for radical changes in housing policy in order to deal with major shortages. Mass building of public rental housing emerged as the main goal of policy (Whitehead, 1993). Moreover, public rental housing would not necessarily be for low-income households alone. Public housing was a 'merit good' that the state was capable of providing, and rights would be extended across social classes. This ideal was short lived in housing policy as the public housing sector became vulnerable to political and financial compromises and also fitted awkwardly with other welfare state policies (see Malpass, 2005). However, it set into motion the mass expansion of local authority housing provision and a mammoth programme of housing construction. Indeed, by the late 1970s more than 30 per cent of housing stock in Britain was local authority rental housing (council housing).

If the importance of housing standards and provision had been the lesson for governments after the First World War, what political parties were beginning to realize in the early post-Second World War years was the significance of tenure. The development of social welfare by the Labour government constituted a fundamental challenge to the legitimacy of free markets and capitalist individualism, and was a de-commodifying force in labour relations and the provision of goods and services. Public rental housing policy, at this time, constituted an important aspect of social provision, even though it functioned unevenly in the welfare state. It is not surprising then at this point, with the extension of state monopoly landlordism considered a prime threat to the hegemony of the political right, that the Conservatives identified housing tenure as critical to the legitimacy of its position. They first needed, however, to get into power.

In 1951 the Conservatives returned to government, but not without making compromises. Housing was put at the head of the political agenda and Conservatives promised to deliver by continuing the mass programme of house building set up by the previous Labour regime. Macmillan, the new minister for housing, summed up the compromise.

> Of course, we recognize that perhaps for many years the majority of families will want houses to rent, but, whenever it suits them better or satisfies some deep desire in their hearts, we mean to see that as many as possible get the chance to own their houses. (Harold Macmillan, Hansard, 1951)

By the mid-1950s the government, under Anthony Eden, committed itself to the ideal of the 'property owning democracy'. This can largely be considered a reaction the expansion of the welfare state ideology seen as a fundamental challenge to a capitalist hegemony. There had been too much effort on allocation according to needs, and far too little on the side of incentive and reward for effort (see MacGregor, 1965; Harris, 1973). While a property owning democracy involved various kinds of property ownership, owner-occupied housing was a more central and malleable target. The Conservatives first sought to reverse public renting policy by increasing the share of housing built for sale to 50 per cent. Home ownership rates continued to increase throughout the 1960s supported by mortgage tax-relief subsidies and a period of growing affluence across social classes.

Housing became embedded in political discourses in this era and politicians more sensitive to the social-ideological impact of tenure. The Conservative ideal of property owning democracy bound home ownership with an image of family, community, freedom and the interests of all social classes through the broader distribution of property. From the mid-1950s onwards a particular rhetoric in policy documents and government discourse emerged which engaged not only with the economic and stabilizing effects of home ownership, but also with its socially integrative and ontological benefits. Although home ownership had been a marginal tenure only fifty years previously, the second half of the century saw it ideologically reinvented as the most natural, normal and intrinsically superior way to live. The values and practices associated with owner-occupation were increasingly bound together with quintessential human qualities as well as the traditional lifestyle of the British. Significantly, discourses of autonomy, control and freedom also evolved in the reinvented conceptualization of owner-occupation. Kemeny (1981, 1986) suggests that the enthusiasm of Conservatives for home ownership reflects a close affinity between the lifestyle and values associated with home ownership, such as thrift, self-help, the ownership of property, independence and conservative principles. The wealth and financial security home ownership potentially offers was emphasized, as was the connection of the individual to their home and family, which is assumed only possible through private ownership.

> It satisfies a deep natural desire on the part of the householder to have independent control of the home that shelters him and his family. ... If the householder buys his house on mortgage he builds up by steady saving a capital asset for himself and his dependants. (Department of Environment, 1971)

By 1975, even though the public rental sector had expanded to around 29 per cent, home ownership constituted 55 per cent of housing. Private rental tenure now accounted for only 16 per cent. At this point the idea of a natural and innate superiority of home ownership was also reinforced by the apparent economic gains available to owner-occupiers. The property price-boom of the 1970s established a more imminent perception of gains made through home ownership which had previously been closely allied to the point of entry and length of time in the market. Discourses on housing as an investment ceased to be figurative or long-term and instead became a matter of immediate importance (Pawley, 1978; Lowe, 1992). Inflation also helped to create particular perceptions about real values and potential capital gains (Bootle, 1996). Arguably the greatest significance of 1970s house-price inflation was the establishment of the 'enduring belief that home ownership is one of the best, if not the best, investment accessible to ordinary people' (Doling et al., 1991, p. 110). It also gave a taste of 'house-price euphoria' that would increasingly infect homeowners in decades to come.

In housing policy, during periods of Labour government in the 1960s and 70s resistance to the principle of home ownership had been in decline. Indeed there was some cross-party consensus with regard to the status quo of the housing system and a growing complicity with the values of prudence and civic responsibility attached to the tenure as well as the advantages that owning your own home offers in terms of opportunities to accumulate wealth. Moreover, discourse on the political left began to accept that prosperity can be achieved and communities can be improved if people are provided the opportunity to exercise their choice in housing. There were also economic concerns as the government was struggling to meet welfare spending demands and sought to reduce spending on public sector housing. The Labour government's 1977 Housing Policy Review reveals the comprehensive acceptance of home ownership as the 'natural' tenure for most people and the potential of individuals to resolve their house-owning issues rather than the state.

> A preference for home ownership is sometimes explained on the grounds that potential homeowners believe that it will bring them financial advantage. A far more likely reason for the secular trend towards home ownership is the sense of general personal independence that it brings. For most people owning one's home is a basic and natural desire.... The widening entry into home ownership for people with modest incomes will help solve housing problems which used to be faced by the public sector, as well as satisfying deep seated social aspirations. (HMSO, 1977)

By the late 1970s the qualities of home ownership that politicians had attached to it had become normalized in the vocabulary of tenure. This coincided with an advantageous condition in the owner-occupied housing sector. Home ownership had expanded amongst younger households at a time of full employment. Households had had limited exposure to interrupted earnings and there were few retired homeowners on low incomes. Furthermore, there were a high proportion of newly built dwellings and images of home ownership were often constructed around newly built estates where problems of disrepair and maintenance were yet to emerge (Murie, 1998). Essentially, conditions shielded homeowners from negative and risky aspects of the market, whilst a moderately healthy public rental system coexisted by its side.

Home ownership had become bound up with discourses of British social tradition and a particular picture of the home-owning citizen which bore little resemblance to the historic housing conditions of the working or middle classes. There had been no tangible evidence that ownership made individuals happier or more satisfied. In other developed countries, urban renting had become the norm in the post-war era, and there was little to suggest that rental tenants in Germany or Sweden were being frustrated in any way.

The Modern Conservative era

Although 1979 has been considered a watershed year in housing policy, the Modern Conservative era arguably marks a period of radical consolidation of the long standing institutional commitment to home ownership, as under the Modern Conservatism of Thatcher's government housing privatization became a focus of policy. The emphasis of the manifesto was more home ownership through tax cuts, lower mortgage rates and special schemes to make purchase easier. Most significant though was the sale of council houses backed by discounts to reduce purchase price and mortgages. The 1980 'right-to-buy' legislation changed the rights of council tenants in a range of ways and the subsequent legislation of 1984, 1986 and 1988 effectively made right-to-buy increasingly attractive while reducing the scope for local variation and implementation. At the same time the role of local authorities in housing was fundamentally restructured with a substantial loss of stock and control. Right-to-buy over the following decades resulted in the sale of more than two million council homes, while restrictions were put on using the capital from the sale of property for replacement building. Further local housing authority stock was moved into the hands of housing associations. The promotion of home ownership thus became part of a wider attack upon municipal ownership and not just a good thing in its own right.

Another significant measure was the deregulation of the credit market through the 1985 Financial Services Act and the 1986 Building Societies Act, which encouraged new entrant credit providers and increased the competitiveness of the lender's market. Increasingly, mortgages became more available, even to 'riskier customers' (see Ford et al., 2001; Munro et al., 2005), and the association of saving up with a building society in order to one day qualify for a mortgage with that lender was undermined by competition between lenders and the new freedom of loan conditions. Over much of the 1980s, first-time buyers constituted around 44 per cent of all buyers who experienced an upward trend in the amount they were borrowing in relation to the price of the property. The effect was that borrowers often had little equity in their properties. The number of mortgages increased by more than 75 per cent between 1980 and 1999 (Wilcox, 2000).

Ideologically, the Modern Conservative commitment to owner-occupation represented more than an attachment to stabilizing, conservative effects or ontological security. It constituted a more considered use of tenure as a social, economic and political tool that would materially and symbolically restructure the meaning of housing as property as well as undermine decommodified expectations and rights. Again, home ownership had become central in political discourse, but this time its impression on the housing system and the fabric of policy thinking, as well as the national psyche, would be indelible. Discourse and policy sought to redefine normal citizenship and family life and irreversibly embed housing practices with market-based, owner-occupied consumption.

> There is in this country a deeply ingrained desire for home ownership. The government believes that this spirit should be fostered. It reflects the wishes of the people, ensures a wide spread of wealth through society, encourages personal desire to improve and modernize one's home, enables people to accrue wealth for their children, and stimulates the attitudes of independence and self reliance that are the bedrock of a free society. (Michael Heseltine, Secretary of State for the Environment, Hansard, 1980)

The 1980s experienced an exceptional housing-boom and home ownership rates increased to around 66 per cent by 1990 while house-prices more than doubled (see Figure 5.2). Much of this boom was put down to the natural desire of individuals to purchase their own homes and achieve greater financial and ontological security which had been facilitated by the changes made in the structure of the market by Conservative housing policy. What Saunders (1990) found evident was the growing

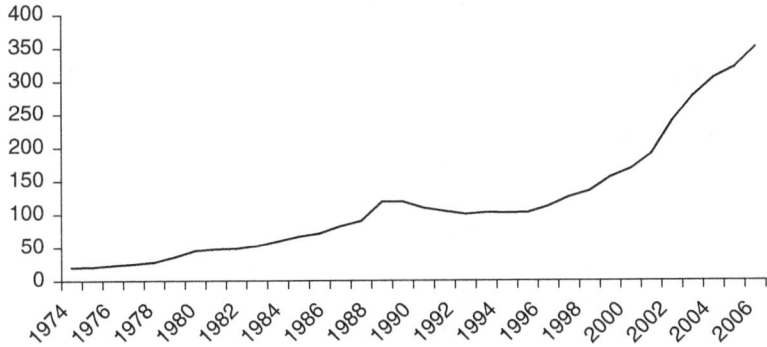

Figure 5.2 UK nominal house-price increases measured as an index, 1993=100
Sources: Nationwide

demonstration of coherent investment and speculation discourses by individual housing consumers in relation to the housing market. House-price inflation had also been associated with the changing dynamics of capital accumulation in post-war capitalism, particularly in relation to 'crises of under-consumption' (see Harvey, 1978). In this case the growth of the home ownership was driven by the relentless search for areas of profitable expansion in an increasingly commodified world rather by rising expectations and changing preferences.

King (1996) asserts that the Modern Conservatives attempted to instigate a particular model more fitting with global trends of late capitalist modernity. This was largely reinforced by house-price inflation and perceived capital gains. The changes in policy and the wholesale support of the transfer of tenure from public to private constituted a total policy where it appeared as if there was no tenable tenure alternative. The effect was symbolic and ideological. Rather than considering housing as a process that facilitates human dwelling, it was increasingly constituted as a physical aggregate of dwelling structures and housing 'properties'. The primary effect of the ideology was the commodification of housing whereby its significance is determined by its economic value and its currency within a market. Housing was no longer a social good that the state was best able to provide, but an object of the market best provided by market agents (Dodson, 2007, p. 75).

While more affluent public housing residents in better quality stock and neighbourhoods were able to take advantage of right-to-buy, for remaining council tenants there were fewer and fewer resources available with more desirable stock sold off. Essentially, the lowest-income sections of council tenants ended up worse off. At the other end of the scale, richer homeowners with better quality houses received most of the benefits (Hamnett, 1999). The outcomes of policy essentially reinforced the reconstitution of housing objects and subjects. Housing users were thus best served as free and self-aware market consumers rather than being oppressed by state imposed mechanisms of provision (Dodson, 2007).

The broadly collective feeling of house-price euphoria among homeowner groups, which reinforced the cycle of over-investment in private housing was brought to a sudden stop by the market crash at the end of the 1980s. Interest rates rose from 9.5 per cent in 1988 to 15.4 per cent in 1990 and house-price inflation was rapidly turned into deflation. Housing property repossessions rose from 16,000 in 1989 to 44,000 in 1990 to 75,000 in 1991. In 1992 households with arrears of 12 months or more topped 150,000. Problems of the housing market and negative equity disproportionately affected the cohorts of households who had purchased dwellings in the late 1980s and early 1990s. The number of property transactions fell from a peak in England and Wales of 2.1 million in 1988 to 1.1 million by 1992. For the next four years transactions remained below 1.3 million (Wilcox, 1997). However, despite housing market set-backs, the normalized status of the tenure meant that support for home ownership in policy and housing aspirations was not crushed. Research suggested that even for those in negative equity there remained a strong desire to own, although aspirations were no longer so closely associated with financial gain (Forrest et al., 1999, pp. 96–97). At the end of the 1990s the cautiousness established in the era of high interest rates and negative equity quickly evaporated and Britain began an even more intense period of home ownership investment.

Although we need to be cautious about making links between macro-ideological structures, political rhetoric and individual discourses, it appears that a key alignment developed between the 1970s and 1990s with a system of values associated with housing and tenure in which the meaning of tenure was polarized. Public renting became fundamentally stigmatized while economic discourses surrounding owner-occupied housing became a definitive feature of individual housing aspirations and public policies. A series of factors including the symbolic polarization of tenure, the advancement of the market and the entrenchment in state ideologies of the importance of owner-occupation set the stage for the development of housing policy for the next century.

The more things change...

The Modern Conservative era established considerable consensus around a form of 'property owning democracy' with two-thirds of housing being owner-occupied. As Gamble identifies (1988), this essentially contributed to discrediting of the social democratic concept of universal citizenship rights in favour of a concept of rights achieved through property ownership and participation in markets. The Labour governments after 1997, headed by Blair and Brown, did little to alter course. Initially, 'New' Labour approaches to home ownership were lukewarm. Indeed, one of the first major steps taken in housing policy, abolishing mortgage-interest tax-relief in 2000 (a process started more than 20 years earlier), eroded the advantages for homeowners. However, Labour policy and discourse soon began to warm up to owner-occupation. Policy documents and policy shifts increasingly located home ownership in discourses of an 'opportunity society', which were reinforced by the apparent affluence generated by the resurgence of the housing market (see Figure 5.2).

Between 2000 and 2005 a series of policy documents and measures set out New Labour's new strategy. The majority of housing policy initiatives focused on expanding the construction of private housing, broadening access to home ownership to more households and further disengagement of the state from the provision of subsidized rental housing. The 2000 white paper 'Quality and Choice, A Decent Home for All', established government concerns with growing housing pressures and the necessity of supporting sustainable home ownership. In 2003, the Deputy Prime Minister's (DPM) Low Cost Home Ownership task-force was set up and was followed in 2005 with a consultation paper with further recommendations for creating stake-hold opportunities for social-renters. In 2004, the Miles Report (UK Mortgage Market: Taking the Long-term View) marked greater involvement of the Treasury with housing initiatives, including setting home ownership targets and encouraging shared equity. In 2005 more explicit steps were taken to embrace home ownership with the DPM Homes for All plan for dealing with housing shortages and the joint proposal, with the Treasury, to extend home ownership by more than one million households by 2011 (see ODPM, 2000, 2005a,b; Miles, 2004). To extend home ownership to 75 per cent of housing has become the objective of Labor policy, which effectively enhances the function of home ownership in the social and economic system.

A key aspect of New Labour's approach to housing is its further marketization, which has in many respects been more intense than in the

Modern Conservative era. The facilitation of the accumulation of housing wealth has become an explicit target of government policy, fitting a more neo-liberal model of household independence and market-based provision and choice. Further deregulation of housing finance has made borrowing cheaper and helped stimulate housing demand and market prices. Home ownership schemes such as HomeBuy, along with other shared ownership and 'affordable' housing schemes constitute a means by which the government has sought to expand home ownership to a wider group of households who would have otherwise rented or have been priced out by market increases. Essentially, there is an aspiration towards enhancing the features of a mass property-owning, asset-based social system (see Chapter 4). What appears significant in government discourses is an alignment with the ideological positions set out by the Modern Conservatives concerning opportunities for individuals to buy their own homes. Even greater emphasis, however, has been put on 'choice' and asset ownership, with Labour, not the Tories, set up as the party of home ownership. This alignment was explicitly set out by Gordon Brown shortly before the 2005 general election.

> The Britain I believe in is a Britain of ambition and aspiration where there is no ceiling on talent, no cap on potential, and no limit to opportunity. And this Britain of ambition and aspiration is a Britain where more and more people must and will have the chance to own their own homes. ... With home ownership expanding into new areas and new groups, today I see Britain as one of the worlds greatest wealth owning democracies where the widely held chance for, not just some, but all to own assets marks out a new dimension in citizenship and makes Britain a beacon for the world. Assets for all, enabling opportunity for all. (ODPM, 2005b)

A central contextual feature of New Labour housing policies and discourse has been the accelerated augmentation in housing property values driven by market activity, as well as a further proportional increase in home ownership. This has been concomitant with intensified deregulation in housing finance, greater household investment in housing and concentration of individual's wealth in their homes. Between 1995 and 2006 average house-prices increased from £65,644 to £199,467 (DCLG, 2006). This has meant that existing owners have achieved substantial nominal capital gains and equity in their homes while potential home-buyers have had to find ways of extending their borrowing capacity. For example, between 1992 and 2002 the required debt to finance home-purchase doubled. Essentially, the market structure of home ownership has been transformed and now involves heavier borrowing and considerable reliance on the market performance of housing property assets (see also Bridges et al., 2004). British mortgage debt is now one of the highest in the developed world (at over £800 billion) and the home ownership rate has reached the 70 per cent mark.

It is important to note that the promotion of private rental tenure also fits within a neo-liberal ideological framework but has been the least successful tenure in the long term. This is essentially due to the critical role home ownership has assumed in political discourses and ideological relations. Renting alternatives have adopted largely supplementary functions in which they support the mainstream owner-occupied system overall. Private renting has in fact seen a small recovery in recent years (from a low of 9.1 per cent in 1990 to 10.8 per cent in 2005) which is arguably due to the effect of over-inflation in the owner-occupied market (as well as the shrinking of the social rented sector) which has prevented many households, who would have normally become first-time-buyers (FTBs), from getting on the homeowner ladder and who remain 'stuck' in the rental sector. Private renting often functions, therefore, as a waiting room for those saving to buy or a limbo for those who fall out of home ownership because of economic failures or relationship breakdowns. In either case it is rarely considered a secure or long-term housing strategy (Knight, 2002).

Public-rented housing has been quite radically restructured into differently managed forms of social rental housing, with large amounts of local authority stock being transferred to housing associations and Registered Social Landlords. As of 2005, 8.2 per cent of housing stock was in the hands of housing associations with 10.7 per cent still under local authority control, compared to 3 per cent and 22 per cent in 1990, and 2.2 per cent and 30.4 per cent in 1981 (DCLG, 2006). This combined social rental sector essentially functions as a safety-net for the housing needs of poorer families. It is a largely residualized tenure and is clearly separated from the mainstream, private market. Many continental European states have effectively sought to control rents and housing cost through their influence in social-sector housing. In Britain alternatively the state has sought to increasingly reduce its role in the housing sector and rely increasingly on a market-based system of provision and pricing.

Emerging features of the homeowner society

The radical reorientation towards home ownership and the rapid augmentation in house-prices in the past 30 years has begun to have destabilizing effects in the housing and social system. An emerging feature within the homeowner market itself has been an 'exhaustion' of home-buyers. In the most recent period, home ownership rates have in fact dipped. This has largely been driven by fewer numbers of younger people entering the market. The decline in young FTBs is illustrated in Figure 5.3. In the past, FTBs made up nearly 50 per cent of annual market transactions. This figure is now down to 30 per cent, constituting a 40 per cent reduction between 1986 and 2005. The total number of English households in home ownership has also fallen since 2005, while the actual number of mortgaged households was in decline between 2002 and 2006 (from 8.47 million to 8.23 million; CML, 2007). Nevertheless, declines do not reflect any change in preferences as the overwhelming majority of households still indicate it as their preferred tenure, which for Pannell (2007) sits rather uncomfortably with declines in owner-occupation among younger households.

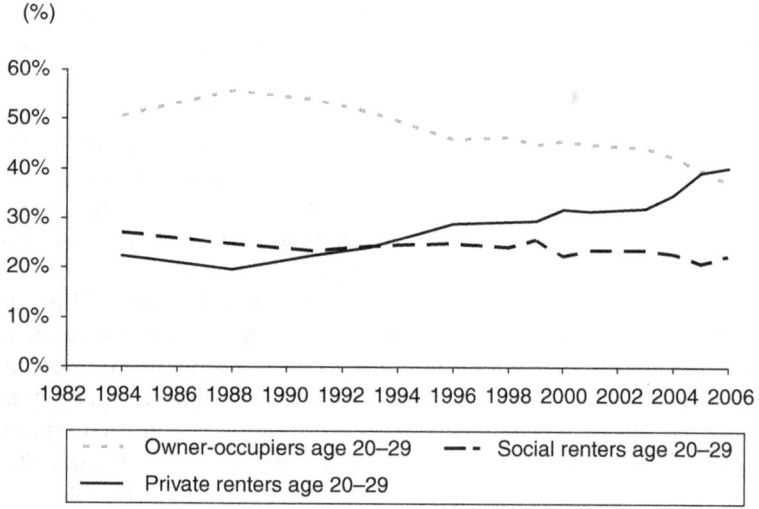

Figure 5.3 Tenure trends of young households in the UK
Sources: Survey of English Housing.

Andrews (2006) explains this fall in terms of how student debt and shifts in income distribution have slowed down tenure transitions. Essentially, many of those born in the 1970s and after have found mortgage-deposits and lending requirements well beyond their saving and income power. Wilcox (2005) analysed the capacity of households aged 20–29 to purchase at the lower end of the market. In the majority of regions, 40 per cent of young adults could not buy at the lowest decile point of house-prices. Many young people, single people (or single-income households), those on low incomes and those without generous parental support face substantial difficulties or may be effectively excluded from home ownership. The desire to become a homeowner, but the inability to do so, has drawn a substantial fault line between younger and older generations and challenges the long-term sustainability of the housing system.

Lenders have engaged with the exhaustion of home-buyers by seeking ways to mitigate risks and get more people into mortgages. New products have been developed to support the changing market and lenders have been switching from simple income multiples to affordability multiples, which look closely at debt servicing capacity, when assessing mortgage applications (CML, 2007). There has been an increasing amount of 100 per cent loans, extended period loans, guarantor arrangements and group mortgages as well as an expansion of near-prime and sub-prime markets (see Munro et al., 2005; CML, 2007). Measuring and managing risk have become central in lending discourses. However, each time lending conditions have improved, more capital has entered the sector, which has simply nudged up prices more and established a new, higher band of affordability.

The inability to enter the market has thrown many young people back onto family resources and has stimulated a rehabilitation of the family economy. Tatch (2006) estimates that 38 per cent of FTBs under 30 got financial assistance from their families in raising a deposit on an owner-occupied home in 2006, up from 10 per cent in 1995. The increase in numbers of parents helping out their children has, arguably, been stimulated by the perception that renting is an inadequate alternative and that children 'must' get on the owner-occupied housing ladder as soon as possible. The costs to parents may be substantial although increasing numbers of older homeowners have been able to take equity out of their own homes in order to assist their children. The dilemma for parents using their own housing equity is that the aggregate impact may render home ownership less affordable overall (CML, 2007).

A vicious cycle may well have formed involving generational transfers of wealth. An increasing number of new homeowners are the children of existing homeowners and are able to make more capital gains through property ownership, which may again be passed on. The government has also become active in supporting homeowners through low-income home ownership schemes, reflecting growing political pressures. Government subsidy has also tended to simply support the buying capacity of lower-end purchasers, pushing up prices.

A significant market feature is an increasing number of existing homeowners seeking to invest in 'buy-to-let' properties. This has involved considerable leverage, and between 1998 and 2004 the value of outstanding buy-to-let mortgages rose from £2 billion to £47 billion (Pensions Commission, 2004). It is estimated that buy-to-let lending grew by another 54 per cent in 2006 (CML, 2007). This sector has arguably become more attractive with increasing sensitivity to potential capital gains and returns. By 2006, buy-to-let purchases accounted for 12 per cent of total purchases, up from 10 per cent in 2005 and 4 per cent in 2002. Second-home owners and buy-to-let investors have effectively extended the limits of house-price inflation and have replaced many priced-out FTBs in the market. Moreover, the resurgence in the private rental sector may be being driven by this dynamic between declining affordability for younger people and the maximization of housing property investment among existing homeowners. A new landlord class is arguably emerging along with significant divides between generations in terms of housing equity and even access to asset-building, owner-occupied property investments.

Brown and beyond

The future of the British housing system is now inescapably bound up with the course of the owner-occupied housing market and reliance on a single tenure considered suitable for all. The domination of home ownership, however, has not been simply a natural outcome of growing affluence and a cultural orientation towards individualism and privatism. There has been clear political sponsorship and active social construction in policy and discourses. This is not to say that this sponsorship has been the only cause. Indeed, there are undeniable advantages and pull factors that attract those who are able to afford it. The issue is that many households, particularly those with low or unstable incomes, have been pushed into home ownership through the ideologically driven policy framework and the stigmatization of renting alternatives. The success of home ownership has essentially undermined the perceived advantages and, effectively, the viability of other tenures (see Chapter 3). This has placed many households and their homes at greater risk to economic fluctuations, and created greater disparities in wealth through uneven gains generated by the property market.

In has not been until the most recent, post-Fordist phase in British social history that owner-occupation has taken on such a central position in the social, economic and political landscape. The Barker Reports on housing supply (2004) and land use and planning (2006) have set an agenda for future housing policy and demonstrate clearly the prevailing institutional conception of housing. The ideological bent is unmistakably neo-liberal and focuses on maximizing the flexibility and freedom of the market in terms of supply and demand. The purpose of policy is thus to maximize market function and housing choice, but the choice has been reduced to one type of tenure. The discursive logic demands that the objectives of sustainable communities and social equality can be principally supported in the housing sphere through enhancing access to home ownership by deregulating the supply and market, and subsidizing purchase for those squeezed out. In his early days in office, Gordon Brown specifically identified housing as central to his agenda on delivering 'opportunities' and a sustainable future. The target is the construction of 3 million more homes in the United Kingdom by 2020, with the central purpose of providing younger people the 'opportunity' to become homeowners.

The idea of housing as a merit good evident in post-war Labour ideologies now seems alien. Some have argued that there is still a commitment to achieve standards in relation to housing and improve general wealth and well-being across society (Groves et al., 2007). The decline in public housing, it is suggested, does not mean an end to housing policy, but rather that the government can pursue its welfare objectives in relation to housing through different mechanisms. It is the ideology of tenure, however, which has arguably framed and guided this evolution. Housing and policy discourses have progressively constructed tenure relations and housing experiences around market objects, which are subject to an economic logic. Relationships between housing and the state, and individuals and housing have thus been restructured along neo-liberal lines. There are inevitable outcomes in relations between the individual and the state in terms of who is responsible for individual well-being and who bears the risks of economic fluctuations. Moreover, the effect of housing markets has been to enhance social inequalities rather than reduce them.

An American home ownership dream

A democratic right

The very natures of rights, identities and aspirations in the United States have long been tied up with discourses on owner-occupied housing. Many European immigrants, it has been suggested, came to the United States to escape the institution of landlordism (see Heskin, 1983). In 1862, the Homestead Act specifically set out home ownership as a prize for those who came to settle and work the land. For Shlay (2006), ideologically, home ownership has been portrayed as a political right seemingly more popular than voting (p. 511). George W. Bush (in 2002) reasserted the significance of the position of the tenure in society, stating, 'owning a home lies at the heart of the American dream. A home is a foundation for families and a source of stability for communities. It serves the foundation of many Americans' financial security'. Institutional discourses have been grounded on the premise that living in a single-family, owner-occupied dwelling is central to a secure and successful life, which for Rohe et al. (2002), is indicative of how deeply seated home ownership and opportunity are in the American consciousness (p. 51). Nevertheless, the modern form of home ownership which developed over the course of the last century bears familiar marks of policy manipulation and economic and political interests. Home ownership only appears to have grown when it has been stimulated by policy initiatives which have been a response to various political and socio-economic developments, rather than being the 'natural' choice of individuals and households.

The US case illustrates a particular interaction between the state and capital with the latter having a pre-eminent position in political discourses. Fears of government intervention are reflected in the constitution which has suggested that the public sector should place very limited controls on private interests. For example, legally, it is only under carefully specified circumstances that the government can prevent construction on private land (Grigsby, 1990). Ownership of land and individual sovereignty are thus legally and symbolically more integrated in the practice of owner-occupied dwelling. Home ownership orientated housing policy has also been considered critical to the maintenance and growth of an infrastructure of developers, financial service providers, planners, realtors and so on, and has thus been politically popular, in part, because of its myriad of constituencies (Buchholz, 2002). Indeed, the maintenance of the economy and the interests of private enterprise have been a central catalyst for pro-home ownership policies that have sustained periods of expansion of the tenure.

Despite rental housing subsidization for low-incomers, there has been strong resistance to the direct provision of public rental housing. Public housing was never developed as a real tenure alternative (less than 2 per cent of housing), as it was once in Britain, and was largely initiated as a measure to stimulate the construction sector, and provided on an unequal and more or less temporary basis for the poor (see Bratt, 1989; van Weesep and Priemus, 1999). House building industries, in coalition with the finance sector and federal government, have successfully marginalized public housing whilst directing subsidy to the private sector (Heidenheimer et al., 1975). Notwithstanding considerable state intervention and the absence of true free market forces, housing discourse and policy has consistently sought to constitute tenants and owner-occupiers as market rational agents

Making the dream

The rate of home ownership at the beginning of the twentieth century was considerably high, but it was not the majority tenure and not characteristically stable. In the first two decades of the century the rate slightly decreased from around 47 per cent to 45 per cent. This was in part due to immigration with populations becoming ever more concentrated in urban areas (Winnick, 1954; Masnick, 2004). Another factor was the affordability of the tenure. Pathways into home ownership reflected a poorly developed system of access to credit and often required substantial amounts of capital up-front (Colton, 2002). The demands of large down-payments (between 50 and 60 per cent) and short-term mortgages (typically 6–11 years) made owner-occupied housing inaccessible to many. The approach of the government to housing was that it was best to leave it to the market, despite demographic and urban pressures and the inefficiency and inequity of the finance system.

The first major political efforts to promote owner-occupation began in the 1920s. The approach was largely propagandist and did not involve considered policy measures to expand access or take-up. Nonetheless, as Vale (2007) notes, 'well in advance of policy initiatives that made widespread home ownership financially plausible, both government and industry had transformed home ownership into an ideological necessity' (p. 39). In the 'Red Scare' that followed the Great War numerous political and civic groups, as well as commercial organizations, began to tout home ownership as a means to politically shore up American society against the evils of socialism and communism. Herbert Hoover as secretary of commerce (1921–1928), and then as president (1928–1932) took on home ownership as a moral issue. The

Own-Your-Own-Home campaign (OYOH), launched by the Department of Labor, was the first major propaganda initiative. Promotional pamphlets were provided for localities that set forth a variety of ways to promulgate home ownership. These included newspaper ads; essay competitions on 'the merits of home ownership'; buttons and badges for schoolchildren; even the composition of waltzes and songs (see Dunn-Haley, 1995). While there were few policy changes supporting the tenure, the government distributed more than 2 million promotional posters to workplaces.

The Better Homes in America movement was inspired by the OYOH campaign, although it was ostensibly a private voluntary organization. Hoover signed up as president of this group, which into the 1930s disseminated information to the public on how to locate, acquire, finance and build a home. Though the focus was 'better homes', the assumption was that a better home was an owner-occupied home. The National Association of Real Estate Boards (NAREB) also became an active lobby group in the 1920s and central to the home ownership agenda. Alongside government campaigns it provided literature and promoted events grounded solidly on a particular ideology of tenure: home ownership built up 'moral muscle' and sent families up the social scale. In NAREB documents and discourses, buying your own home could put the 'MAN back in MANHOOD' by enabling you to be 'completely self reliant and dominant'. Women gained too: 'To install your wife in a home of her own is a convincing demonstration of your affection and consideration for her comfort and happiness'. Once installed, the wife would gain 'the joy of possession that relieves housework of its monotony' (Folsom, 1922).

By the end of the 1920s government sponsorship of owner-occupation encompassed a broad cross-section of voluntary and commercial groups 'all dedicated to extending home ownership, and to keeping the government out of the business of providing European style housing subsidies' (Vale, 2007, p. 31). The booming economy of the 1920s led to a surge in the housing market and millions of units were added to housing stock annually, increasing home ownership rates. The 1929 stock market crash, and subsequent banking failures and economic depression, led to a 4-per cent drop in owner-occupation. In the early 1930s, half of homeowners defaulted and there were around a thousand mortgage foreclosures a day (Listokin, 1991). The 'Savings and Loans' banking system also contributed to economic decline as only local savings could be used for mortgage loans making the supply of funds fragmented. When people stopped saving, with high inflation undermining cash assets, banks had little capital to fund further mortgages. While the government had encouraged as many families as possible to become homeowners, the strategy had been rhetorical and no measures had been taken to offset mortgage risks among a broader income class of home purchaser.

The New Deal for homeowners

The economic depression was accompanied by social unrest and there were again fears among industrialists and politicians of communist activism. The extent of the economic depression required action and provided a platform for reformers to initiate radical interventions that would reshape policy and the housing system. Although housing had not effectively been a state responsibility, under Franklin Roosevelt in the 1930s it became a focus of attempts to realize social and economic changes. With the previous embedding of ideology however, interventions continued to support home ownership.

In the New Deal interventions (1933-1943) the government readdressed its role in welfare and established a comprehensive network of assistance for households across income groups. Restructuring and subsidizing housing finance for home-purchase was central to this and involved a system of government backed mortgage guarantees and greater federal regulation of lending. While there was some displacement of the function of the market, this approach to social welfare sought to support the private sector rather than replace it. The Federal Home Loan Banking system was established in 1932 and the passage of the National Housing Act of 1934 established the Federal Housing Administration (FHA). The 1930s also saw the establishment of the Home Owners' Loan Corporation, the Federal Savings and Loan Insurance Corp (FSLIC), the Federal National Mortgage Association (Fannie Mae) and the Reconstruction Finance Corp (RFC; see Grigsby, 1990).

The new system radically improved the flow of mortgage finance and conditions for borrowers. The FHA guaranteed mortgages and regulated fixed-term low interest-rates, while Fannie Mae replenished the supply of lendable money for mortgages in the primary market by issuing securities in a secondary market. In addition, government insured mortgages established stability and accessibility in the housing system which made 'the dream' of home ownership possible for a larger number of families. As well as guaranteeing loans for home purchases, the FHA provided up to $2,000 in loans for 'repairs, alterations, or improvements' to existing dwellings. In the first three years of the Better Housing Programme, one in eight homeowners received a 'home-modernization loan'. The average loan of around $400 covered projects like repainting home exteriors, installing new heating systems and electrifying kitchen facilities.

At the same time as making home ownership affordable, federal policy sought to boost economic growth and employment. This was achieved through private housing development and also construction projects aimed at clearing slums and building rental housing for poor families. The Public Works Act in 1933 and the United States Housing Act of 1937 established a small public housing sector. The aim, however, was to create employment and support the construction industry rather than establish a comprehensive stock of public rental housing.

Federal housing policy, necessitated by private housing market failure, marked a substantial intervention by the state and eroded the free market model. Nevertheless, a home ownership orientated system based on federal mortgage guarantees provided stability without de-commodifying the housing system. Capitalists strongly resisted the provision of public housing during the depression, fearing it would compete with private rents and house values. To accommodate the private market, legislation required local housing authorities to eliminate a substandard dwelling unit for each new unit of public housing built. In this way the overall supply of housing was not increased, since an increase could drive down rents in the private housing market (Bratt, 1989, p. 56). Public housing was also limited to very-low-income households and eviction of above-income families was authorized. A small amount of subsidized rental housing for the poor thus continued to trickle through, but inevitably the focus was home ownership. In 1950 construction started on only 32,000 public housing units compared to 2 million private units (Listokin, 1991). While the immediate effect of policy in the 1930s had been slow, home ownership began to grow dramatically in the 1940s and 1950s (by almost 20 per cent between 1940 and 1960) (see Figure 5.4).

Rapid growth in the owner-occupied sector was stimulated by a number of policy-based and socio-economic factors (see Masnick, 2004). Tax-relief on mortgage interest, initially introduced in 1913, provided considerable subsidy on investment in housing property. The development of a secondary mortgage market also created greater incentives and an improved credit supply. Government backing of mortgages made the long-term costs of home ownership more affordable to a broader range of households, which was enhanced by the post-war economic boom and boosted earnings, along with other multiplier effects. In the late 1940s low-cost, guaranteed mortgages for war veterans were introduced, along with other services to facilitate entry into home ownership. In addition the first federal low-income home

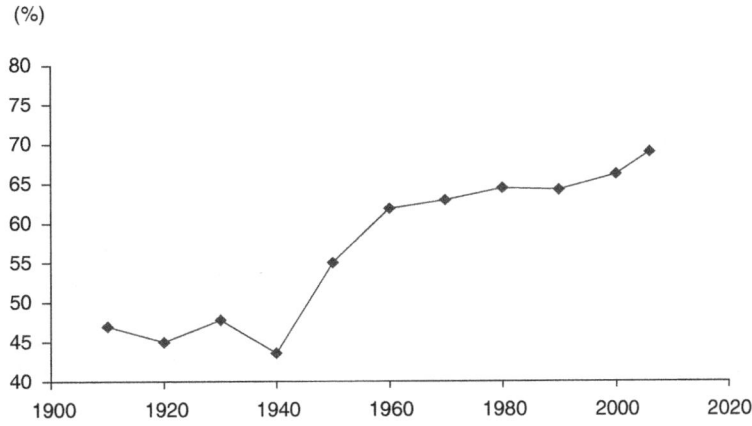

Figure 5.4 US home ownership rates 1910–2006
Sources: US Census Bureau.

ownership programme was inaugurated (Section 502) but was only targeted at rural areas.

The opening up of cheap land through improvements and reduced costs in transport and infrastructure effected housing consumption along with improved access to suburban development. Housing demand was further enhanced by changes in family formation in the baby-boom period. Slum clearance and urban renewal also diminished the availability of affordable rental housing in urban areas. This combination of push and pull factors fundamentally reshaped housing around a modern form of suburban home ownership fitting with a post-war image of family life and civic participation.

The 1950s thus marked the beginning of majority home ownership and the socio-cultural consolidation of the tenure in social discourses. The ideology embedded before the depression concerning the superiority of home ownership was restored, although post-war discourses were not so naive concerning financial risks. The association of social problems with bad housing in rental districts also helped re-embed tenure perceptions. Vale (2007) argues that the legacy of the pre- and early post-war promotion of home ownership has been the establishment of an enduring fantasy among citizens and policy makers that the only thing thwarting the United States from becoming a nation of 100 per cent homeowners inheres in the 'character flaws' and lack of 'responsibility' of low-income households (p. 40).

The War on Poverty

Despite the embedding of home ownership ideology, the tenure expanded by only a few per cent between 1960 and 1990. Although programmes were developed and the tenure was supported, home ownership was no longer considered the primary means to improve social conditions, especially for low-income, urban households. The interaction of social and economic transformations in public policy in the 1960s largely enhanced the stability of rental housing and there was a marked shift in the focus of government subsidy and approaches to welfare housing policies. Demographic pressures included rising numbers of single-only and single-parent households, following changes in divorce and family formation, which led to greater urban pressures. Another critical feature of the 1960s was socio-political unrest and growing demands for civil rights. Government discourses began to address the need to improve social equity and the quality of life in central city neighbourhoods, especially for black communities. A 'War on Poverty' was set out which, among other things, incorporated improving housing conditions. The approach involved federal subsidization of both home ownership and rental alternatives.

Home ownership in the 1960s continued to be fuelled by the long-term, low-interest mortgages of the federal housing loan system and sweetened by mortgage-interest tax deductions, but primarily enjoyed by white, middle-income households. Black households found entry to home ownership particularly difficult due to institutional prejudices in lending practices where home-loans in black and mixed race inner-city neighbourhoods were redlined (see Masnick, 2004). This led to a declining representation of racial minorities in the owner-occupied sector (see Table 5.1). Following

Table 5.1 Home ownership rates by race in the United States

Race	%
Non-Hispanic whites	74.3
African-Americans	48.0
Hispanic Americans	47.6
Asian-Americans and others	53.7

Source: US Census Bureau, 2007.

concerns about poverty and racial unrest, along with ideologically charged assumptions that the expansion of home ownership creates a more loyal citizenry and generates social, political, economic changes in neighbourhoods, the Section 235 of the 1968 Housing and Urban Development Act was introduced to expand urban owner-occupation among low-income and racial minority families. It constituted a major federal initiative and between 1969 and 1979 helped some 500,000 households buy their own homes.

The programme was introduced under the Housing and Urban Development Act of 1968 and provided subsidies to reduce interest rates on privately originated home mortgages. The necessary size of deposits was also substantially reduced for the households who qualified. These conditions opened home ownership to thousands of households that had been effectively excluded by financial constraints. Section 235 also had the support of the private house building industries and other private constituencies and service providers. However, shortly after the programme went into operation it became evident that the role of the private sector and the responsibilities of the department of Housing and Urban Development (HUD) were insufficiently thought out and poorly aligned. It became evident in the first few years that there was an inadequate provision of counselling services, uneven funding commitment, ineffective management or spread of risk, and some rather unscrupulous activities among agents and private sector actors (see Bratt, 2007). By 1979, around 90 thousand federally supported loans (18 per cent of the total) had been foreclosed. As a measure to expand access to home ownership, Section 235 is remembered as somewhat of a failure and it was inevitably cut in 1987.

Federal rental housing subsidy, however, faired considerably better. A limited programme of subsidized rental housing had grown after the war as part of the process of urban renewal, and as a free market housing policy had poorly served the needs of renters. By 1960, 425,000 subsidized rental housing units were being constructed annually. In 1961 Kennedy signed the Housing Act in to law which created the first FHA insured programme for low-income rental housing. Rental housing subsidies initially took the form of interest rate relief for non-profit and limited-profit organizations on the construction of rental housing for 'moderate-income' families. Essentially, policy sought to assist the construction industry, the underdevelopment of which was thought to be the cause of poor housing conditions and inadequate rates of production. Subsidized rental construction expanded rapidly, and by 1975 2.4 million rental units for low-income households were being constructed annually. Beneficiaries were low-income households who were not poor enough to qualify for the very limited supply of public housing. Despite state support, the social rental sector remained a residual one (see Grigsby, 1990; van Weesep and Priemus, 1999). Subsidization of housing construction was extended to for-profit building companies as well as the home-owner sector in 1968.

In the early 1970s, approaches to rental subsidy began to move to users. As urban housing problems were considered ostensibly overcome, policy discourses asserted that the market would now be capable of meeting housing needs with subsidized low-income households functioning as market actors. In 1974, following some experimental programmes run by the HUD, 'Section 8' housing vouchers were introduced (later to become the Housing Choice voucher). Subsequently, qualified low-income applicants who could find standard accommodation in the private sector were reimbursed for the difference between an administratively determined 'fair market rent' and the amount they were deemed able to afford.

Federal support and mortgages markets

What unified rental and owner-occupied housing subsidy approaches of the 1960s and 1970s was the way in which low-income families were treated as rational market subjects, which legitimized market solutions. Housing received considerable federal subsidy, yet individual recipients still had to operate in markets and deal with private agents and providers. In the private owner-occupied market the government was also active in manipulating conditions. The rise in interest rates to double figures in the 1970s, and the slow-down in the flow from savings into the mortgage market constituted a threat to the housing system. The government consequently extended the role of federal finance organizations.

Capital shortage problems in the 1930s had been the rationale for establishing a federal housing loan system. The government then introduced a package of measures including fixed-rate fully amortized mortgages. Mortgage securitization also made it possible for other financial institutions to buy mortgage loans in a secondary mortgage market which facilitated a broader flow of capital. Fannie Mae held a virtual monopoly on the secondary mortgage market after its inception in 1938, and was made into a private corporation in 1968, with responsibilities for guaranteeing government-issued mortgages transferred to the Government National Mortgage Association, (Ginnie Mae). In 1970, the Federal Home Loan Mortgage Corporation (Freddie Mac) was introduced in order to further develop the secondary market.

While Fannie Mae guaranteed loans which were then securitized into mortgage-backed security bonds, Freddie Mac bought mortgages on the secondary market, pooled them and sold them on as mortgage-backed securities (MBS) to investors on the open market.

Although these institutions became independent and their operations have become more convergent, they are classed as Government Sponsored Enterprises (GSEs), and as such pay lower interest rates compared to other financial institutions. This is because of the assumption 'in the market' that the government will step in if there are any difficulties (Poole, 2003). They can thus offer lower MBS interest rates with advantages passed on to borrowers through cheaper and securer mortgages (see also Haffner, 2005). The regulation and standardization of housing finance was considered to be at the heart of the efficient mortgage system. However, state sponsorship appears more central to practices of securitization than market competition (Poole, 2003). The federal mortgage system has effectively subsidized the owner-occupied housing system and undermined the free market, but in ways that have maintained market relations.

The revival of home ownership policy

The post 1960s period is characterized by an economic and social polarization in the housing sector. Further house-price inflation motivated those who could afford it to purchase their own homes and invest in moving up the housing ladder into bigger and more expensive housing (Masnick, 2004, p. 310). However, it was increasingly difficult for many poorer households to afford down-payments and monthly repayments generated by the inflating market. The types of low-income households who had become homeowners in the 1940s and 1950s found entry conditions much more adverse. While securitization was a success, the 1980s witnessed a marginal decline in home ownership (by 0.2 per cent). It seemed that although homeowners were considerably subsidized there was no significant movement into the tenure. Meanwhile, urban rental neighbourhoods remained segregated and were increasingly occupied by marginal and low-income families.

Housing tenure had begun to form a key dimension of social inequality, with homeowners benefiting from tax deductions and gains on their property while urban social rental housing became increasingly stigmatized. In the 1990s, however, inequalities generated by tenure differences were rediscovered in political discourses, which drove a realignment of policy around home ownership. The discourse asserted that the solution to urban problems and social inequalities generated by tenures was not to restructure inequalities between tenures, but to expand home ownership to include more and more low-income and non-white households.

In 1990, interest in low-income home ownership policy was revived by the HOPE programme (Home Ownership and Opportunity for People Everywhere). It particularly provided opportunities for residents in public and project based subsidized rental housing to buy their own homes, and was partly inspired by the 'success' of the right-to-buy policies in the United Kingdom. It inevitably had a limited impact as the scale of social rented housing was so small already and subsequently offered home ownership opportunities to the households least able to afford it (see Bratt, 2007). The major policy realignment which had a substantial impact came with the Clinton administration in the early 1990s. The governments' desire to increase the overall home ownership rate was set out clearly in the open letter sent to the HUD secretary. There was also an evident ideological appreciation of home ownership as a means to achieve social equality and social inclusion in the 'American dream'.

> Today I am requesting that you lead an effort to dramatically increase home ownership in our nation over the next six years.... Your program should include strategies to ensure that families currently underrepresented among homeowners – particularly minority families, young families, and low-income families – can take part in the American dream (letter from Bill Clinton to HUD secretary Henry Cisneros, 3 November 1994).

The approach was, as usual, ostensibly market based and sought to enhance the stability and affordability of owner-occupied housing. The programme had four goals for home ownership: to make it more affordable, to eliminate barriers to it, to enable families to better manage responsibilities and rewards, to make it easier to complete the paperwork involved in buying your own home (US Department of Housing and Urban Development, 1994). Fannie Mae, the FHA and Freddie Mac were brought on board a programme which aimed to lower required down-payments and recognize multiple income sources in qualifying for a housing loan. The programme also sought to end discrimination in marketing and lending which had led to highly differentiated rates of black and white home ownership. The policy focus did not involve radical reform in funding or legislation, but sought to address issues of access for lower-income groups who had normally been excluded from the housing market. It also involved vigorously enforcing fair housing and banking laws that were already on the books (Frey, 2001). The target was to increase home ownership to a rate of 67.5 per cent by 2001. The level actually reached 67.8 per cent. The increase was especially strong for minorities. Underlying the logic of policy and the methods used was the discursive assumption that a main cause of social inequity was the inability of households to build wealth and assets (see Retsinas and Belsky, 2005). Housing policy was thus linked to a broader agenda that sought to help families build up their savings and transfer them into other sorts of assets.

The Bush administration at the beginning of the twenty-first century embraced home ownership, placing it even more centrally in political and policy agendas. The policy also followed the principles of social inclusion of the Clinton initiatives. As well as increasing low-income owner-occupation generally, a particular aim was to increase minority home ownership by 5.5 million families by 2010. The integration of the ideal of home ownership with the natural rights of citizens and the objective of social inclusion was again explicit.

> The goal is that everybody who wants to own a home has got a shot at doing so. The problem is that we have what we call a home ownership gap in America. Three quarters of Anglos own their own homes, and yet less than 50 percent of African-Americans and Hispanics own homes. That ownership gap signals that something might be wrong in the land of plenty. And we need to do something about it. (George W. Bush, June 2002)

The approach of the Republicans was arguably more interventionist and subsidy orientated than that of the Democrats. The American Dream Down-payment Act (ADDA) was introduced in 2002. Measures specifically addressed the high cost of individual down-payments by attempting to reduce this burden on low-income families. The fund established with this Act sought to subsidize access to home ownership for 40,000 low-income families annually. Non-white families were a particular target. Concomitant measures taken on the supply side included $2.4 billion tax credit for developers to build affordable single-family housing as a means to deal with the lack of affordable housing units. Another element of the policy involved addressing the complexity of purchase, with efforts made to find means to educate FTBs and protect them against unscrupulous lenders. A further measure was extra funding for Self-help Home ownership Opportunity Programmes (SHOP). This assistance scheme for non-profit, community organizations (for example, Nehemiah and Habitat for

Humanity who have been operating since the 1970s) provides land and resources for families willing to contribute their own 'sweat equity' in order to become homeowners.

Under the Bush administration house-prices and owner-occupancy rates boomed and by 2004 home ownership rates had reached 69.2 per cent. In 2006 policy was developed further in order to greater augment the scope of the tenure through the Expanding American Home ownership Act, which provides the FHA with increased flexibility for mortgage down-payment requirements and tailored housing finance. In the summer of 2007 there was however, a fundamental crash in the sub-prime housing finance sector which to a large extent derailed policy approaches to expanding home ownership. The rate of sub-prime borrowing advanced rapidly in the 1990s to around $2.1 billion annually (see Hurd and Kest, 2003; Munro et al., 2005). Sub-prime borrowers are usually those who are refused access to federally discounted, fixed-rate mortgages (often because of low or insecure incomes, or poor credit ratings) and are forced to borrow at excessive interest rates (on 'exotic' loans). Following interest rate increases the number of foreclosures on sub-prime and other stretched borrowers began to balloon in 2007. The subsequent panic in financial markets revealed a broad network of bad debt mediated by sub-prime securitization reaching across global financial systems. The FHA responded by enhancing its refinancing programme for an estimated 240,000 households who were in default on their loans. Measures taken, however, have only covered households with good credit histories.

Waking up from the dream

In terms of the ideological dynamics of housing policy, Shlay (2006) suggests that it is not entirely evident whether federal policy came to reflect prevailing popular culture or whether desires for home ownership became the ideological manifestation of these political forces (p. 513). Similarly for Vale (2007), the growth of the tenure has been neither accident nor inevitability, but rather 'has been nurtured by generations of public policy, which were in turn proceeded by concerted efforts to instil an ideology grounded on the belief in the moral value of the owned home' (p. 15). Certainly, the American dream of home ownership has been historically bound up with a settler-frontier heritage, but is not determined by indigenous traits. The ethical doctrine of the 'American Dream' is itself argued to have emerged as a symptom of loss and identity confusion during the Great Depression (Decker, 1992). The idea that home ownership constitutes a significant discourse in a nation of migrant origin is a more convincing proposition.

While home ownership has always held a central course in the housing system, it has only proliferated when it has been pushed by government manufactured incentives and where conditions have been favourable. In the 1990s and 2000s the tenure has become central to government discourses and the direct target of subsidies to encourage expansion. This may be due largely to intensified neo-liberalization in socio-economic relations where home ownership has taken a more prominent role structurally in mediating household wealth accumulation in the form of housing assets, which form the basis of self-care and reliance on market services (Sherraden, 2003; Retsinas and Belsky, 2005). The idea is not to necessarily generate greater social equality through housing policy, but to give all, especially those racial communities excluded from home ownership in the past, better access to property assets from which they can help themselves. Indeed, mortgage-interest tax-deduction, for example, disproportionately benefits the richest homeowners (see Bourassa and Grigsby, 2000) and costs the government $76 billion a year (in 2006). Essentially, it supports higher house-prices rather than entry into home ownership. The government, however, has been reluctant to erode the advantages of the social ideal of home ownership.

> My approach to broadening access to home ownership focuses on empowering people to help themselves and to help each other. ... The strength of America lies in the honour and the character and goodwill of its people. When we tap into that strength, we discover there is no problem that cannot be solved in this wonderful land of liberty. (George W. Bush, June 2002)

In the American context, discourses in favour of public solutions to inadequate housing conditions and the failure of the private sector have been consistently undermined by the logic of market ones. The effective mobilization of the vested interests of house building, financing and retailing industries in conjunction with federal governments hostile to public services have been particularly influential. The government has directed massive sums of public money to homeowners through the subsidized mortgage system and mortgage-interest tax-relief, as well as to rental tenants and corporations through subject and object subsidies, but has consistently resisted de-commodified forms of assistance. What has been most consistent in discourse and policies therefore, is the logic of capital and the market.

Shlay (2006) suggests that the strength of home ownership discourses have effectively crowded out housing policy alternatives, and pushed more and more marginal households into the tenure. Facilitating asset-building and increasing involvement in property ownership among lower-income and ethnic minority households, along with market deregulation, has become central to government policy. The idea that cheaper borrowing for housing can help build wealth in low-income communities (for example, Retsinas and Belsky, 2005) is, however, ideological and central to the legitimacy of neo-liberal socio-economic restructuring. With de-industrialization and declining employment stability, welfare security has become a central concern to governments and individuals, but appears to be reorienting towards decidedly individualized forms, and in particular housing equity.

For sub-prime borrowers and other low-income mortgagees conditions are riskier and less advantageous. Such homeowners are more likely to find housing in poorer quality neighbourhoods, face greater risks of costly repairs and have access to lower quality amenities (Shlay, 2006). Inevitably, they are more likely to fail as owner-occupiers and make far fewer gains. Nevertheless, the emphasis put on property ownership by the state has made it appear for poorer families that increased housing debt is necessary in order to achieve greater security.

It now looks like the US house-price boom is at an end. In 2006 the number of units being sold began to fall (by 11.2 per cent from a year earlier). Conditions have been further exacerbated by interest rate increases and the credit market crunch following developments in the sub-prime market in the summer of 2007. House-prices have started to sink, although the distribution of falls is uneven. A continued decline in property values will fundamentally challenge the basis of housing policy of the past decade, which has assumed that families will only build wealth through participation in housing markets. It is the poorest and most marginal homeowners that suffer most as they are more likely to have to sell their homes and realize losses should economic circumstances change or interest rates go up further.

The Great Australian Dream

Australian dreaming

The development over the last century of the home ownership system has been central to the 'Australian dream' and a specific target of policy and political rhetoric. Of the three 'nations of home-owners' considered in this chapter, Australia is arguably the one that demonstrates the most consistent orientation towards the tenure. It has been suggested that Australians have always preferred private housing to other forms of investment and have sought to make themselves more comfortable by building larger houses. This contributed to a process of suburbanization which was strongly associated with a particular type of single-family housing on its own land with a garden, which in turn was associated with achieving higher standards of living and the aspirations of a working man's paradise (see Butlin, 1964; Stretton, 1970; Paris, 1993; Snooks, 1994; Beer and Blair, 2000). There are also spatial considerations as the realization of a 'quarter acre block' has been easier to realize for working-class families due to the availability of land and a lack of resistance to urban sprawl. Nevertheless, building a nation of owner-occupiers has not been as 'natural' a development as the image of a 'suburban paradise' would suggest. The drive towards mass home ownership has been strongly aligned with the dynamics of political hegemonies.

Kemeny (1986) argues that home ownership has dominated in Australia as a direct result of government engineering because of its close affinity with a range of conservative political beliefs which have motivated political sponsorship (p. 251). Indeed, home ownership has been directly nurtured by considerable subsidy in numerous forms and guises over the century (see Yates, 2003). However, the discursive consensus formed between the political left and right concerning the tenure strongly reflects Australia's particular socio-political pathway and construction of welfare–labour relations, or as Castles describes it (1985), 'workfare' system (see Chapter 4).

At the turn of the twentieth century home ownership constituted around half of housing stock, much of which was owned outright. The status of private rental tenure, which essentially made up the remaining stock, was in decline in line with global economic trends. There were also concerns with problems of slums and slum landlords. The government was beginning to recognize the need to replace private renting and, at the same time, was seeking to increase immigration. Home ownership offered the most attractive solution. Mortgages were considered a means by which home ownership would stake residents to the country (Troy, 2000). An initial step taken to achieve this aim was the War Service Home Scheme in 1919 which sought to reward those who had served in the Great War with easier access to home ownership. The main problem faced by the authorities in promulgating home ownership was how to expand practices of owner-occupation among the working classes whose ability to obtain credit was limited. As in Britain, in order to promote housing purchases they needed to make potential buyers more competitive than private landlords. This required developing an infrastructure of lending for home-purchase. This would involve subsidizing savings banks and building societies in order to divert funds into the owner-occupied sector.

In the mid-1920s, under Prime Minister Bruce, a scheme to encourage lower middle-class private house purchase was introduced through the 1928 Commonwealth Housing Act. At a regional level, measures included, in South Australia for example, the Advances for Homes Act of 1928, by which the state bank was funded to make loans available for home-purchase, the Mortgages Relief Act of 1931 to lengthen the period of loan repayment, and the Building Societies Act of 1941, guaranteeing the availability of bank loans for home-purchase. Even the setting up of the South Australian Housing Trust in 1936 had provision for the sale of homes to tenants and eligible tenants. Similar Acts across different states effectively institutionalized and normalized borrowing for home ownership throughout the 1920s and 1930s. Nevertheless, the impact on tenure growth during this period, while notable, was essentially limited.

Menzies and the home-owning society

Housing policy had played a largely peripheral role in political debates during the 1930s. However, in 1942, Menzies, (Prime Minister 1939–1941, 1949–1966), while in opposition, took hold of housing tenure policy as a key political issue, calling for a concerted effort to increase home ownership. Menzies' rhetoric embraced the qualities of home ownership and identified its potential in the process of nation building. He argued that 'one of the best instincts in us is to have one little piece of earth with a house and garden which is ours, to which we can withdraw, in which we can be among friends, into which no stranger may come against our will'. He also suggested, in view of the conflict at the time, that homeowners were more likely to fight for the nation, as patriotism 'springs from the instinct to defend and preserve our own homes'. It was further proposed that after the war home ownership would make people less susceptible to foreign ideologies, more committed to their communities and less likely to 'engage in industrial and social activities that would threaten the security of their investment' (Menzies, 1942; see Brett, 1992). For Troy (2000) the intention was more politically divisive. The notion was that once they had a target, some equity to hang on to or to strive for, householders would behave and think like capitalists (p. 720). For Kemeny (1986), the expansion of working-class home ownership was seen as a major antidote to communism by giving individuals a stake in the system. Indeed, there was a considerable consensus on the right formed during the 1940s concerning the potential 'effects' of home ownership. Political discourses constructed a particular notion of the home, its natural position in society, its relative merits for the nation and its significance to the individual.

> Invariably, the man who owns his home is an exemplary citizen. His outlook on life is immediately changed from the moment when the first nail is driven into the structure that is eventually to become 'his castle'. In reality, it is a symbol of achievement, purpose, industry and thrift. The homeowner feels that he has a stake in the country, and that he has something worth working for, living for, fighting for; something he has never had in the past, something he has to look forward to in the future. (Dunstan on the Housing Bill, Victorian Parliament, 1943)

The creation of the Commonwealth Housing Commission (CHC) in 1944 and subsequent Commonwealth State Housing Agreements (CSHAs) in 1945 have been identified as the key points of legislative transformation in the housing and home ownership system (ABS, 2001). However, private landlordism at this time came under considerable attack in terms of both policy and discourse. It has been suggested (Hill, 1959) that the Landlord Tenant Act (originally a war time measure to control rents) was the most important legislation in driving the switch to home ownership. There was virtually no private rental accommodation built between 1947 and 1954, while at the same time, one-sixth of existing privately owned rental stock was sold off to owner-occupiers. The Act effectively restricted the building of rental accommodation in a time of housing shortage and thus demonstrates the conviction at the administrative level to support home ownership at the expense of landlordism (p. 6). Kemeny (1986) similarly identifies a strong discursive resistance to the ethics of landlordism which contradicted individual rights to home ownership.

The increase in home ownership was rapid and dramatic. As well as government sponsorship, a series of factors contributed to the continued surge in home ownership consumption: the establishment of a financial infrastructure; increased prosperity; a post-war surge in immigration and acute housing shortages. Economic growth was another considerable factor (see Paris, 1993). Essentially, home ownership grew under ideal conditions along with policy mechanisms which, on the one hand, undermined private renting and, on the other, underpinned private purchases. This sits awkwardly with claims that home ownership has long stood as the natural predisposition and the Australian dream. Tenure patterns suggest that working-class home ownership was not especially popular before the war and only boomed during critical conditions where ownership was the most expedient means of finding housing (see Figure 5.5).

In the political sphere Menzies and his centre-right Liberal party held onto power which has supported claims that home ownership did indeed have an ideological effect in subduing leftist discontent and forming a hegemonic consensus over individual rights and property ownership. However, although Menzies did specifically target affluent workers in an expectation that tenure practices would reshape the landscape of political allegiances, Liberal party election success was not a consequence of political transformations among the home-owning working classes. Troy (2000) suggests that, in fact, many suburbanites began to agitate for more and better services as 'the security they had gained from home ownership created notions of entitlement' (p. 725). Developments in the Australian context do not suggest that home ownership has been a driving force of political conservatism (Winter, 1994; see Troy, 2000). Indeed, in Sydney and Melbourne between 1950 and 1980, where suburban home ownership had been nurtured strongest, most labour seats in the House of Representatives remained Labour.

There was no discernable difference between the level of owner-occupation and the propensity to vote for either of the major two

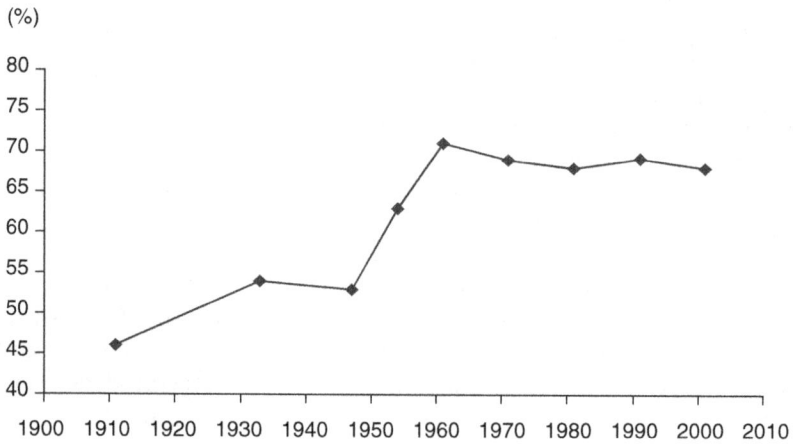

Figure 5.5 Australia home ownership rates 1911–2001
Sources: Australian Bureau of Statistics, 2001.

parties.... Those who were homeowners before the Menzies initiatives voted Conservative and continued to do so because it was in their interest. Those who became homeowners after 1949 were more likely to come from traditional 'labour households' and those who were renters 'knew' that, historically, Labour Governments were more likely to look after them. (Troy, 2000, pp. 728–729)

While there is evidence of an ideological link between discourses on housing policy and political interests, Kemeny (1981, 1986) arguably overstates the effect (although the material effects are also important). There was some consensus across the left and right in the early postwar period over home ownership as the best form of housing. Indeed, Menzies had found considerable support among the labour-union movement for his preference for owner-occupied suburban family housing. In the mid-1950s, even the communist unions (for example, the Waterside Workers Federation and the Building Workers Industrial Union) campaigned for the release of funds to build owner-occupied housing, and for further control of interest rates as a way of stimulating the economy and overcoming housing needs.

Throughout the 1950s and 1960s suburbanism and owner-occupation became fundamentally normalized in family and social relations. On the left intellectuals maintained a strongly apathetic stance to suburban living, taking it to be intrinsically parochial, self-centred and materialistic (see Rowse, 1978). Labour movements, however, sat very comfortably with privatistic housing policies. Property ownership has thus been said to have taken a particular place in the Australian political landscape in the reconciliation between individualism and collectivism, as a link to liberal citizenship, a mark of social membership and an entry ticket to political participation. However, how much individuals have consciously embraced this ideological notion of citizenship and ownership is more questionable (see Donoghue et al., 2002). Among working-class owner-occupiers there has not been simple acquiescence to the promulgated superiority of the tenure, but more a recognition that households are better off materially, with more space for children and themselves and greater independence and security (Richards, 1990). What is more significant discursively is the formation of housing objects and subjects in market terms, where the obligation of the state is to ensure a market supply of housing commodities rather than supply housing itself to families.

The relationship between labour unions, political hegemony and welfare has been identified as forming a specific pattern in the Australian context, and home ownership, arguably plays a key position in this framework. For Castles (1985, 1998) labour unions have often fought for higher pay and access to owner-occupied housing instead of demanding greater government provision of universal welfare services, as has been the case in Europe. In terms of a 'workfare', instead of welfare state model (see Chapter 4), the expansion of home ownership diminishes reliance on the government for welfare services (where workers rely more on resources derived from improved wage-earning conditions and housing assets which gain in value), and prevented the proliferation of de-commodified social relations. Left wing parties have not been bound up so strongly with obligations and public welfare ideologies, especially in the case of housing. Consequently, public rental housing was not strongly supported or developed in Australia as it was in Britain during the expansion of the welfare state. A marginal stock of public housing did emerge after the 1940s but has not exceeded 6 per cent of national housing stock.

Pragmatically for the state during the 1950s and 1960s, housing constituted a mechanism to regulate growth, immigration and family formation (Troy, 2000). There was a strong concern following the Pacific war that the nation was vulnerable. Policy sought to populate the country to help resist a foreign take-over ('populate or perish'). Couples were encouraged to have children, thought to be enhanced in post-war policy discourses, by facilitating owner-occupied suburban family housing. Furthermore, single-family housing was increased or decreased relatively easily as a means to stimulate consumption and domestic demand (p. 720).

Home ownership incentives were enhanced throughout the 1950s, 60s and 70s in the form of preferential interest rates and housing grants for FTBs. Many lenders could lend for housing in return for special taxation treatment. Preferential loans for houses were not transferable which meant that once committed, households were locked into their new home. Lending subsidy was also directed at loans for new buildings. In this way home ownership policy had a substantial impact on economic demand (see Bourassa et al., 1995; Yates, 2003).

Post-Menzies home ownership

In 1961 home ownership reached over 70 per cent. Governments began to rethink housing into the 1970s and 80s with some debate over whether home ownership was such a good thing after all. Growth of the owner-occupied sector led to rigidities in labour markets as well as over-investment in housing property, which inhibited the country's economic performance. There was also concern with over-sizing of homes, suburban spread and the need to rationalize and consolidate housing in the cities. Also by the 1980s it was becoming clear that tax benefits provided to homeowners as an indirect housing assistance was poorly targeted and overwhelmingly benefiting the rich (Flood and Yates, 1987). In 1986, the Federal Government deregulated the finance industry and effectively removed many advantages in terms of preferred access to funds and controlled interest rates. It was also apparent that the Direct Assistance Scheme for Home-buyers (introduced in the 1960s) was, rather than facilitating home ownership, only advancing the entry by a few years of households who would have entered the market anyway (Bourassa et al., 1995). This scheme was suspended in 1990.

Despite the waver in government enthusiasm for home ownership in the 1980s, in the late 1990s the ideal of a property-owning society was revived by the Howard government. Howard's Liberals have, however, focused more on property ownership in terms of economic liberalism. Housing has become increasingly significant as an economic investment with a large proportion of the population (almost a third) owning two or more housing properties. At the same time, growing numbers of households have found themselves excluded from the owner-occupier housing market by levels of house-price inflation stimulated by over-investment (Baxter and Macdonald, 2005).

Following Menzies' image of a home-owning Australia, Howard encouraged Australians to see themselves as members of a 'share owning democracy'. While housing has not been as central on the political agenda as share ownership, home ownership has been easy to stimulate and remains central to the strategy of the Liberal Party. In 2000 direct assistance for homeowners was re-introduced in the form of a First Home Owners Grant (FHOG). This grant has no means testing, no restriction on the value of the property, and costs the state about AUS$1 billion a year. There was a subsequent boom in housing property values, especially in terms of house-price to income ratio, which represents a much more substantial change in household equity. Household debt has also increased in line with low inflation, low interest rates, augmenting rates of real income, and an increased availability of mortgage finance (Yates, 2003). Outstanding mortgage loans have increased from 45 per cent of total household liabilities in 1990 to 69 per cent by 2001. Net equity was also down from 89 per cent in 1990 to 74 per cent in 2001 (Australian National Accounts Balance Sheet, ABS, 2002).

There have been a number of problems associated with the targeting of direct home ownership subsidies (Productivity Commission, 2003). First, assistance has gone mainly to those who would have purchased a home without the assistance provided by the grant. The home-buyers grants have thus largely assisted middle to high-income earners rather than low-income ones. Second, the introduction of an additional $7,000 loan to encourage the purchase of newly built properties resulted in increasing prices and making housing more unaffordable. Third, many parents purchased investment homes in their children's names, although this loophole has since been changed (p. 150).

There are significant differences in effects on citizenship, rights, obligations and competence between property owning and home-owning, but their convolution in the most recent era of housing and economic policy reflect discursive transformations. Menzies lauded security, continuity, predictability and community in home ownership, seeing it as a means to build social capital by giving individuals a stake in the country, whereas Howard's notion of property owning implies more mobile and speculative features. It is built on the premise that property ownership will encourage people to be more neo-liberal and market orientated, which is assumed, in turn, to make them more dependent on governments who favour free-market policies.

It is arguably the reorientation of individuals towards 'housing market commodities' that is most salient in the most recent incarnation of Australian home ownership ideology. Individuals are now encouraged to invest and speculate in order to build up enough equity to provide security for themselves and their families. However, dependence on the market and inequalities in the housing system, structured by preferable subsidies, are beginning to challenge stability. Substantial imbalances have emerged along with pronounced differences in the financial advantages enjoyed between renters and owners, and poor and rich homeowners. The tax system provides most assistance to outright owners who can often receive around five times more benefit from indirect assistance (specifically from the positive benefits of net imputed rent and capital gains exemptions) than mortgaged home purchasers (Yates, 2003, p. 20). Affordability problems that these imbalances generate between different generations and income groups have meant that since the 1990s owner-occupancy rates have begun to fall, especially among younger age groups. Home ownership rates among 25–34 year olds dropped by 10 per cent between 1981 and 1996 (see Baxter and Macdonald, 2005). The government response has been predictably neo-liberal and sought to enhance accessibility and affordability problems in the housing market rather than seeking to develop other tenures or restructure subsidies. Despite the more neo-liberal government approach, political rhetoric concerning the embedded place of home ownership in society has continued to follow the logic of the Menzies era.

But young Australians and older Australians too, still aspire to home ownership. Why? Because it gives them a security in life, a security that gives them a little piece of our country. It is a bit like 'The Castle', their little piece of turf they can defend against all comers and gives them security and their family security. And we should encourage and nurture home ownership. This is something that is important not just in an economic sense but also I believe in a social sense. (Peter Costello, Australian Treasurer, Launch of the Great Australian Dream project, 14 August 2006)

The developing role of home ownership arguably follows the logic of the 'workfare' system under emerging global conditions where there is increasing pressure on welfare spending, intensified economic competition, and growing concern over ways to support the growing proportion of the retired population. In this context there are pressures to expand the home ownership further in order to develop the capacity of and 'asset-based' welfare system (see Chapter 4). The centrality of home ownership in Australia has already been recognized as a central feature of the pension and welfare system. The OECD report on 'Coping with Population Ageing in Australia' (1999) stated that retirement income is comprised of three main elements in Australia: old-age pension; superannuation pension funds; and voluntary savings which include homeowner assets as the central component. This has led to calls for the Federal government to explicitly declare home ownership a pillar of the retirement system and to expand the sector further through even more tax concessions and subsidy for FTBs (Real Estate Institute of Australia, 2005). However, the OECD also estimates that Australian housing was overvalued by 52 per cent compared to 33 per cent in the United Kingdom in 2003, suggesting reliance on owner-occupied property for retirement provision may be a rather risky strategy.

Conclusion

In light of policy developments and social discourses underlying the emergence of home ownership in Britain, the United States and Australia, it is difficult to assert that a model of Anglo-Saxon homeowner society constitutes a particularly meaningful category in terms of policy frameworks and housing system pathways. Moreover, identifying relationships between discourses and policies is fundamentally challenging as policies reflect the intersection of numerous factors including pre-existing frameworks and approaches to finance and subsidy, as well as production and consumption practices. Owner-occupation also appears uneven in hegemonic strategies and outcomes in each society.

While I have sought to illustrate that there are substantial differences between these societies in how they have achieved mass home ownership, there are a number of ideologically convergent features. The first is that home ownership demand is primarily the result of discursive processes and policy development rather than a 'natural' phenomenon. Second, there is an apparent relationship between housing discourses, tenure policy and hegemonic features. Third, the ideological significance of home ownership has been transformed in tenure discourses and policy practices from a concern with building socially conservative hegemonies to a reorientation of households towards the market that follows neo-liberal principles. What are most divergent between these societies are the frameworks and policies by which home ownership has been advanced. Types of subsidies, finance systems and government measures all vary radically. In the last decade, all have sought to drive the take-up of owner-occupation, but while Britain and Australia developed various rafts of shared ownership schemes and incentives (Berry et al., 2006), the US focus has been the mortgage system and assisting deposits (Retsinas and Belsky, 2005).

What are most salient to ideological processes are the intersections of discourses with policy moves that promote home ownership. Inevitably, the promulgation of home ownership constitutes housing objects as market ones, and human subjects as rational market consumers. The constitution of houses as market objects demands that the most effective form of provision depends on the freedom of markets, and that state interventions which undermine the market, such as the provision of public housing, is undesirable. There are ultimately implications for the construction of the state as a provider of goods, the viability of de-commodified services and the roles of households and housing assets in the realization of individual security and well-being.

Although the lines drawn among social contexts, government discourses and housing and policy practices have been crude, the objective has been to establish connections between these rather elusive and often incompatible empirical dimensions. In Chapter 7 I contrast approaches in these societies more comprehensively, considering convergence and divergence in ideological processes, and the significance of differences in policy measures. Ultimately, I advance a more consistent model of Anglo-Saxon market-based home ownership in terms of diverse modes of homeowner society discernable in other groups of societies such as East Asia.

6
East Asian Homeowner Societies

Introduction

While the consideration of 'homeowner societies' has been dominated by Anglo-Saxon contexts, home ownership has also expanded rapidly in recent decades across a group of newly industrialized East Asian societies. In the Asian Tigers, including Singapore, Hong Kong, South Korea and Taiwan, as well as the 'big tiger', Japan, levels of GDP per capita have reached levels comparable to Western societies while property values and home ownership rates have rapidly advanced since the 1970s (Agus et al., 2002; Lee et al., 2003). Housing policy orientated towards the expansion of owner-occupation has taken a privileged position within these regimes and become central to ideological relations in the process of economic growth and modernization (Ronald, 2007a). As in Anglo-Saxon societies, home ownership has been embraced as the 'natural' tenure, even though the achievement of high home ownership rates involved considerable policy manipulation. Just as an 'Englishman's home is his castle' a Japanese home, for example, is talked about in terms of 'one castle, one country, one master'. In both contexts such phrases have become emotive, associated with home ownership and mobilized in the normalization of tenure.

Nevertheless, East Asian, Tiger societies differ substantially from Anglo-Saxon homeowner societies, not only in terms of housing objects, systems and practices but also in relationships among housing systems, social hegemonies and welfare regimes. The aim of this chapter is to illustrate that while home ownership has played a central role in East Asian socio-economic development, it has not been ideologically orientated towards promoting citizenship rights based on property ownership or constituting individualized neo-liberal subjects. Housing policies have primarily constituted housing as a market object and orientated housing subjects around patterns of family consumption and family-based welfare. However, home ownership discourses have not been dominated by individualism, but have instead emphasized particular forms of social-mainstream subjectivity. The relationship between neo-liberal governance and market subjects is not as significant as in Anglo-Saxon cases, as East Asian welfare capitalism relies on more hegemonic social practices based on rapid economic growth.

Housing policies and systems of provision and finance are characteristically diverse among the East Asian societies, as are welfare systems, political organization and patterns of modernization and urbanization. However, an East Asian welfare approach has arguably emerged that can be defined in terms of a 'productivist' welfare regime orientated towards achieving greater social equity and satisfying welfare needs through economic growth (see Jones, 1993; Goodman and Peng, 1996; Holliday, 2000; Walker and Wong, 2005). Home ownership appears to be a feature of this regime type, and the role housing plays in each society is similar, following a pattern of strong state intervention, but with market based consumption (Doling, 1999, 2002; Ronald 2007b).

We consider in this chapter the three most diverse societies within the East Asian group in terms of the structure of housing and welfare systems. These countries also represent examples of system types and regime subcategories established within the region (Deyo, 1992; Doling 1999, 2002; Holliday, 2000). The three countries are Japan, Hong Kong and Singapore. Fundamentally, all three societies have developed ideologies around home ownership, which serve power relations between the state, families and civil society, based on the growth and stability of housing-property-assets. The nature of housing policy, owner-occupied housing objects and the centrality of home ownership in each society however varies substantially.

The analysis begins with the consideration of the development of welfare regimes in East Asian Tiger societies which have challenged assumptions formed in Western contexts. Institutionalized systems of social security and welfare have, historically, been rather underdeveloped, which has led to the neglect of the group in the conceptualization of welfare states. However, this is argued to be because of the rather narrow Western view of welfare states (Holliday, 2000; Groves et al., 2007). What characterizes East Asian approaches to welfare is the role the family plays as a welfare provider, which has increasingly relied on access to housing properties which have increased in value as economic growth has been achieved. As in the preceeding chapter, I relate social contexts to policy discourses and practices in order to provide a narrative outline of developments. Three diverse pathways are established that are all orientated towards an ideological view of the superiority of home ownership. The growth of owner-occupied housing has historically supported an emerging set of relationships among housing, social provision and state hegemony.

East Asian welfare 'regimes'

Consideration of welfare relationships in East Asia provides some insight into the significance of housing and specifically home ownership in relationships between the state, market and family. The understanding of development of advanced capitalist societies and patterns of differentiation in welfare systems has been dominated by Esping-Andersen's analyses of welfare capitalism (1990, 1999). The economic success of the Asian Tigers, however, has provided a considerable challenge to the assumptions concerning welfare regimes as none of these countries fit neatly into the established categories. Indeed, economic development in these contexts has not been accompanied by the comparable development of 'welfare states'. Since the 1980s a debate has emerged concerning the character of East Asian social and welfare systems and their incongruence with threads of Western welfare capitalism. They have been argued to be unique or hybrids, to constitute an Oriental, Confucian or even Asia-Pacific type (see Rose and Shiratori, 1986; Jones, 1993; Goodman and Peng, 1996; Esping-Andersen, 1997; Walker and Wong, 2005).

Relationships between the state, capital and economic growth have been profoundly different from Western societies, being instead based on the 'developmental state', where the government prioritizes economic goals in cooperation with the corporate sector. For Wade (1990) these East Asian societies have been economically successful because of the 'government market' in which states take major roles in ensuring specific industrial sectors have developed in ways consistent to perceptions of national interests.

> Using incentives, controls, and mechanisms to spread risk, these policies enabled the governments to guide – or govern – market processes and resource allocation so as to produce different production and investment outcomes than would have occurred in either free market or stimulated free market policies. (p. 27)

While Johnson (1982) refers to the idea of the developmental state to describe the form of corporatism evident, Schaede and Grimes (2003) refer to 'economic nationalism' in conceptualizing the mutual coordination of policy and markets between government ministries and industrial sectors. In the developmental state bureaucrats and political leaders are compelled to get on and organize growth using whatever methods are to hand. Henderson and Appelbaum's (1992) classification of industrial societies contrasts 'market ideological' countries, such as the United States in terms of prioritization of free markets, with 'plan rational' countries in East Asia where the state sets national goals and intervenes in order to direct the economy as a whole. Doling (1999) identifies a further distinction as both market rational and plan rational societies are characterized by forms of corporatism, but in each the form is different. East Asian societies are characteristically more authoritarian and hierarchical in the imposition of the state agenda.

The welfare systems that developed in line with plan rational capitalism have been essentially minimal due to the centrality of economic growth in the formation of social policy. Holliday (2000) therefore suggests that East Asian societies constitute a distinct group, or 'productivist regime', that can be added to Esping-Andersen's welfare capitalism typology. This is theoretically possible because of Esping-Andersen's claim that the category of welfare capitalism can be applied to those capitalist states so strongly affected by their social policy as to be identifiable as welfare states. Among the Tigers, social policy is strictly subordinate to the overriding policy objective of economic growth, and everything else flows from this: minimal social rights with extensions linked to productive activity, reinforcement of the position of the productive elements in society, and state–market–family relationships directed towards growth (p. 708).

While East Asian regime typologies have been asserted, there has been little reference to different class or power relationships (Kemeny, 2001, p. 59). Understanding of Western regimes is based on class and corporate conflicts which determine levels of goods and services provided in de-commodified forms by the state. The role of trade unions and the political left has not been as significant in the formation of political hegemony in Tiger economies, and it has been difficult to align political power and welfare provision. Essentially, states have managed to maintain power and legitimacy during radical periods of economic growth without having to provide comprehensive welfare services that alleviate the uneven effects of capitalism. Walker and Wong (2005) argue that the 'welfare state' is very much a Western construction and that East Asian economies often shy away from a negative connotation of welfare, instead preferring a discourse of 'workfare' (see Chapter 4). There has also been considerable variety in the state–market mix and the point at which states intervene.

In the dynamics of welfare capitalism of Tiger societies, the role of housing and families within the social structure is critical. Families are often more central in the 'welfare mix', covering gaps in state provision by providing social insurance for their members. The housing system has been very important for families in many societies in facilitating welfare care and services. The ability of families to procure owner-occupied homes that gained in value has often been the basis of welfare for members in terms of shelter, as well as financial reserves to draw upon in case of hardship. Housing, especially owner-occupied homes can thus provide the financial base for retirement and feature strongly in exchanges between generations where care in old age is often provided reciprocally in terms of cohabitation and inheritance.

State approaches to housing thus feature in the East Asian productivist welfare regime as there is considerable reliance on family housing resources and assets (Doling, 2002; Ronald 2007a). This aspect is not unique and is also particularly evident in the patterns of home ownership and family provision in the high-rate homeowner societies of Southern Europe that also have lower levels of social spending among industrialized societies. However, the role of housing systems is more integrated in Tiger economies. The state has been exceptionally active in the management of housing production and consumption, which has been central to economic growth. Ultimately, macroeconomic growth and micro-consumption of housing properties are tightly bound together in the overall system of housing and welfare in East Asian societies, which strongly differentiates the role of home ownership in this region from other contexts.

The three cases I now consider arguably constitute the most diverse housing systems in the East Asian group, but all demonstrate a core commitment to developing owner-occupation orientated housing systems. Japan has been economically developed substantially longer than the other societies in the region, and home ownership was at the heart of post-war housing policies. Hong Kong and Singapore are both former British colonies and have been influenced in different measure by aspects of British housing policy. Singapore became independent from Britain almost 50 years ago and developed an intense and highly controlled system of 'public-home ownership'. Hong Kong, alternatively, was influenced longer by British housing policy discourses. It demonstrates a more managed approach to housing system development and has a large public rental sector. Nevertheless, there was substantial commitment to expanding owner-occupation in the 1980s and 90s, and home ownership remains central to the development of the system.

Singapore and Hong Kong as public housing orientated societies have been categorized as different from each other and very distinct compared to other Tiger countries (Deyo, 1992; Doling, 1999). In South Korea, Taiwan and Japan past approaches to housing have focused on state intervention rather than public provision. Within Holliday's East Asian welfare regime typology (2000), there are three subgroups. The case societies in this chapter constitute leading examples of each of these types. The nature of these divisions is discussed further in the following chapter. The concern here is to first demonstrate the diverse nature of home ownership in theses countries, which provide a fundamental challenge to the notions of homeowner society established in Anglo-Saxon contexts.

A Japanese nation of homeowners

Housing, modernity and the social-mainstream

Japan's transformation into an advanced, industrial-urban society was remarkably rapid, and the housing system has been an important element in this metamorphosis (Hirayama and Ronald, 2007). Despite current levels of owner-occupation and the attachment to the idea of home ownership in popular discourse, Japanese patterns of owner-occupied dwelling largely developed in the process of socio-economic restructuring following the second World War. At the end of the 1880s barely 15 per cent of Japanese lived in cities. By the end of the 1980s around 80 per cent of Japanese lived in urban areas, the majority of whom owned their own homes, and the Japanese economy was the second largest in the world. The transition from feudal farmer, to urban tenant to homeowner society is essentially more radical than in any Western society, but has resulted in a similar embedding of home ownership in the ideological and social system. This development is here considered in terms of a discursive socio-historical context and key policy innovations.

The emergence of home ownership in Japan begins with transformations in the nature of households. There is a conceptual integration in the Japanese word 'ie' as a primary referent for both houses and families. The 1898 Meiji civil code put into law a particular set of rights and obligations concerning *ie*, under which the family head was provided with privileges and powers necessary to fulfil obligations to society and the Emperor, as well as maintain the name, assets and social status of the family for the next generation (see Morishima, 1988; Koyano, 1996). In the late nineteenth century, Japan underwent a revolution in which the feudal government was replaced by the Emperor and a modernizing regime that sought to socially and economically develop the nation. The shape of the household subsequently became a discursive battleground for traditionalists and modernizers seeking to guide the trajectory of social development (Sand, 1998). On one side, conservatives aimed to consolidate a particular discourse on traditional household organization. The concept of house in this case embodied buildings, land and families in terms of continuity across generations. On the other side, modernist reformers sought to encourage a more Western form of nucleated family orientated around child-rearing and middle-class norms. Critically, the household patterns that emerged demonstrated aspects of both discourses. They were later moulded further by developments in the housing system (specifically the early post-war period) into a standard type and associated with home ownership.

In the inter-world-war period, increasing numbers of households migrated to the cities forming more nucleated household units. Land transactions, which had been permitted since 1868, began to have an impact on the commodification of land making private housing purchase possible (Yamada, 1999). Nevertheless, the proportion of rental housing grew most substantially, and accounted for more than 70 per cent of housing in urban areas by the 1940s (89 per cent of housing in Osaka and 73 per cent in Tokyo; Ministry of Health and Welfare, 1941). Although residential conditions in cities were poor, urban residents were generally passive and there had been little resistance to the demands of militarist governments. It eventually became necessary to deal with growing pressures however (see Hayakawa, 1990; Sorensen, 2002; Waswo, 2002; Hein et al., 2003). In 1939 – a year after the Welfare Ministry was created – a specialist housing agency was formed, and in 1941 a state-funded Housing Corporation was also inaugurated to provide more rental units. Socio-economic reorganization, however, following military defeat in 1945, moved construction and owner-occupied housing further up the agenda.

War damage, largely caused by bombing, required approximately 4.2 million new housing units. Initially, however, housing was not a priority and greatest effort was put into industrial recovery. By the mid-1950s housing construction was becoming central to recovery and an engine of economic growth. The thrust of housing policy became more interventionist and focused on supporting the construction sector, on one side, and enhancing family self-reliance, on the other. Consequently, the expansion of home ownership became the main feature of policy. In terms of subduing private landlordism, the Rent Control Ordinance was introduced (1946), following earlier rent control initiatives (1936, 1940), which eroded the management base of private rental supply. In addition, in 1949 a heavy tax was levied on private landlords for one year, which further helped undermine the system. In terms of promoting home ownership, during the early 1950s the 'three pillars' of post-war housing policy were established: the Government Housing Loan Corporation (GHLC; 1950), the Public Housing Act (PHA; 1951) and the Japan Housing Corporation (JHC; 1955). The GHLC provided middle-income households with fixed low-rate mortgages, while the JHC was founded in order to promote and construct multi-family estates for middle-income families in cities. The PHA subsidized public rental housing for low-income families, constructed, owned and managed by Local Authorities. The balance between these institutions, however, was not even and the provision of GHLC loans was the government priority. The provision of public rental housing was not envisioned as a long-term solution to housing issues. It was seen as a steppingstone to other tenures for young low-income families, and over time was increasingly residualized and maintained for those categorized as 'worthy poor'. The ratio of public-rented housing to total stock was never large and peaked at 7.6 per cent in the early 1980s (Table 6.1).

A boom in housing was driven by rapid growth in home ownership, sustained by government policy, and associated with economic growth (Miyake, 1985). Critically, priority was given, in housing subsidy, to working households who were best able to secure their own private accommodation. Such households were perceived in policy discourse as the most economically productive (Hirayama, 2007). Owner-occupation orientated policy was thought to encourage self-help and the greater reliance of households on social networks rather than the

Table 6.1   Housing tenure in Japan

Year	Owned houses (%)	Public rented houses (owned by local government) (%)	Public rented houses (owned by public corporation) (%)	Private rented houses (%)	Company houses (%)	Total housing units
1968	60.3		5.8	27.0	6.9	24,198,000
1973	59.2	4.9	2.1	27.5	6.4	28,731,000
1978	60.4	5.3	2.2	26.1	5.7	32,189,000
1983	62.4	5.4	2.2	24.5	5.2	34,705,000
1988	61.3	5.3	2.2	25.8	4.1	37,413,000
1993	59.8	5.0	2.1	26.4	5.0	40,773,300
1998	60.3	4.8	2.0	27.4	3.9	43,922,100
2003	61.2	4.7	2.0	26.8	3.2	46,862,900

Source: Statistics Bureau, Housing Survey of Japan and Housing and Land Survey of Japan.

state. This strategy was considered most likely to enhance economic development and stability and therefore linked economic and social objectives in policy and ideology. Home ownership also proved an effective means of driving economic growth and was largely considered an aspect of economic rather than social policy. While cities continued to expand rapidly (the urban population rose from 37.7 to 63.9 per cent, from 1950 to 1960) the construction sector continued to catch up with housing shortages. Over the same period, the economy developed at an exceptional rate (average annual growth of 10 per cent GDP from 1955 to 1973).

Although the focus was economic, the objective of developing a core, social-mainstream class of owner-occupiers also reflected post-war socio-political strategies. The concept of a 'social-mainstream' encapsulated traditional discourses of social homogeneity with modern ones concerning advanced industrial society. Moreover, home ownership was central ideologically as it enhanced aspects of a unified middle-class identity. The home ownership system divided society into an inside and an outside with a 'social-flow' of people from rental housing on the outside to an owner-occupied housing-ladder system on the inside (Hirayama, 2003, 2007). The housing-ladder system defined the pattern of the life-course with households entering through condominium purchase and working their way up to detached family houses. It also defined aspirations and the ideal of *'mai homu'* (my own home), or being a homeowner. Essentially, the emergent housing-ladder system had a strong hegemonic impact in defining social inclusion, and there was an increasing flow into the centre as the number of homeowners increased. Although it had been the minority tenure before the war, home ownership was arguably normalized and embedded in middle-class aspirations. By the early 1960s the rate of urban owner-occupation had exceeded 60 per cent from pre-war levels of less than 30 per cent.

The increase in demand for owner-occupied housing drove house-price inflation and, subsequently, the augmentation of property assets. This contributed to the consolidation of home ownership ideology. As a growing asset, an owner-occupied house not only seemed to provide security for the current generation, it also promised security for future generations who would inherit it, involving a build-up of wealth across generations (Hirayama and Hayakawa, 1995). It thus became integrated into the developing ideal of *ie* as it reinforced the significance of the house, family heritage and continuity through the generations via inheritance. Land price inflation also fuelled the 'land myth' and 'fetishisation of space' where land has a precious and essentialized status, expected to increase perpetually in value (Mizuoka, 2004).

By the late 1960s the 'standard-family model' had become the fundamental basis of housing provision, and epitomized the new nucleated form of *ie* that aligned with an ideal of Japanese post-war social and economic modernity. It was comprised of a breadwinning husband, a homemaking wife and two children. There were subsequent spatial impacts in the organization of residential spaces and urban environments. Multi-family apartment-block estates proliferated in the 1950s and 1960s and were associated with modern families and more Westernized ways of living (Waswo, 2002). While the JHC began the construction of these estates, private sector production soon expanded, and apartments were increasingly built for sale rather than rent. Increasing numbers of standard families and levels of home ownership drove a spatial modernization with housing design moving from traditional forms towards systems incorporating concrete and prefabrication. In this way housing policy drove physical as well as social changes with new owner-occupied homes physically representing modernity and economic growth (Ronald, 2007b). The post-war civil code also abolished the *ie* system in legal terms which impacted socio-cultural practices.

Government support for home ownership was supplemented by the company welfare system. The company system and Japan's 'enterprise society', considered a central part of Japan's economic success, developed in the early twentieth century. In this model the company acts as a form of family for employees, rewarding their loyalty with a secure system of lifelong-employment, age-based wage increases and a small raft of welfare services (see Sato, 2007). Company welfare packages after the war included direct (cheap rental housing) and indirect (housing loans) housing subsidies for workers. At its peak in the 1960s, company rental housing constituted almost 9 per cent of all housing. Company housing provided a means for new families to establish themselves outside the parental home while saving up to purchase their own home. In this way it constituted a steppingstone to home ownership rather than a long-term rental alternative. Companies also provided subsidized company housing loans for employees, which supplemented a portfolio of borrowing (including GHLC, bank and family loans) necessary for a family to get into owner-occupation.

The owner-occupied housing-ladder and social-mainstream were strongly associated with the growing sense of social equality and prosperity in post-war Japan. By the mid-1970s around 90 per cent of Japanese rated themselves as middle-class (Cabinet Office, 2004). The formation of this home-owning, middle-class mainstream can be strongly linked with political formation. The Liberal Democratic Party (LDP), a party of establishment conservatives, came to power in the mid-1950s and continues to hold it (excluding a short period in 1993). Growth in the numbers of 'middle-class-feeling' homeowners (Hirayama, 2007) essentially supported social stability and discourses that served the hegemony of economic expansion, which supported the LDP and its political objectives. In this case, tenure biased policies were not political tools by which the right and left appealed to different groups of voters. Moreover, although home ownership appeared a conservative force, there was arguably little sense of citizenship rights or 'property-owning democracy'. Owner-occupation orientated policy was thought to encourage self-help and greater reliance of households on social networks rather than the state. This strategy was considered likely to enhance economic development and stability and therefore linked economic and social objectives in state policy and ideology.

During the 1960s some major improvements were made in welfare provision, specifically in terms of healthcare and pensions. Nevertheless, even though Japan was economically catching up with the West, its social security spending levels continued to lag. In 1970, while Sweden spent 18.6 per cent of GDP on social security and Britain 13.7 per cent, Japan spent just 5.3 per cent. Further moves were made to improve welfare provision (by the Tanaka administration) in 1973 and the social security budget was raised by more than a quarter. However, the building-up of welfare was, shortly after, sidelined again in favour of a 'Japanese style welfare state' in which emphasis is put on systems of welfare beyond the state. The Ohira government of 1979 asserted the desire to build a welfare society based on 'retaining a traditional Japanese spirit of self-respect and self-reliance, human relations... and the traditional system of mutual assistance' (Ohira Masayoshi, National Diet, January 1979, cited in Shiratori, 1986). The gist of policy discourse thus moved away from patterns of development in Western welfare states, and reverted to traditional practices of mutual aid within the family and community, and employee and firm (Rudd, 1994). Consequently, practices of self-help encouraged by home ownership, as well the resources represented by housing-property-assets, became more critical to the system. The government pushed families to build up and draw upon their own wealth to cover for family needs, and viewed housing assets as an individual safety-net. In this way the Japanese housing and welfare system was, arguably, able to facilitate modernization and growth in the Japanese economy without recourse to de-commodified goods and welfare services. This pattern would be repeated across many newly industrializing countries in East Asia.

From boom to bust

In the environment of early post-war Japan, social and economic conditions made owner-occupation realistic for large segments of the population, even if younger or lower-income households could not afford a home immediately. Government housing loans effectively provided access to necessary funds. However, house-price inflation gradually became a characteristic feature of the housing system. The pattern of steady increases in house-prices was briefly interrupted in 1973 by the oil crisis. As a way of getting the economy back on track, the state looked to the housing system as a means to stimulate growth. Housing policy became more aggressive with more pressure exerted to encourage people to purchase their own homes with GHLC loans. Over the next ten years the GHLC launched a series of programmes to extend home ownership. These included the Step Repayment System (1979), in which repayments were lowered for the first five years, the

Two-Generation Mortgage (1980) which allowed the children to take over their parents' mortgage and extend the repayment period, and the Supplementary Loan system (1985) in which additional loans were added to the main one. A cycle was formed in which the improvement of lending conditions encouraged house acquisition, which expanded demand for owner-occupied housing, boosting housing prices, and when it became difficult to acquire a house lending conditions were again improved (Hirayama, 2003; Oizumi, 2007). While the policy stimulation of home ownership contributed to rapid house-price inflation, there was also a speculative bubble in land. Companies and banks increasingly invested in land, which was considered a 'safe' investment, and used to secure loans for other investments (see Kanemoto, 1997).

The 1980s saw the most substantial rises in the prices of properties, especially in metropolitan areas. Housing affordability became an escalating problem with the number of people taking GHLC loans unable to make repayments for more than six months increasing 10.8 times, from 1,382 in 1975 to 14,888 in 1985 (Statistics Bureau, 1986). Between 1980 and 1990, average housing costs in Tokyo increased from 24.8 million yen to 61.2 million yen for a condominium, and from 30.5 million yen to 65.3 million yen for a ready-built single-family house. Price–income ratios rose from 5.0 to 8.0 and from 6.2 to 8.5 times for a condominium and a ready-built, single-family house respectively (Ministry of Construction, 1995). Critically, increasing funds, both commercial and domestic, were pushed into the sector. By 1990 the total land value of Japan was three times that of the United States and Japanese property assets accounted for almost 20 per cent of global wealth.

In 1989 the Japanese economic system reached a peak, largely driven by over-investment in, and the overinflation of share values (the Nikkei stock index tripled, in 1985–1989, to constitute 44 per cent of the world equity market) and, crucially, in land and housing property (which had been used as collateral for other borrowing). The subsequent bursting of the economic bubble threw this system into turmoil. The following decade, to become known as the 'lost decade', saw the disintegration of the housing-ladder and the integrity of the housing system. Homeowners were not only faced with harsh new economic realities, but also a new social context in which the certainties of the old order began to unravel (see Eades et al., 2000).

The 1990s began with a sharp decline in share values followed by a collapse in the nominal values of housing properties (see Figure 6.1).

176 *The Ideology of Home Ownership*

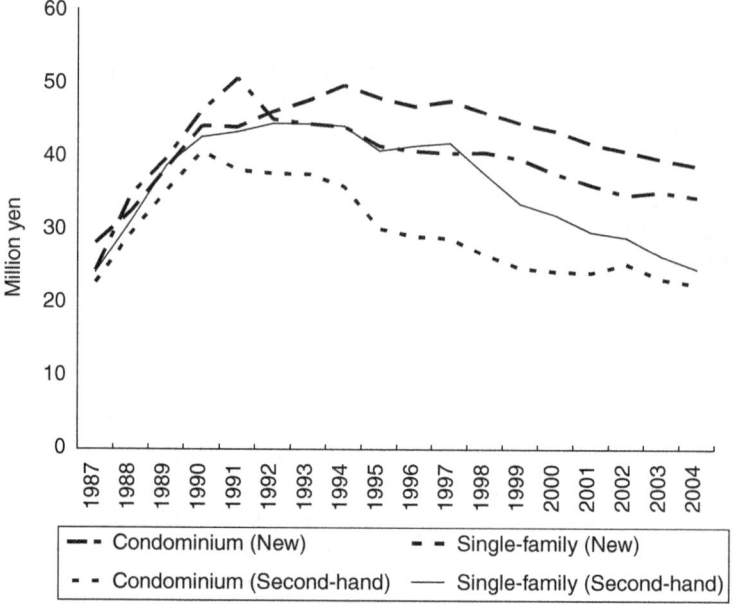

Figure 6.1 Nominal housing prices of homes with GHLC loans within a 70km radius of central Tokyo 1987–2003 (million yen)
Source: Hirayama, 2007.

The stock market lost more than 80 per cent of its value by 2003 from its peak in 1989, while, in most cases, urban property values dropped by 40 to 50 per cent. Urban owner-occupiers consequently experienced major capital losses on their primary assets.

The economic downturn also revealed problems with the home ownership system that had been disguised by the prolonged augmentation in property values. The construction sector, in the post-war years, had applied new building technologies and materials, but still promoted a 'scrap and build' approach where housing is torn down and rebuilt every 30 to 40 years (see Oizumi, 2007). Housing policy also provided a number of advantages for households purchasing new housing units in order to encourage construction. The GHLC encouraged construction by excluding loans on dwellings more than 25 years old and providing longer repayment periods for buyers of new housing. The effect was that older housing units dropped rapidly in value once they were erected, while property prices were maintained by increases in land values. As the construction sector had been an engine of economic growth in the past, when the economy went into freefall, housing policy focused on the promotion of construction. Despite early post-war shortages, a housing surplus had been achieved by the end of the 1960s with vacancy rates advancing ever since (from 7.6 per cent in 1978, 9.8 per cent in 1993, 12.6 per cent in 1998, and around 14 per cent in 2003). Effectively, practices of housing over-supply along with the failure of older properties to keep their value, driven by the housing system, became dysfunctional during the 'lost decade' and contributed to the further erosion of property values (Ronald and Hirayama, 2006).

Essentially, the state logic concerning home ownership policy focused on its macro role as economic driver when the economy went into decline rather than the micro role of housing as a stabilizer and reserve of asset security for families. While problems in the housing system contributed to the overall disruption of the socio-economic fabric, shifts in society reciprocally eroded the integrity of home ownership relations. Key factors included rising unemployment rates (from 2.1 to 5.6 per cent, in 1990–2001), casualization of working conditions and the contraction of company welfare provision and job security. Declining fertility rates (falling to 1.29 children per woman, in 2004) and considerable societal ageing (around 19 per cent of the population aged 65 or above by 2000) also contributed to destabilization. Increasingly, households began to manifest more diversified types. The proportion of houses with a couple and children living together decreased from 46 per cent in 1970 to 32 per cent by 2000, while single households rose from 11 per cent in 1970 to 28 per cent in 2000 (Japan Statistical Association, 2001).

After 1990 home ownership was unable to support the formation of standard families on standard life courses as it once did, and practices of home-owning, social-mainstream identification unravelled. In 1978 over a quarter of those aged between 25 and 29 and nearly half of those aged between 30 and 34 were homeowners. By 1998 this had dropped to one in eight for the former group and around one in five for the latter, whilst the overall level of home ownership (which was expected to expand) stayed about the same. Whereas home ownership was once integral to the formation of standard families and family formation was central to the expansion of owner-occupied housing sector, after 1990 the failure of housing values and the erosion of the housing-ladder undermined the stability of families, which became increasingly fragmented. The decline in the volume and integrity of standard families concomitantly disrupted the housing market. Essentially, the housing-ladder system and home ownership dream failed to bond society together as it had in the years of post-war construction.

Reorientation

The effects of the 'lost decade' were reinforced by the Asian economic crisis of 1997 which pushed the recession beyond 2000. The 2000s have, however, marked a government reorientation in housing, economic and social policy, and seen new emergent housing strategies among households along with new social and economic patterns. It has been evident that, despite the failures of the housing market and housing system in the 1990s, a commitment to home ownership persists in housing preferences and ideologies. The state also remains rooted to private home ownership orientated policy and has in fact reinforced its approach to family self-reliance.

The state's response to a decade of economic stagnation was to reassert the project of modernization. This time it adopted the language of global competition and Urban Renaissance Policy has been used to drive change (Saito and Thornley, 2001). New policies and rhetoric have initiated practices in which housing systems and urban conditions for people capable of competing in global markets are nurtured. The standard family and the standard life-course are no longer central to policy making. It is effectively the housing needs of professional middle-class individuals that are increasingly being focused upon, with lower-income families neglected.

Deregulation and marketization have been the watchwords of twenty-first century government approaches. Housing has been a specific target. The state's central role in the housing system is being gradually dismantled and even more freedom is being given to the private sector. The Urban Development Corporation (originally the JHC) has been restructured into the Urban Renaissance Agency and no longer supports social rental housing projects, and it plays only a limited role in housing provision. The Government Housing Loan Corporation has withdrawn from the primary market (since 2007), leaving housing finance to the private sector. The GHLC now has a function similar to that of Fannie Mae in America, concerned with the development of a secondary mortgage market. The private banking sector is expected to replace the GHLC in the primary market, although it is apparent that private banks will be more likely to transfer economic risks onto homeowners and will serve the needs of low-income borrowers less effectively (Oizumi, 2007). The social-mainstream family is no longer being supported by housing policy and households are expected to become even more economically self-reliant. Increasingly, homeowners are being exposed to greater risk as the pillars of the housing system are pulled away to be replaced by a more market orientated approach.

Homeowners themselves have become more realistic about the potential of property price increases and have developed more pragmatic approaches to the home as a centre of family continuity and intergenerational family-assets. Evidence has suggested that there are changing expectations with new generations becoming more geographically mobile and independent, making inheritance of family-owned land problematic, and putting more emphasis on negotiated social contracts over welfare exchanges and asset transfers (Izuhara, 2002; Ronald, 2004; Ronald and Hirayama, 2006). Recent housing market developments indicate localized house-price recovery, suggesting that even though the standard life-course and housing-ladder have been eroded, there is still a commitment to housing-property-ownership among most families (Hirayama, 2005; Ronald and Hirayama, 2006).

It appears that the discourse established in the previous 'golden era' of growing home ownership levels and house-price inflation, may have undermined the viable development of other tenures. As in Western homeowner societies, housing consumption discourses are dominated by an economic logic resistant to rental tenure as a normal or reasonable long-term housing solution, and cultural associations with owner-occupied housing have become embedded (Ronald, 2008). Research into meanings and housing discourses in Asian contexts is embryonic. However, early indications are that while there is alignment in terms of commodification, the content and emphasis of homeowner ideologies is more variable (Ronald, 2006).

In contrast to Western homeowner societies, the characteristic features of Japanese home ownership have been, first, the scope of state institutional intervention in the housing system in order to ensure that households can access owner-occupied housing. Second, the focus on housing has underpinned a more commodified approach to welfare, as households have been encouraged throughout the Fordist period of economic development to draw upon their own reserves and to rely on the augmentation of housing assets. This contrasts to the development of de-commodified welfare relationships in European contexts. It is important to note that until 1980s, mass housing construction was supported by material concerns with the poor conditions of dwellings and rapid urbanization, which had been resolved much earlier in Western contexts.

Housing regimes in Japan and European contexts thus emerged in the 1990s on a strongly differentiated basis.

The current trajectory of housing policy in Japan indicates that the ideology is modifying or evolving. The intervention role of the state is being reconsidered and there is increasing reliance on liberal-market approaches. At the same time, in Japan and other East Asian societies, there has been some socialization of welfare (Peng and Wong, 2004), with greater emphasis on comprehensive public welfare services and increased welfare spending. These trends and the changing role of home ownership ideology in East Asian contexts are considered in the next chapter. It is first necessary to consider further the diversity of approaches to home ownership across East Asian societies.

Home ownership in Hong Kong

Between public rental housing and home ownership

Although it appears difficult to consider Hong Kong as a mass-homeowner society because of the relatively moderate rate of owner-occupation and the availability of public rental housing, since the 1980s there has been a transformation in housing and a rapid changeover from majority renting to majority owner-occupation. In 1976 the home ownership rate was only 23 per cent. By 1997, thanks to a deep and comprehensive package of reforms and government programmes, this had reached 52 per cent. At this point the new government, following the transfer of status from Crown colony to Special Administrative Region (SAR), promised to develop home ownership further, expanding the rate to 70 per cent of housing by 2010 (see Lee, 1999; Chan, 2000; Lau, 2007). In the early 2000s the policy was readdressed in light of the crash in the housing market following the impact of the Asian currency crisis of 1997–98. Nevertheless the home ownership rate stood at 58 per cent in 2006, whereas the level of households in public rental housing was around 30 per cent. The state has been particularly effective in taking policy measures that control the flow of housing and the relative balance between public-renters and homeowners. What has characterized the housing system in Hong Kong therefore has been the management of both the expansion of home ownership and the maintenance of a strong public rental housing sector.

The origin of the housing system is substantially different to Japan as is the geographic, social and political context of development. Hong Kong is a densely populated city-state that has socially and economically developed from a remote trading colony of 600,000 people at the end of the Second World War to a global economic hub of around 7 million people by 2006. Mass immigration from the mainland during the 1950s and 1960s initially drove the urbanization of the region with the formation of large squatter settlements and rising population density. In 1954 a basic public program of building was set out to clear the public hazard of squatter areas and to meet the housing shelter needs of some lower-income households. The next major move in the development of housing policy came about in 1965 with a move to improve the quality of public rental housing. Significantly, in 1973 housing organizations merged to form the Hong Kong Housing Authority (HKHA) and a new ten-year housing programme involving further redevelopment and the building of new towns was laid out. The role of the HKHA has been central, not only to the development of housing but in social policy and economic strategies of the government more broadly.

The HKHA's main objective since the 1980s has been to support the stable expansion of home ownership. This has been achieved by instituting numerous programmes and subsidies to get better-off households in rented housing (especially public housing) into owner-occupation. Nevertheless, the promotion of owner-occupation has not involved the abandoning of public rental housing policy and the necessity of a social rental sector remains anchored in government thinking and economic planning. The role of the HKHA has been more than interventionist and constitutes what has been described as a 'state management' approach (Lau, 2007). State management has involved the co-ordination of social housing provision for lower-paid workers, on one side, and the expansion of home ownership on the other.

The role of public rental housing in home ownership ideology

What sets the Hong Kong housing system clearly apart from others in East Asia is the significance of public-rented flats, which constitute about 30 per cent of housing. The initial stock of social rental units for lower- income families were developed after slum clearance and rebuilding programmes of the 1950s and 1960s. The government has been active in the construction of a large volume of public housing into the 2000s. Even though the public rental housing sector is of comparable size to those in European social democratic regimes, Hong Kong public rental housing is not provided on the basis of universal welfare rights. Indeed, even though the state functions as a social landlord for a large swathe of the population, the approach seeks to resist the development of de-commodified relations (Yu, 1997). While the main purpose of social renting housing is to provide housing for low-income workers, it has also provided a means to clear illegal squatter areas and allow for social and economic development of sites in key urban areas.

Policies have been devised to restrict entry of well-off households into public rental housing and get better-off public tenants out of the sector (Chan, 2000; Lee and Yip, 2001; Lau, 2007). There have been numerous means and tests implemented to regulate entry into and exit out of public rental housing. After 1987, households living in public rental housing for ten years or more had to declare their incomes every other year to determine continued eligibility. Those who failed to declare or exceeded the subsidy limit (calculated against a Waiting List Income Limit) were forced to pay double the amount of net rent (net-rent-plus rates; see Lau, 2007). In 1992, 34 per cent of public rental households resident for ten years or more were paying double net-rent-plus rates, representing 11 per cent of HKHA tenant households. Since 1994 tenants with household income between two and three times the Waiting List Income Limits are required to pay 1.5 times net-rent-plus rates. Those earning three times more pay double. To further encourage those paying higher rates to leave public housing they have been given priority status in public-home ownership schemes. This has largely been an effective strategy and there has been a considerably high take-up from which the state has recovered 31,133 flats from well-off tenants between 1988 and 2003.

Chan (2000) has seen this move as an ideological one, and part of the overall strategy of promulgating home ownership. It is suggested that the strong anti-public-renting and pro-home ownership discourse that developed along with policy actions has served the interests of government macro housing management strategies. Well-off public housing tenants have been increasingly portrayed as 'free riders' who should vacate their flats and buy their own homes. Occasionally, the HKHA will single out a very rich tenant and present the case in the media. 'The implication is that the lack of public rental housing is due to the selfishness of well-off tenants who will not move out. Tenants are penalized for abusing social resources and not purchasing their own home as soon as they can afford to (or more exactly, bear the heavy mortgage burden)' (p. 41).

This is not to say that the government has sought to empty out social housing. Indeed, the state has explicitly recognized the necessity of

East Asian Homeowner Societies 183

supporting the needs of lower-income households. The HKHA rent policy thus not only reflects a desire to move richer tenants into owner-occupation but also an understanding of the financial position of poorer tenant households, especially over their lifecycle.

By allowing tenants an option to stay in their public rental housing units by paying higher rents when they are in a good financial position or to revert to normal rents when their income drops, will do far more good that evicting them. (HKHA, 1993)

The existence of one of the largest public housing services in the world (46.2 per cent of housing in 2006 including 29.7 per cent in public rental flats and 16.5 per cent in subsidized owner-occupied flats (see Figure 6.2)), has not been considered contradictory to capitalist interests. Critically, public rental housing in Hong Kong sits along side the home ownership system. They are not seen as ideologically antithetical as they have been in Anglo-Saxon societies. This is because public housing has been considered necessary for developing human capital and has functioned as a form of social wages that fosters economic development more broadly (Castells et al., 1990). At the same time public housing has been a means to manage the private sector growth and has been adjusted (especially since 2000) to support stability in private markets.

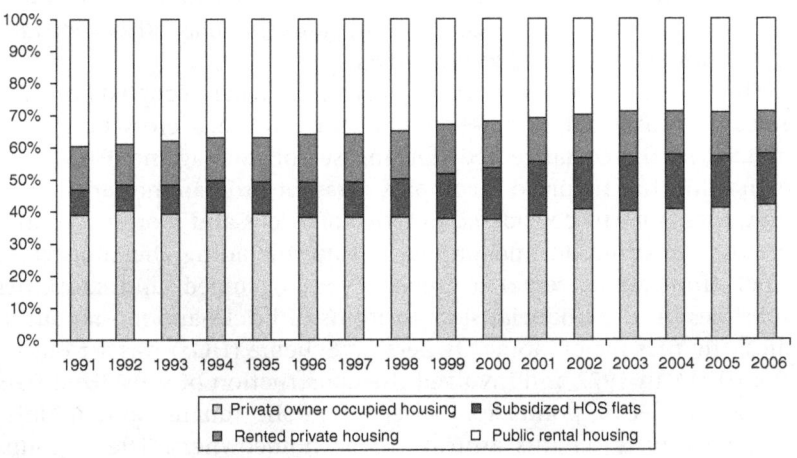

Figure 6.2 Tenure rates for permanent residential housing in Hong Kong
Source: Hong Kong Housing Authority, 2006.

Essentially, public rental housing has been perceived as having a social function that supplements economic objectives and does not promote forms of collectivity resistant to market consumption.

Managing home ownership

Ideologically, the rationale of home ownership promotion is two-fold. On one hand is the imperative to support private developers who constitute a powerful lobby and are seen as central to economic growth. Owner-occupied housing development has been an important source of state revenue and it has been estimated that in peak market years, about one third of government revenue came from related sales (Chan, 2000). On the other hand is the perceived necessity to make households independent of de-commodified services, which is achieved through the purchase of private housing units which function as investment assets and a reserve of welfare and financial resources.

There is essentially an underdevelopment of social security beyond public housing services. Hong Kong did not have a retirement protection scheme until 2000 (Mandatory Private Provident Fund), and even this provision has appeared inadequate to working-class retirement needs. Home ownership has consequently received popular support from nearly all sides. The state has been able to shift the onus of welfare responsibility onto individuals and enjoyed the revenue benefits of property market growth. The corporate sector has made considerable profits from housing and investments in development, and homeowners have, in many cases, made apparent gains that may offset shortfalls in pension provision and welfare cover.

The HKHA has been the primary driver of owner-occupied housing. Sales of subsidized owner-occupied housing have cross-subsidized deficits in the social rented housing sector. Management of home ownership has involved a complex array of programmes and subsidies: these may be considered in terms of bricks-and-mortar subsidies on the construction and provision side, including the transfer of stock from public rental to public owner-occupied, and consumer subsidies on the financial side. In terms of bricks-and-mortar subsidies, the first major Home Ownership Scheme (HOS) was set out by the HKHA in 1977 and involved the construction of subsidized flats designed as exit points for better-off public tenants and middle-income private tenants aspiring to be homeowners. These groups have essentially formed a sandwich class of those with incomes not high enough to enter the private market easily, but too high to justify public rental housing provision.

The Private Sector Participation Scheme (PSPS) was later introduced to involve private developers in the process of providing flats for sale at below market rates for target groups. In the late 1980s policy measures were extended with greater pressure on well-off public-renters to vacate (pushed by higher rents) and more opportunities to get into home ownership through improved supply and finance of government-subsidized owner-occupied flats. The HKHA also became financially autonomous and set out a long-term housing strategy (1987–2001) focused on the expansion of home ownership. By 1996 the number of subsidized owner-occupied units accounted for 10.6 per cent of housing (50 per cent total home ownership). By 2001 the rate was 16.6 per cent while the total home ownership was 55 per cent (see HKHA, 2006).

Access to subsidized built-for-sale flats has not been universal with, usually, substantial eligibility requirements, subsidy limits or defined total numbers of places. There have also been restrictions on public housing sales programmes in terms of conditions for resale to reduce speculative behaviour and provide greater security. Before 1997, HOS homes could only be resold in the first five years to the housing authority at the original price, and from then until the tenth year at prevailing HOS prices. Only then could it be sold in the free market subject to the payment of a proportionate premium. Conditions were relaxed in the late 1990s to create an active secondary HOS market, with freedom to sell on condition that the original portion of the discount was paid back to the HKHA. Transactions in the secondary market are similar to that in the open market. However, purchasers in the secondary market assume the liability to pay the premium back to the housing authority if they sell on the open market in the future. About 87.7 per cent of HOS/PSPS purchasers have chosen to stay in their flats.

On the finance side of promotion and subsidization, the Home Purchase Loan Scheme began in 1988. In this scheme borrowers can opt for an interest-free loan over the same period offered by banks, or a monthly non-repayable subsidy for 48 months. This subsidy was increased in 1995 to increase take-up and get people out of public rental flats. The Sandwich Class Housing Loan Scheme for middle-income households was also introduced in 1993. There were clear income brackets in this scheme and borrowers could borrow up to 25 per cent of purchase price or a fixed price of 550,000 HKD (whichever is lower) for a property newer than 20 years and not worth more than 3.3 million HKD. Interest-rates were set at 2 per cent (compared to a market average of 10 per cent in the mid-1990s) starting from the fourth year from when the loan was made. In 1998 a new Home Starter Loan Scheme was also introduced.

Within the overall strategy to transform households into homeowners the transfer of public rental housing has featured in more recent years. In 1997 a Tenant Purchase Scheme (TPS) was introduced, making it possible for 250,000 selected tenant households to buy their public-rented homes at discount. This policy was packaged as an additional choice to the HOS. The discount was graduated with sales made at 12 per cent of assessed value in the first year of the offer, 21 per cent in the second, and 30 per cent thereafter. Although the aim was to speed up take-up, phases also softened the market impact. In the first phase there was a 74 per cent take-up.

The housing authority has also provided mortgage guarantees and banks were able to provide loans on more favourable terms (see Lau, 2007). Those waiting for public rental flats were given more options to directly enter public built-for-sale units, while public rental blocks were converted to owner-occupied ones when needs arose. Although not everybody had the option to buy their homes, the orientation of policy in the late 1990s was increasingly directed towards enhancing the transfer of stock between public rental and public-homeowner sectors. While the overall public housing sector only increased from 46.1 to 46.8 per cent between 1996 and 2001, the proportion of rental units declined from 35.5 to 30.1 while the owner-occupied part increased from 10.6 to 16.6 (HKHA, 2006).

The myth of home ownership

As in most societies where owner-occupation rates and house-prices have boomed, there are also strong associations between tenure preferences and indigenous culture in Hong Kong. The orientation towards home ownership, however, was more significantly grounded in policies established by the British colonial government following housing privatization in the United Kingdom under Thatcher. These policies were reinforced perceptually by the rapid acceleration in property values that accompanied economic growth in Hong Kong in the 1980s and 90s, and politically by regimes which sought to resist the de-commodifying influence of public housing provision and enhance private development. Consequently, the rise in the demand for home ownership over recent decades is, as Chan (2000) suggests, 'neither a reflection of some natural desire of the people nor a reflection of Chinese culture, as generally believed. It has been socially constructed via a home ownership biased housing policy, in a specific socio-economic context mingled with a traditional Chinese culture' (p. 30).

Indeed, the policies which produced large numbers of cheap flats for sale initiated a frenzy of housing investment in Hong Kong. Nominal housing values subsequently increased nine-fold and rents quadrupled between 1985 and 1997 (see Forrest and Lee, 2003). Rises in property values heightened sensitivity to tenure issues and further fuelled the demand for private housing purchase.

While claims that home ownership boomed in the 1980s and 90s because of 'Chinese culture' appear spurious, patterns of consumption have followed a particular ideology and mythology surrounding owner-occupation and housing investment. Lee (1999) suggests that each society demonstrates an evolving consumption culture of housing, and there is evidence in Hong Kong of the influence of local values and family practices. The primary outcome was the emergence of a culture of housing speculation. In the key years of market growth, flat-hunting, home purchases and related activities became a significant part of social and cultural life. For Chan (2000) there was not only demand for 'home ownership', but demand for investment opportunities in housing. Increasingly, a house was not a home – but a speculation or investment (see also Cheng, 1997). People were prepared to queue for several days to buy flats, and some buyers were prepared to pay several thousand dollars just for a place in the queue. Opening days at private housing developments were the focus of large-scale promotions with celebrity events and carnival-like activities. Many housing estates were sold out within days and often in advance of completion. Hong Kong's transformation into a homeowner society was thus characterized by a particular view of housing commodities and market consumption.

> There is a popular saying that house-prices are like an accelerating train – you should get on the train as soon as possible otherwise you will never make it.... In this situation the home ownership ethos is cultivated in which people believe that they should purchase their home as soon as possible, or invest in housing as much as possible. Everyone believes that a fortune can be made as long as he or she can afford to buy a flat. (Chan, 2000, p. 34)

An associated feature of housing speculation consumption has been the role of the family. Families acted in the property boom as a network of mutual support and mobilized considerable financial resources to support the maximization of private housing investment. Rising prices put pressure on all working family members to provide funds for the purchase of a flat. In Western contexts it has been argued that families organize themselves in this way because of mutual advantages (Finch, 1989). However, Lee (1999) asserts that the concept of family banking is inadequate in capturing the significance of kinship ties in Hong Kong. 'The basic denominator of family help is always familial bondage, duty and responsibility, followed by the prospect of reciprocity, while the consideration of mutual advantage is always last on the list' (p. 145). Essentially, family mobilization around owner-occupied housing investments has been tied more to reciprocity between generations. This arguably aligns with the organization of self-reliant families under poorly supported welfare regimes, which rely on assets which can be exchanged for care or carried over to descendants, building up across generations. The system has also been considered rather unequal because of differential treatment of family members. As daughters move out of the home to join a new family after marriage, they often lose any rights to property they have invested in. Also, when an eldest son marries, his sisters may have to move out to make space in the 'family house', and lose out on the property.

Other values which have driven the particular culture of housing consumption may have originated in migration practices in the region. Lee (1999) identifies that older people have endured considerable hardship, making them tough and pragmatic and endowing them with a strong desire to improve living environments. Whether such qualities constitute discourses that are unique to Hong Kong is difficult to ascertain. What is more convergent with other East Asian societies is the normative status of family self-reliance, or at least the pervasive acceptance that the government is not responsible for individual welfare.

As Hong Kong's population is primarily immigrant in origin and not as homogenous or rooted in the country as many other societies, the promotion of owner-occupied housing has been considered a force for building stable ties to the area. In terms of institutional home ownership discourses, the state's imperative has been the building-up of social and cultural capital among residents. 'The government's goal is to encourage home ownership in the community. Home ownership helps to foster social stability and a sense of belonging and to provide personal financial security' (Housing Authority, 1997, p. ix). Housing policy has thus been an aspect in which the government has sought to bolster values and behaviour aimed at promoting social belonging in a territorial and geographical sense (Le Grange and Yip, 2001).

What is arguably more significant for the state in its approach to home ownership is the propping up of the middle classes, and providing opportunities for this class to build up wealth. Home ownership has been strongly implicated in defining new social and class groups and marking the broad and subtle differences between them (Lee, 1999). The pursuit of cultural capital through home ownership by the lower service class and intermediate class is argued to be a prime reason for the growth of the tenure. For Lee, home ownership now represents both an economic and cultural capital and has been part of dynamic change in the social structure. Housing property consumption has become definitive in contemporary forms of status-identity, and supported traditional family relations and asset-building. This has sustained state hegemony and justified the focus of policy on economic growth rather than welfare spending.

On one side, policies that have supported the promotion of home ownership reflect socio-political objectives and ideologies concerning the social effects of tenure. On the other, discourses also appear to reflect the social origins of inhabitants. It has been easy, ideologically, to bind home ownership with cultural tradition in Hong Kong because of the association of homes with families, the interdependency between family members it enhances and the ties with locales it reinforces. However, as tenure preferences and owner-occupied housing consumption have been dominated by investment ideologies and a modernized urban form of social life, it is difficult to account for the growth of home ownership with traditional ideals of rural Chinese houses. The formation of home ownership ideology and homeowner ideologies has essentially been driven by quite drastic policy initiatives which follow the political objectives of state approaches to welfare and economic growth, which have combined with family practices and values shaped by social conditions.

Adapting to global conditions

At the transfer to SAR status in 1997, home ownership featured in regime promises made by the new Chief executive, Tung Chee-hwa, to improve social and economic conditions of households. The approach to home ownership has, however, been distorted since 1997 following the volatile economic transformations brought on by the Asian Economic Crisis. In 1998, Hong Kong started to record negative growth in GDP. Unemployment also began to grow, peaking in 2003 at 7.9 per cent. The impact on the economy, and specifically the housing market, derailed state management objectives in the owner-occupied housing sector and undermined the discursive pattern of home ownership ideology that had previously dominated.

By mid-2000 property prices had dropped to 50 per cent of peak prices in 1997 (which had increased by 66 per cent in 1995–1997). The number of households defaulting on mortgages grew from 0.29 per cent in June 1998 to 1.19 per cent in May 2000 (Cheung, 2000). By June 2000, 170,000 households were in negative equity (*Hong Kong Economic Journal*, 2000). While conditions were very hard on families and decimated the assets built up, the economic downturn also began to disrupt the effectiveness of the housing management system. Applicants for HOS housing dropped to 29,000 in 2000 (from 112,000 in 1994), and around 25 per cent of flats up for sale could not find buyers. Conditions were exacerbated by building quality scandals on HOS estates. Essentially, the passion for home ownership in the high-interest-rate, price-decline period between 1998 and 2004 was subdued.

Conditions called for a radical rethinking of housing policy targets. The new strategy that emerged in the 2000s involved a more pragmatic and less interventionist approach to tenure balance. This involved the abandoning of home ownership targets, the reduction in output of public built-for-sale flats, and reduced assistance for new home-buyers. This entailed turning 16,000 units intended for the HOS into social rental flats (between 2000 and 2004), and, more significantly, shelving plans for 29,000 new flats a year between 2000 and 2004.

The HKHA arguably became more concerned with the impact of the falling property market on the economy than the transfer of households into owner-occupiers. Home ownership policy was not reversed but some drastic measures were taken in order to bolster the system by addressing over-supply. These adjustments reflected the calls of private developers to reduce provision of HOS housing in order to stabilize prices in the owner-occupied market overall (Lau, 2007, p. 64).

The downturn in property values has strongly impacted macroeconomic conditions. In the public sector, the HKHA, which had been self-financing since 1992 – largely down to revenue from HOS sales – made losses in 2003–2004. In the private development sector, which had been a major contributor to government coffers and a driver of GDP growth, there was steep decline, which enhanced the overall economic effect of the crisis. As Hong Kong was the most economically exposed Tiger economy, due to its dependence on international trade, and as housing was so embedded in the economic system, the impact was considerable. The recession revealed the vulnerability of house-price values to the whims of global capital. The government's commitment to home ownership has, inevitably, been unsettled by economic events over the last ten years. However, home ownership ideology has been persistent, and since 2004 there has been notable market recovery. Public rental housing is seen as an important safety-net and form of social wages, but the intention is still to develop the private side. The policy focus has become stability in property values, achieved through controlling overall private housing and land supply, minimizing government intervention and supporting general economic growth (Chiu, 2006, p. 16).

'Public' owner-occupied housing in Singapore

Universal home ownership

Singapore arguably constitutes the most extreme case of homeowner society and home ownership ideology among any industrialized society. Overall, around 85 per cent of the population lives in state subsidized housing provided by the public housing authority, more than 90 per cent of which is 'public' owner-occupied flats held on 99-year leases from the state. Including private sector owner-occupied housing, largely made up of privately developed condominiums built on land leased from the state, home ownership constitutes around 92 per cent of all housing units (see Figure 6.3). What is meant by home ownership in this case is, consequently, qualitatively different from other societies.

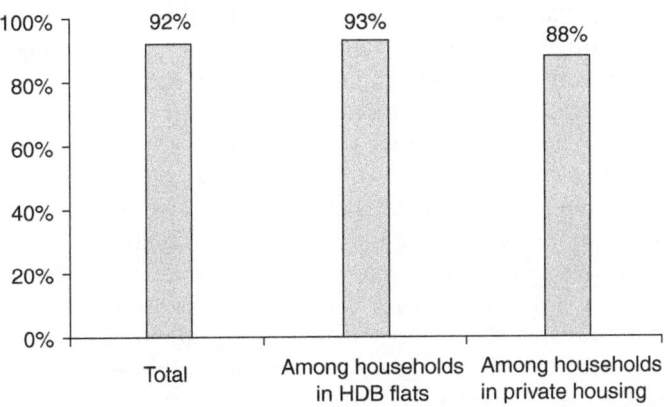

Figure 6.3 Home ownership rate of houses by dwelling type in Singapore
Source: Singapore Department of Statistics, 2005.

The government essentially holds a monopoly on land and housing, creating a condition described as 'universal home ownership' (Chua, 2003). The high rate of owner-occupation has been engineered through state control involving the compulsory purchase of land, the institutionalization of a state controlled saving system and an equally state monopolistic system of housing provision and finance. Moreover, the growth of home ownership is also radical, expanding from 29 per cent in 1970 to 92 per cent by 2000. While there has been considerable demand for owner-occupied housing property, it has been the intensity of political sponsorship that has ensured the orientation of the system so strongly to a single tenure.

Like Hong Kong, Singapore is an island city-state that has undergone rapid economic and demographic growth since the Second World War. In the past 40 years alone the population has increased from two million to four and a half million people. A national public housing programme began after limited self-government was achieved in 1959 (see Wong and Yeh, 1985). The newly elected parliament that took over the functions of the British Colonial Office (independent from Britain in 1963, separated from the Federation of Malaysia in 1965) saw housing as a central means of building up the society and procuring public support. The national project to replace the impermanent structures of squats and congested urban shop-houses with modern ones with proper sanitary facilities symbolized the administrative efficiency of the fledgling government and enhanced its legitimacy among the newly enfranchised electorate (Chua, 2003, p. 766). It was also thought to create jobs in construction and speed up capital formation. The People's Action Party (PAP), which formed the new government, was very successful in its housing and economic expansion programme. So successful, in fact, that it has held a substantial majority in parliament ever since. Critically, a large part of this success has been put down to the 'universal' system of home ownership.

The PAP leadership is argued to have developed a perspective on housing tenure which asserts that home ownership promotes social rootedness and conservative attitudes, from the ideology that developed among post-war British Conservatives (Tremewan, 1994). Other influential discourses established a set of assumptions about the socioeconomic impacts of tenure which became salient to socio-political conditions. In the 1960s, after rapid industrialization began, left-leaning trade unions became active in Singapore. For the state, home ownership was perceived as a mechanism for taming the working masses. By seeking to make the vast majority of workers homeowners there would be demands on them to make regular mortgage payments. These could only be met with a regular income achieved for workers through greater compliance with the state economic agenda.

As in Hong Kong, the public provision of housing for low-income workers was understood as a necessity for both social welfare and the growth of industry. The Singapore government, however, sought to provide cheap housing in owner-occupied forms in order to cement a sense of belonging and provide a stake in the country for the workforce (largely of migrant origin). It also enhanced worker dependency on a system geared towards capital growth. Chua (2003) argues that it became imperative to the PAP, therefore, to support the expansion of a public owner-occupied housing sector which would include as many of the working and voting population as possible.

In the interest of extending and securing its political popularity and legitimacy, the government kept raising the income-ceiling of eligibility to transform an increasing proportion of the citizens into homeowners. Buoyed by the euphoria of the uptake and a political belief that owner-occupation gives individual citizens a stake in the nation, which encourages nationalism, the government eventually made '100 per cent home ownership' and a 'home-owning democracy' its political aim (p. 766).

The leader of the PAP and Prime Minister from 1959 to 1990, Lee Kuan Yew, was archetypal among the British educated, middle-class administrators who filled the power gap after independence. His commitment to the ideology of home ownership established in Britain was explicit, as was his confidence that it would be central to social stability and political power in the emerging city-state.

> My primary preoccupation was to give every citizen a stake in the country and its future. I wanted a home owning society. I had seen the contrast between the blocks of low cost rental flats, badly misused and poorly maintained, and those of house-proud owners, and was convinced that if every family owned its home the country would be more stable.... I had seen how voters in capital cities always tended to vote against the government of the day and was determined that our householders should become homeowners otherwise we would not have political stability. My other important motive was to give all parents whose sons would have to do national service a stake in the Singapore their sons would have to defend. (2000, p. 116–117)

Home ownership was also critical to the social welfare system overall. Singapore has not been regarded as having a 'welfare state' and needy Singaporeans have been helped through a handful of financial assistance schemes based on short-term relief, focused on resisting the formation of a dependency culture (Yap, 2002). People have been expected to rely on their own savings and assets, the accumulation of which, the government has institutionally supported through two interrelated mechanisms. One is the Central Provident Fund (CPF), which is a type of providence account into which employers and employees contribute equally, based on a percentage of monthly salary (see Low and Aw, 1997). Contributions can accumulate in the CPF and be cashed in later life to support retirement and welfare needs. Critically, CPF savings can be alternatively or concomitantly transferred into down payments, stamp duty, and mortgage repayments for owner-occupied public housing units, which constitute the second mechanism of state supported savings. The role of CPF accounts in paying off housing loans has been critical to the growth of the owner-occupied sector and they together constitute the main asset-base for the provision of welfare. They constitute a commodified form of social security based on individual wage rates and investment activities in public owner- occupied housing property.

From the outset the Singaporean government has sought to resist the development of a welfare state made up of de-commodified services and instead retain a principle of self-reliance. The current Prime Minister, Lee Kuan Yew's eldest son, Lee Hsien Loong, reaffirmed this in his 2005 budget speech.

> We must not breed a culture of entitlement, encouraging Singaporeans to seek government support as a matter of right, whether or not they need it. The better off must help the poor and disadvantaged – the sick, the elderly, the disabled and the unemployed. In many developed countries, the state takes on the responsibility, but this is invariably financed through high taxes and levies on businesses and those who are working. Our social compact is rather different. It is based on personal responsibility, with the family and community playing key roles in supporting people through difficulties. The state will provide a safety net, but it should be a last resort, not a first resort and should focus on the minority who need help most. We thus avoid state welfare, which will erode our incentive to achieve and sap our will to strive. (*The Straits Times*, 19 February, 2005)

Building a system of universal home ownership

The system of public-home ownership is very peculiar to Singapore. There are arguably a number of conditions upon which the government has been able to achieve such a high level of control of the housing sector. The primary institution which has facilitated development of the system is the Housing Development Board (HDB). The HDB was established in 1961 and started by producing the first basic high-rise flats. In 1964 construction began of basic three-room flats (with two bedrooms), which were the mainstay of the early public housing system. In the same year the HDB began to encourage eligible households to 'buy' a 99-year lease on their public flats and thus become a type of owner-occupier. The decision to 'sell' public housing was unprecedented (Chua, 1997, 2003). Within a decade renting became the lesser preference among Singaporeans eligible for public housing. What was critical about the public form of home ownership was that a system evolved in which public housing units on fixed-term leases could be exchanged within a market (albeit tightly regulated by the government). By 1971 the resale of public-leasehold housing units was permitted. Such housing units thus constituted an exchange commodity, with a value that could increase (or decrease) and provide a container of equity and wealth for the family who sheltered within.

Another basic requirement of the system was government control over land. In 1966, the Land Acquisition Act gave eminent domain to the state in buying up land for the ostensible purposes of national improvement. Land was taken off private owners at below market rates, which allowed cheaper provision of public housing on this land. By the early 1990s the state owned around 90 per cent of the total land. Chua (2003) identifies that the system of selling leases to properties on state-owned land facilitated rapid system expansion. With each cycle of construction the state was able to recover costs in order to finance the next cycle (p. 769). In a public-rented housing system, the collection of rents would never be sufficient to support such expansion. Between 1970 and 2000 the HDB housing stock grew from 120,138 units to 846,649 (see Table 6.2).

The final key element of the system has been finance. The HDB not only provides housing but also mortgages and mortgage insurance for purchasers of new and used public owner-occupied flats. In 1968 the government approved the transfer of savings in CPF accounts into public owner-occupied properties. Owner-occupiers were thus able to transfer credit built up in the compulsory saving scheme, which is the

Table 6.2 Singapore housing indicators

Year	Residential dwelling units (Thousands)	Residential property Price Index (4Q 1998 = 100)	Type of Dwellings			
			Private houses (%)	HDB flats (%)	Condominiums and private flats (%)	Others (%)
1970	305.8		13	37.5	3.3	46.2
1975		12.8				
1980	467.1	33.5	9.3	70.0	3.5	17.2
1990	781.1	56.4	7.1	79.3	6.3	7.3
1996	874.8	173.1	7.0	81.7	8.0	3.3
1998		100				
2000	1,046.2	132.8	6.5	80.5	11.0	2.0
2005	1,133.9	118.2	6.2	78.2	13.9	1.7
2006	1,140.3	130.2	6.2	77.8	14.3	1.7

Source: Singapore Government, Statistical Highlights.

primary source of social insurance, into a 'housing account' with transfers allowed for both down payments and mortgage repayments. The CPF savers could use up to 80 per cent of their savings for public owner-occupied housing, while the remainder could be taken as a lump sum at 55. In this way the CPF cross funded the HDB, or in other words, the government was able to borrow directly from individual's savings rather than take commercial loans for development activities. The process constituted an internal transfer between government departments with favourable terms for all parties, without involving the conventional banking system (Lin and Tyabji, 1987). This transfer network in turn supported the system of individual housing consumption which formed the basis of asset-based welfare.

The objective of government control has been to ensure that, on one side, the liquidity of housing commodities is maintained in order to support property values, while on the other ensure that housing does not become the object of over-speculation. In order to achieve this there has been careful control of HDB housing flow and capital gains made. Initially, resale conditions where considerable. Owners who had owned for five or more years were only allowed to sell to those meeting HDB eligibility requirements (this was reduced to three years in 1973). At the end of the 1970s a 5 per cent levy was introduced to reduce windfall profits as well as to ensure that subsidies for a family buying another HDB flat was less than that on their first. In the 1980s the housing market began to mature along with the satiation of basic housing needs. There was, subsequently, further easing of restrictions on the public-home ownership system. In 1981 the CPF-Approved Residential Properties Scheme started to allow CPF savings to be used for private housing mortgage payments. Also significant was the easing of eligibility requirements for entry into the resale sector of public owner-occupied housing. By 1989 citizenship requirements and income ceilings were adjusted for resale flats and after 1991 singles over 35 years old were also eligible (HDB housing was available only to family households before that).

During the mid-1990s sales and loan practices moved closer to market ones. The progressive deregulation of the HDB market was accompanied by an increase in the number of transactions in resale flats. In 1979 there were fewer than 800 resale flats (3 per cent of the total market of public owner-occupied flats), in 1987 there were 13,000 (37 per cent), in 1999 60,000 (64 per cent), and in 2004, 31,000 (68 per cent). The development of the resale market and a drive to maintain housing demand became a government imperative in the 1980s and 1990s. The public-home ownership system inevitably relies on an inflow at the bottom end of the market which pushes up values. Falls in values would devalue the nation's capital formation embodied in the housing stock. Furthermore as public housing flats largely constitute the main family-asset, falling house-prices jeopardize the financial security of households, especially those nearing retirement.

The state has thus endeavoured to maintain home ownership consumption through a series of divisive measures. These have mainly been focused through the manipulation of a housing-ladder. This has been achieved in one way by improving the quality and size of stock over time. In construction, three-room flats gave way to a stock of four- and then five-room ones, and in the 1990s an 'executive condominium' (semi-private) was introduced for the upper-middle housing market. By progressively building better quality housing the state has sought to encourage resale and movement up the ladder as improvements in housing at one end eroded values of housing down the ladder thus compelling the upgrade as a means to preserve investments (Chua, 2003).

At the very bottom of the public housing-ladder are low-rent flats which are small in size with a very low income-ceiling of eligibility. Low-income home ownership is then encouraged by the HDB buy-back scheme which buys back older flats, refurbishes them and sells them on to lower-income families entering the market. New flats are also affordable as HDB housing is provided at near cost prices which are low due to the cost of land to the state. Mortgage interest-rates of HDB are also pegged very close to CPF interest-rates and reflect the rates at which the HDB borrows from the government. After a number of years in a public housing property the 'owner' is allowed to sell to an eligible household at a price agreed by the actors without HDB intervention. Capital gains are retained by the vendor (tax free until 1990), who can then buy one more HDB flat (eligible households can purchase two subsidized flats in a housing career and thereafter at market rates). These measures have been essential to a trickle-down of older and smaller flats to lower-income families. This has structured a ladder, up which public housing residents climb through a series of investments, accumulating increasing equity and property wealth on the way.

Social objectives

There are a range of social objectives of home ownership in terms of how the state has perceived and constituted tenure relations. First, public-home ownership controls have been a means of preventing the formation of low-income immigrant ghettos. Under ethnic integration policies, racial limits have been set for HDB neighbourhoods. Social control can also be exerted through the housing system and authorities can fine errant residents, cancel applications and evict families. Motorists who fail to pay parking fines may not be given keys to new flats until they pay up (Phang, 2007). Second, immigrants with permanent resident status have become regarded as a new market driver. Households selected for permanent residency have been allowed to buy resale flats at market prices.

The family orientation of Singapore's approach to housing has been a consistent aspect of policy. There are numerous social and ideological dimensions, the most obvious being the relationship between the building of family wealth in owner-occupied housing assets and family-based intergenerational welfare exchanges. Subsidies introduced in the 1990s focused on supporting the family function of asset-based welfare. Subsidies took the form of CPF home buyer grants of 30,000 dollars for purchases of resale HDB flats close to the households' parents or married children. This was later increased to 50,000 and an alternative 40,000 dollar loan was introduced for those who didn't intend to live near their parents/married children in order to stimulate demand more generally. It has been argued that subsidizing proximate family dwelling reduces social costs for childcare and building of elderly care centres (Chua, 2003). It also stimulates demand and supports the housing-ladder.

Singles do not qualify for new HDB housing and unmarried mothers have been ineligible for both new and resale HDB property.

The state has also used the housing system to stimulate household patterns in other ways. In 1987 the pro-natal Third Child Priority Scheme aimed to assist bigger families with HDB flat purchases, while in 1994 a Small Families Improvement Scheme was introduced to encourage low-income families to limit their family size to two children. Incentives included educational bursaries and housing grants paid into the CPF accounts of mothers, which can be used to buy a three- or four-room HDB flat (see Phang, 2007).

What has been clear about the universal approach to home ownership in Singapore is the considerable power it has given the state, or more specifically the PAP, which has held power since independence. Arguably, the housing situation has contributed a dependency of families on the state. This effectively transforms citizens into 'clients of the state' (Chua, 1997, 2000; Yu, 1997). In such cases the exercise of electoral power becomes more divisive as it is in the interests of citizens to elect the party most able to maintain high levels of state provisions. Self-interests thus constrain citizens' bargaining position with the state. When support for the state has been withdrawn, for example, in wards that have failed to register a high ratio of PAP votes, the government has been able to manipulate the electorate by undermining neighbourhood improvement programmes which enhance housing values. The government normally assists in programmes to bring existing housing stock up to comparable standards with new estates, which are critical in maintaining property values. Decisions concerning neighbourhood improvement programmes are coordinated through management councils, or 'town councils', chaired by ruling members of parliament.

This is not to say that the home ownership system has made the state all powerful. Indeed, the state has become increasingly dependant on the system itself and the housing demands of voters. On one hand the state is compelled by demands to maintain property value increases. Even though home ownership is practically universal, a market of new entrants must be created continuously at every stratum of housing types. 'Without such transactions, the ability of homeowners to realize capital investments will be severely jeopardized, affecting in turn the political legitimacy of the ruling government and, in general, the state that has encouraged the citizens to become home-owners' (Chua, 2003, p. 778). On the other hand, demands made by housing consumers become paramount in the interests of the government. For example, there has been a growing influence of young, university educated singles, who have argued articulately about the unfairness of the family focused public housing policy and gains missed out on. Since the early 1990s, political pressure has been enough for the government to advance the eligibility criteria for singles. Moreover, competition within this group has been influential in driving up prices, which has given home-owners better capital returns.

Maintaining property values

Until the mid-1990s, under conditions of low inflation and market value increases, the filtering down process had largely been effective. The cycle of purchase-resale-repurchase was central to the success of the system, but was also vulnerable to shifts in economic conditions. If one element slips out of alignment the apparently 'virtuous' cycle is disrupted. The system then becomes better conceptualized as a rigid 'monopolisation' of housing provision (Chua, 2003). After a small disruption in the mid-1980s the system came under more considerable destabilization in the late 1990s, in the aftermath of the 1997 Asian Economic Crisis. This shake-up exposed considerable fragility in the system which was already being eroded by the over-supply of housing. It also revealed the unique condition of ideological power relations surrounding home ownership in Singapore. Chua (2003) points out that for the state the monopoly position proved to be a double-edged sword. While the success of the system bolstered its legitimacy and made the vast majority of voters (who were homeowners) dependant on government policy, the government was also expected to shoulder the responsibility for declines in public housing prices. Failures in house-price increases would create financial hardship for the vast majority of the population. 'Failing to shore up the falling prices would thereby damage the PAP government's foundation of political legitimacy' (p. 771).

After 1997 housing demand and house-prices began to decline abruptly. Unemployment also began to grow, exceeding 5 per cent by 2002. These two trends were related for the state as under conditions of rapid economic growth there had been mass immigration and almost full employment, and so there was little need to develop social safety-nets. Home ownership property assets were thought to function as an adequate safety-net, but were also being eroded by economic conditions. It thus became imperative for the government to maintain property values. The government halted land sales and introduced subsidy for purchase by singles. Nevertheless housing prices declined further into

1998 and 1999 and conditions worsened with growing numbers of unsold units (by 2002 there was 17,500 unsold units).

Issues of surplus have long been a concern for the government in trying to maintain housing-asset values. However, there have been clashes with political objectives. In the mid-1980s, at a time when the state needed to contain supply, especially of lower-end flats, output reached its maximum (70,000 units a year). Production was driven by political motivations as the PAP lost substantial votes in the 1984 elections. Increasing public housing was thought to be both an economic pump-primer as well as politically popular (Krause et al., 1987). Subsequently, in 1986 and 1987 there was a minor recession as house-prices declined. Public housing production was then reduced to 20,000 units per annum in a conscious effort to support prices and prevent a surplus from forming again.

Housing inheritance also became an issue for the government as its effects are enhanced when there is a monopolization of housing production. The usual result of multiple suppliers is 'normal' cycles of overproduction and devaluation which creates investment risks for buyers. Chua (2003) identifies that in a state monopoly situation the need to maintain property values for all becomes the responsibility of the producer. As inheritance undermines the normal flow of house-purchasers and constitutes a potential source of surplus, it thus becomes a problem for the producer. 'Under that condition, if each newly married couple were to get a flat then logically, over the longer term, the flats held by parents would eventually be vacant, thus creating a general surplus and bringing prices down across the board' (p. 773).

Housing policy, welfare strategies and discourses of the family have essentially been intertwined to constitute a rather unusual relationship. The state has become particularly concerned with controlling movement within the housing system in order to maintain values, which constitute family welfare safety-nets. Housing objects at various levels of discourse are constituted as market goods, family goods and public goods. The relationship is highly contrived, but the necessary ideological outcome is that individual subjects are consumer subjects defined in a market and the family is thrown back on itself to actively provide for its own needs. The government, however, is still constituted as a competent housing provider, although this has been challenged by oversupply and shifts in economic conditions which have undermined the state's ability to maintain the system.

Shaping up the housing monopoly

In the 2000s the problem of maintaining property values has reshaped government strategies and ideology. Arguably, the government no longer sees public-home ownership simply as a means to encourage a sense of national rootedness, promote conservatism, and stimulate political popularity by providing voters with subsidized property investments. It does, however, still constitute the basis of housing policy. Home ownership now fits into a more complex set of mechanisms and objectives and is no longer primed around its initial function to drive urban and economic development, and improve housing conditions. The main focus of policy changes has been the preservation of the home ownership system through measured deregulation. The aim appears to be the maintenance of a level of protection of homeowner property assets. The choice to achieve this through greater marketization is arguably driven by the growing influence of neo-liberal discourses as Singapore has entered a new stage of economic development.

At the end of the 1990s mortgage services were remarkably underdeveloped due to the domination of the HDB (Bhaskaran, 2003). The sector's linkages with capital markets were weak and unsophisticated and the secondary mortgage market underdeveloped. The government has since sought to develop the financial-market side of the system. Commercial banks held 47 per cent of the housing loan market by 2003 (up from 41 per cent in 2000). Since then the HDB has stopped providing loans for those ineligible for concessions in order to support increase in the market share. There have also been steps taken to develop securitization (Phang, 2001, 2007).

While the HDB downsized in line with declining demand for new flats, there is persistent reliance on the HDB and CPF in maintaining the stability of housing assets. The CPF has first claim on a property in the case of a default which protects the CPF savings of the purchaser. New flats are now pegged to average household income levels to ensure that 90 per cent of all households can afford 70 per cent of a new four-room flat. In 2002 caps were placed on CPF withdrawals for housing to reduce risks of over-concentration in the sector and over-egging on the housing side in terms of asset and saving portfolios.

Over-investment in housing and declining housing values have exposed many households to unexpected risks and undermined their ability to draw upon their assets for care and healthcare needs in retirement. Lim (2001) projects that 60 to 70 per cent of 50–55 year old cohort will not have sufficient funds to meet government stipulated minimums for retirement. The Singapore system has generated an extreme condition of asset-rich-cash-poor older households with most people retiring having 75 per cent of their retirement wealth in housing (McCarthy et al., 2002), provided that housing values increase in real terms. The social security of older residents in Singapore appears dependant upon the performance of their housing-property assets.

The steps the government has taken to both marketize as well as soften the risks of over-investment in housing property suggest that the role of home ownership in state strategies continues to be central. The government may well continue to release control of the sector and thus its accountability. Nevertheless, the state also remains committed to promoting home ownership to support the value of existing homeowner-assets which provides considerable leverage over citizens as, historically, individuals have been ready to accept increased consumption of commodified goods over political change, the expansion of universal rights and de-commodified services.

Conclusion

These three East Asian cases appear fundamentally different. Not only in terms of the policy structure but also in terms of essential differences in the organization of home ownership. There is, for example, a considerable difference between Honk Kong high-rise flats and the single detached units most Japanese homeowners inhabit. In Hong Kong, flats function much more effectively as exchange commodities involving networks of mobile family members in buying, selling, letting and exchanging. Research in Japan has suggested that a sense of permanence attached to the land is more central in home-buyers discourses (Ronald and Hirayama, 2006). In the case of Singapore, nine out of ten homes are owner-occupied, but on land normally leased from, and in units financed by, the state. Nearly all owner-occupied housing is public housing and market exchanges are strongly regulated by eligibility criteria. Indeed, the notion of 'public-home ownership' in Singapore challenges very basic conceptual assumptions about 'private' tenure.

Other key differences concern the very natures of the three nations. Japan is a large, industrially mature nation with a mostly homogenous population, whereas Hong Kong and Singapore are small city-states that have urbanized even more rapidly, with large immigrant populations and a long history of colonial occupation. In Singapore there has been a longer period of independent policy development compared to a stronger influence of British housing policies in the Hong Kong, which may partly explain differences in approaches to public housing. In both cases the role of home ownership developing social capital and embedding a sense of belonging are far more important to housing discourses than in Japan.

The impact of the home ownership system is also strongly variegated at the macroeconomic level. The outstanding loans to GDP ratio in 2001 was 71 per cent in Singapore compared to 39 per cent in Hong Kong, and 35 per cent in Japan (Renaud, 2004). Whereas the housing market was strongly affected by global financial shifts in Hong Kong (specifically after 1997), Singapore and Japan were more protected (Chiu, 2006). Moreover, responses to the financial crisis have led to even more differentiation in housing system trajectories. Singapore has sought to protect the home ownership system through measured deregulation and greater temperance in housing investment in order to provide greater stability, which may be motivated by the centrality of property ownership in supporting asset-based welfare. Hong Kong has suffered some of the worst losses in real estate values and drastically cutback on subsidized owner-occupied housing. Authorities sought to stimulate demand by managing supply, which may be motivated by demands to support the private development sector and macroeconomic recovery. Japan, has historically attempted to deal with economic stagnation by stimulating construction. In the 1990s little was done to protect individual property values, with housing seen primarily as a macroeconomic pump-primer. Since 2001, state strategies and discourses have become focused on deregulating and neo-liberalizing the housing sector, and socio-economic policies have begun to disengage with traditional models of standard families and self-reliance.

Although state approaches and the embedding of home ownership policies appear very different, there is greater convergence across Japan, Hong Kong and Singapore in an ideological conception of home ownership as a means to pursue economic and social objectives. There have been particular concerns with legitimating 'growth-at-all-costs' economic strategies and the authority of a dominant single political party. Building a sense of individual wealth and supporting a strong state hegemony around the primacy of economic growth have thus been more critical to ideological dynamics. Home ownership discourses and practices are strongly embedded in both of these processes. Furthermore, this constitutes a departure from the neo-liberal mode of housing discourse and ideology identified in Anglo-Saxon societies (Chapter 5).

The constitution of housing as a market object remains critical to ideological relations in both East Asian and Anglo-Saxon homeowner societies. However, the prominent role of the state in the housing system does not appear to have contradicted the constitution of market subjectivities in Tiger countries. Indeed, owner-occupied housing units seem to have some salience as social or public goods, although less so for Japan. They are central to participation in a social-mainstream, although ownership does not extend individual rights or engender political inclusion. Market exchangeability is a characteristic of housing objects, and policies and discourses have effectively constituted them as such, but without recourse to ideologies of individualism and neo-liberal forms of governance. The ideological implications are considered further in the following chapter. I also establish a more integrated comparison of ideological patterns across homeowner societies and illustrate aspects of convergence and divergence in the roles home ownership plays.

7
Comparing Homeowner Societies

Introduction

Inevitably, putting together a comparative social and ideological analysis is a pragmatic and imperfect process due to issues of interpretation, incompatible comparative measures and specifity of context and pathway differences in housing systems, among many other things. Nevertheless, it provides a basis for the consideration of the diversity of practices and discourses that have shaped institutional structures and actions that, critically, constrain individual interpretations and choices. In Riceour's (1981) 'depth hermeneutics' ideological analysis begins with a social analysis concerned with the social-historical conditions within which agents act and interact. Chapters 5 and 6 considered social-historic conditions in terms of policy developments and discourses, and socio-political contexts in six countries in two sets of home ownership orientated societies. The task now is to try to make sense of developments in home ownership systems, practices and discourses between societies.

The aim of this comparison is to identify significant points of convergence in ideological structures and social outcomes of home ownership within and between groups of homeowner societies. This does not mean I seek to assert universal truths about the role of housing policy and housing discourses or imply that there are irresistible forces at work, driven by globalization, which are moulding a convergent pattern of social and economic organization across societies. The concern is making sense out of divergence assuming that the forces of globalization, economically and culturally, interact differently with localized features in each society which may structure potentially greater diversification (Doling and Ford, 2003). While I assert there is some regularity within groups of societies which are bound up with patterns of social development and the organization of welfare, I also suggest that the effects of intensified globalization on housing markets and social systems lead to differentiated responses. In some West European contexts the proliferation of home ownership and housing market intensification may result in greater orientation towards neo-liberal ideologies which structure state 'rollback' and the advancement of markets in the welfare mix, whereas in some East Asian contexts the intensification of housing markets combined with the experience of economic destabilization in the late-1990s is contributing to the advancement of public welfare spending and social-security policies, although state approaches to housing remain varied.

The first part of the comparison deals with apparent divisions across Anglo-Saxon home ownership systems. While we consider key aspects of diversity, the trend in recent decades has been towards considerable convergence around a particular model of property-based citizenship and social inclusion, which constitutes housing objects, individual subjects and the relationship between housing and dwelling in market terms. It is, moreover, related to processes of individualization and neo-liberal restructuring of governance, markets and welfare practices. The second part addresses the diversity in housing systems and social and policy development across East Asian societies. Again, we identify a unifying pattern in ideological terms as, despite the multiplicity of measures, housing systems in East Asian societies have erred towards similar social relations based on subdued citizenship rights and limited public welfare commitments balanced with strong family ideologies and facilitated access to property assets. This has fit with a productivist welfare regime formation in which neo-liberal features are more restrained. Essentially, productivist welfare regimes have also constituted housing objects as market ones, although the state has occupied a clear and central role in facilitating them. Moreover, while subjectivities are market-consumer orientated they are less individualized or discursively individualistic.

Convergence and divergence in the Anglo-Saxon model

De-commodification

The development of the housing systems in Britain, the United States and Australia demonstrate considerable diversity and challenges a notion of uniformity within an Anglo-Saxon market-orientated model of home ownership, or that there is consistency in housing approaches across the liberal-welfare regime. Harloe's (1995) tentative assertion has been that in market-capitalist regimes, where there are greatest opportunities for capital accumulation, there is least likelihood of de-commodification. However, in terms of the welfare system and the role of housing within it, each country demonstrates variation in levels of de-commodification.

While Britain as a liberal regime has largely formed a hegemonic orientation towards the freedom of markets and possessive individualism, there have been sustained periods when labour movements and left-wing governments have successfully nurtured de-commodified forms of public rental housing. In the post-war period, along with the expansion of the welfare state and in response to massive housing shortages, a comprehensive system of social rental housing was established. The post-war expansion of home ownership thus occurred in parallel with public housing sector growth, which established greater de-commodified relations in the housing market. Moreover, until the 1980s, both private and public sectors supported the housing system in unison with around 33 per cent (Local Authority and Housing Association) social rental housing at its peak. The social rental housing sector in Britain thus stands out among the group of liberal homeowner societies. Although Britain had followed a pattern of post-war development similar to other European welfare states, the 1980s marked a substantial turn in housing policy and tenure discourse towards a model of 'homeowner society' that was already well established in countries like Australia and America.

Although, de-commodified housing provision was championed at one time by Labour governments, public housing provision never constituted a considered measure by which the political left sought to undermine private home ownership or commodified relations more generally. Housing policy in the welfare state was not central ideologically. However, the reverse case is more evident as housing was central to Conservative policies in the 1950s and 1980s which sought to undermine the social-collective features of housing objects and their de-commodified consumption. New Labour policy and discourse since the late 1990s has persisted with the commodification of housing (for example, ODPM, 2000, 2005a and 2005b).

Although the British social rental housing sector atrophied to 19 per cent by 2005, the parallel figure was only 6 per cent in Australia and 2 per cent in the United States. There has been consistent resistance to the development of public welfare services in the United States, with housing as no exception. While, there has been considerable government subsidization to facilitate cheaper housing for poorer households in the rental sector, it was initially distributed to construction companies in the private sector rather than in forms that would de-commodify consumption or promote dependency on the state. This is not to say there has been no public housing, and a small residual stock has been provided as a very basic safety-net for the poorest households. The stock is so small however, that only 29 per cent of those eligible for federal housing-assistance actually have access to it (see van Weesep and Priemus, 1999). There has been a strong anti-welfare ethos premised on discourses asserting that social-economic stability relies on private, free-enterprise and individual self-reliance. State welfare has thus largely been distributed as temporary 'assistance' for 'needy' families. The Roosevelt reforms of the 1930s and Johnson's 1960s measures represent points where the deterioration in conditions required considered intervention. The nature of intercession, however, has rarely challenged the interests or principles of private enterprise and market relations. During the 1970s and 1980s housing subsidies for the poor were in fact enhanced, but only in the form of individual based 'assistance' to be used in the private rental market. Critically, vouchers were introduced in a form that constituted tenants as rational consumers while housing objects were embedded in markets.

Despite the resistance to public welfare, since 1994 (and especially after 2002), owner-occupied housing has become the target of new subsidies. Home ownership thus constitutes a form of welfare housing in this context to the extent that subsidies focus on families from low-income groups and ethnic minorities, and housing policy is seen as means to redistribute the advantages of the tenure to more needy households, advancing social inclusion. Nevertheless, considering home ownership in the American context as welfare is misleading because, first, enhancing the owner-occupied housing market tends to exaggerate social inequalities between owners and non-owners as well as between different sectors of homeowners, and stretch the resources of lower-income families further. Second, the basis of provision is commodified and does as much to enhance market dependency and vulnerability to economic fluctuations as to ameliorate them. Third, home ownership subsidies inevitably boost private sector companies and growth of the economy.

The nature of housing welfare and de-commodification in Australia however, follows yet another pattern different from that in Britain and the United States. While the influence of labour movements has been considerable, the strength of the political left has not forced through substantial welfare housing measures. A hegemonic consensus has formed, following the logic of the 'workfare' system, asserting that access to private home ownership is important to working-class interests and a source of collective solidarity. Indeed, home ownership was seen to expand expectations of workers' rights (Troy, 2000). While the features of Australian welfare are not as de-commodified as the British case due to labour movement strategies demanding better salaries rather than social wages (state subsidized services and goods), they are also not as focused as the American system on private enterprise, or as resistant to goods and services provided on the basis of rights and in competition with markets. What appears more universal in the development of home ownership is therefore, a characteristic acceptance that it facilitates greater self-reliance and an opportunity for households to accumulate wealth, while encouraging social stability and economic growth.

Ideological divergence

Beyond de-commodification, other aspects of divergence among these three societies appear more profoundly ideological. Ideology can here be considered in terms of two dimensions: tenure discourse and hegemony. By tenure discourse I here refer to the meanings and values associated with tenures which have influenced policy preferences. Although we argue that we should be cautious of claims of a cultural tenure predisposition, there appears a strong alignment between the United States and Australia around a 'tradition' of housing self-provision tied up with the immigrant-settler origin of both nations. Home ownership has been integrated with a 'national dream' which mythically epitomizes a way of life and values of a society. These dreams, as we have demonstrated, have often been borrowed in political rhetoric to support social policies, although there does appear to be a discursive assumption that home ownership gives individuals a 'stake in the country' and is important in processes of nation building. On the other hand, it is more difficult to square the British case with the homeowner-dream. The experience of tenure transfer is more extreme with only 10 per cent home ownership a century ago (compared with 45–50 per cent in America and Australia) and a large and relatively successful post-war social housing-program. The British case is more ambiguous when it comes to tenure ideologies and it is only in recent decades that social rental housing and the mythical realm of the council estate has become so stigmatized (see Gurney, 1999b).

The stigmatization of renting in general and public rental housing in particular is a point of ideological convergence between societies, although, only a recent one. Indeed, public renting was a central part of state housing strategies in Britain until the 1980s, and in the United States, construction and user subsidies for private rental housing dominated policy between 1960 and 1990. In the last two-decades housing policies have effectively consolidated housing relations around discourses and practices that constitute housing objects as private commodities that are most effectively provided by markets and consumed by purchase rather than rent. The same practices have simultaneously, and potentially irrevocably, undermined the status of housing as a merit good that can be best supplied by the state.

Hegemony is an ideological dimension that has been, initially, at the heart of tenure policies. Between the world wars, in all three societies, a consensus formed mooting the expansion of working-class home ownership as a potential antidote to both declines in the private rental sector, on one side, and labour unionist agitation, social unrest and demands for the expansion of citizenship rights, on the other. There was also an assumption that home ownership would concomitantly improve civic responsibility and encourage support for conservative political parties. This assumption can also be couched more divisively as enhanced dependency on waged labour and property relations (engendered by mortgage requirements) was argued to encourage bourgeois ideologies of property ownership, and supported false consciousness. While there is little convincing evidence that owner-occupation has political effects or 'improves' citizens (see Chapter 2), politicians and planners have, arguably, pursued tenure policy strategies with the intention of consolidating conservative hegemonies, or at least undermining collectivistic ones. In the post-war years it was clear that Macmillan and Eden specifically identified housing policy in Britain as a means of building a conservative hegemony, just as Menzies had in Australia. In the United States however, the conservative aspects of home ownership were not so evident in political contestation. Although home ownership represented a 'bulwark to bolshevism' in the 1920s, American political parties have never looked to home ownership as an equipoise of political power to the same extent evident in political discourses in the other Anglo-Saxon homeowner societies. Arguably, home ownership sits comfortably in the ideologies of both dominant political parties, and housing welfare intervention strategies have featured both private rental and private-ownership housing (see Table 7.1). What are more characteristic in the United States are priorities given to the interests of construction, real estate and finance companies, and resistance to public housing as a normal sector (Heidenheimer et al., 1975).

Table 7.1 Key aspects of Anglo-Saxon home ownership systems

	Britain	United States of America	Australia
Home ownership rate[1]	70%	69%	68%
Social/public rented housing	Housing Assoc 8.2%, Council Housing 10.7%	2%	5%
Private rented/other housing	11%	29%	27%
House-price increase 1997–2005	154%	73%	114%
Mortgage-debt/GDP ratio	73%	69%	82%
Key events for Home ownership Policy	1923 and 1924 Housing Acts: subsidy for private and public construction 1945–1950 Labour Welfare State: Local Authority mass public-housing construction 1955 Conservatives set out Property Owning Democracy, homeowner construction increases 1974 First restrictions put on Mortgage Interest Tax Relief (MITR)	1932–1942 Federal Housing Association, Federal Savings and Loan Insurance Corp, Reconstruction Finance Corp and Federal National Mortgage Association (Fannie Mae) established 1944 'GI Bill': veteran home-loans introduced 1949 Housing Act, Section 502 1965 Housing and Urban Development (HUD) dept elevated to cabinet agency	1918 War Services Homes Act 1928 Commonwealth Housing Act 1931 Mortgage Relief Act 1936 Australian Housing Trust 1941 Building Societies Act 1944 Commonwealth Housing Commission 1945 Commonwealth-State Housing Agreements 1947 Landlord Tenant Act 1964 Home Savings Grant Act

	UK	US	Australia
	1980–1988 Right-to-Buy legislation 1985–1986 Housing finance deregulation 2000 MITR finally abolished 2000 White Paper: 'Quality and Choice, A Decent Home for All' 2003 Low Cost Home ownership Task Force 2005 Plan to expand home ownership to 75% 2006 Home Buy	1968 Fannie Mae privatized (Ginnie Mae takes over public functions), Section 235 1970 Federal Home Mortgage Corp (Freddie Mac) 1987 Section 235 ends 1990 HOPE 1994 Clinton requests expansion of home-ownership 2002 American Dream Down-payment Act, Funding extended for SHOP 2006 Expanding American Home-ownership Act	1982 Home Deposit Assistance Scheme 1983–1990 First Home Owner Scheme 1986 Federal deregulation of finance 2000 First Homeowner's Grant introduced and in 2001 increased for those building or purchasing a new home
Measures to support owner-occupation	– Mortgage market deregulation – Right-to-buy for social-renters – Shared-ownership and low-income home ownership schemes	– Securitized mortgage market through GSEs making credit cheaper for homeowners – Mortgage guarantees – Tax Relief on Mortgage Interest – Subsidized down-payment and self-help schemes	– Mortgage market deregulation – Homeowners grants for first-time-buyers – Substantial tax advantages for owner-occupiers, especially un-mortgaged ones, and buy-to-let

Note: [1] Tenure Figures for 2005.

Sources: AHURI, 2005; American Survey of Housing, 2005; Australian Bureau of Statistics, 2002; DCLG, 2005; FNA, 2007; OECD, 2005; US Census Bureau, 2006.

Convergence

Despite international differences in the evolution of home ownership policy and ideology, housing and regime approaches have demonstrated growing convergence in recent years. Specifically, Anglo-Saxon homeowner societies have experienced greater housing market and finance deregulation, further decline in social rental housing sectors, greater expansion of home ownership, and increasing orientation towards an asset-based form of welfare system.

Theorists have attempted to identify core processes of transformation in housing systems across Western societies. McGuire (1981) puts forward a 'housing policy cycle' based on the experiences of twelve countries. The first phase begins with acute housing shortages (following the Second World War for most countries). The next stage is characterized by a drive to increase the number of housing units and achieve more capacity. The next stage seeks to improve quality and standards of amenity. Finally a point is reached where basic needs are met and the state consciously begins to reduce the financial burden assumed for housing. This is done by first eliminating indiscriminate subsidies and second by encouraging home ownership including sales to sitting-tenants. Boelhouwer and van der Heijden (1992) identify a similar pattern of development. In a number of Western European countries, policy focus shifted from an initial need to alleviate housing shortages to a concern with housing quantity and, subsequently, to a concern with housing quality. This has been followed by a growing interest in reducing the pressures of public spending on housing. While salient as generalizations to overall patterns of development in many Western housing systems, these approaches do not capture the nature of increased convergence in home ownership orientated policy around a specifically neo-liberal welfare model in recent decades.

Although the historic alignment between housing systems and decommodification in the homeowner societies I have discussed is rather uneven, specifically in terms of the role of housing policy in liberal welfare regimes, there has been in recent decades an evident realignment. Essentially, Harloe (1995) implies a process of 're-commodification' across a number of Western societies, with a shift away from social housing and towards home ownership. In the societies we have considered, shifts in housing policy are clearly convergent with a specific tenure policy model that aims to expand the tenure to as many households as possible, especially lower-income ones who have traditionally relied on private-renting or state provision, while shrinking the social rental housing sector to a residual. Furthermore, it is bound up with an intensification of international economic flows and the restructuring of global housing finance. The purpose of the private rental sector is to fill the gaps, supporting a housing-ladder into home ownership.

We may therefore, provisionally identify three steps in development of home ownership policy in an Anglo-Saxon homeowner 'model'. The first step was taken in all three societies in the 1920s and 1930s and represented an initiation of state intervention. This period also coincides with a global decline in systems of private landlordism. Intervention involved accepting a government role in the housing system, identifying home ownership as the most appropriate tenure for both economic and socio-political reasons (to expand the private housing sector and deal with collective welfare demands), and establishing a framework of financing and construction to support the growth of the tenure among the lower-middle and working classes. This step was usually balanced by some elementary public housing provision for the very poor. The second stage involves a form of moratorium in state support of home ownership, or at least a fragmentation of housing policy strategies involving other tenures. This occurred in Britain in the early post-war period and involved the mass construction of public rental housing by Local Authorities. In the United States it developed during the 1960s and 1970s which saw substantial state resources go into private rental housing as a means of dealing with the housing needs of low-income families. In Australia the moratorium is least extreme, but was evident in the 1980s when authorities began to question the purpose of home ownership subsidy and to withdraw direct assistance and tax allowances. The third stage that these homeowner societies have entered most recently may be considered a period of 'total home ownership policy' representing a point in the status of the tenure where it is almost universally considered the 'best' or 'natural' way to consume housing. The viability of rental tenures is simultaneously undermined by a whole set of discourses surrounding ontological and economic insecurity. This shift arguably began in Britain in the 1980s under Thatcher and the 1990s in the United States and Australia where it signified a less radical shift. The strength of commitment to home ownership has been reinforced by the house-price euphoria of cohorts of households who have experienced rapid house-price inflation.

While home ownership ideology may have initially served an ethos of bourgeois property-ownership, it now sits more centrally with discourses of market subjugation. The ideological reorientation of home ownership becomes primarily neo-liberal and restructures responsibilities for welfare among the state, the individual and the market. Neo-liberal governance involves a restructuring of risks between the state and individuals which facilitates state withdrawal. Policy practices and discourses assert that households are best off attempting to accumulate individual reserves through investment in their own housing properties in order to ensure economic security, and that the market is the most effective means of facilitating this (Chapter 4). In this way home ownership practices help shift emphasis from the government to the market. The process is not simply hegemonic but involves a multiplicity of discourses that restructure dwelling subjects around housing objects in terms sympathetic to the operation of markets. Discursive processes involved in home ownership relations in Anglo-Saxon societies constitute homes as commodities and summon up particular types of market-investor subject (Chapter 3). While government actions reflect, constitute and reinforce such discourses, individuals have, to varying degrees, embraced the restructuring of housing practices around market 'risks' (constituted as choices and opportunities) and realigned expectations of citizenship rights and state responsibility for individual well-being and thus their own subjugation to neo-liberal market relations.

A critical aspect in Anglo-Saxon homeowner societies is that the discursive constitution of housing as a market good undermines the viability of housing as a de-commodified good and the state as a housing provider. A dimension of difference between societies is the extent to which housing was previously de-commodified. The process of commodification is ostensibly stronger in the British case due to the historic embeddedness of social housing, and as such 're-commodification' may mark a more radical shift in ideological relations between individuals and the state. In the United States and Australia, housing commodification has been more embedded and there has, therefore, been less concern with resisting de-commodified practices in home ownership policy. This situation is apparent in comparisons of subsidization measures for homeowners. Whereas the United States and Australia have provided incentives and subsidies that undermine market mechanisms (including subsidized federal mortgages, mortgage interest tax-deductions and first-time-buyer's grants), conditions for low-income home ownership in Britain are more commodified and state subsidies more complementary to market competition (see Table 7.1). Discounted purchase of public housing and shared-ownership have thus been primary incentives.

Significantly, Anglo-Saxon home ownership systems, while diverse in terms of pathways and policies, have become similar in terms of housing finance mechanism and practices, which have become increasingly dynamic and sophisticated. Systems were increasingly marketized and deregulated in the 1980s and 90s along with a shift from non-price to price rationing which helped expand mortgage and housing finance. Subsequently, economic globalization and the intensification and deepening of flows and ties between local and international markets accelerated and expanded the reach of housing finance systems. Expansion was also in part due to increasing sector competitiveness and supported by the redistribution of risks from intermediaries to borrowers and third parties. A number of diverse factors related to market access and flexibility have also enhanced market competitiveness: growing numbers of loan insurance mechanisms; valuation systems based on current market value of properties; high loan to value ratios and long duration loans; foreclosure laws which allow relatively quick repossessions (Stephens, 2003, p. 1014). Housing markets in the Anglo-Saxon group have consequently become more dynamic and volatile following mortgage market liberalization and deregulation, characterized by speculative booms and busts. Critically, the eminence of market discourses through deregulation and the promotion of home ownership have become manifest in economic mechanisms and practices.

Despite global finance mobility, credit and mortgage systems have maintained considerable distinctiveness (see Lea et al., 1997; Stephens, 2003), especially in terms of intermediary systems and mortgage products where local lenders have freedom in regulating funds, and take advantage of tax exemptions and subsidies. Nevertheless, patterns of housing demand, financial deregulation and home ownership policy commitments, led by Anglo-Saxon housing markets and policy regimes, have promoted neo-liberal ideologies in more social democratic states who are increasingly submitting to the global discourses that assert the need for greater market freedom and national competitiveness (Doling et al., 2003). Economic deregulation and liberalization in housing markets originating in liberal regimes, despite associated volatility and risk, thus represent an increasingly powerful international policy hegemony.

The constitution of citizenship rights in Anglo-Saxon homeowner societies also appear to have aligned around an influential set of core tenure meanings and values. Evidence suggests that, in particular, values of economic prudence, security, status, permanence and adulthood and so on, have become embedded with owner-occupied tenure (see Chapter 3), and, more importantly, these values have supported powerful discourses that assert that home ownership is 'natural' and associated with 'better' households and a superior type of citizenship (see Kemeny, 1981, 1992; Forrest et al., 1990; Richards, 1990; Winter, 1994; Murie, 1998; Gurney 1999a). However, individualization and privatistic ideologies are also enhanced by home ownership practices, and erode citizenship rights to public goods to the extent that discourses promote private self-reliance rather than state provision. Anglo-Saxon home ownership thus tends to undermine 'universal citizenship' in favour of a form of citizenship achieved through property ownership.

My analysis has sought to demonstrate the significance of home ownership tenure policies and the special role they play within a group of economically liberalized countries. Social, economic and ideological aspects are by no means unique to this group and may be found in different measures across other societies with high rates of home ownership. I have sought to question assumptions about the natural basis of tenure preferences and alternatively suggest that there are ideological foundations to the proliferation of owner-occupied housing premised on a consideration of power relations. It can further be suggested that a form of tenure imperialism has emerged in recent decades which has asserted a rather singular view of how to live, what to build and which policies are better.

The difference between Anglo-Saxon homeowner societies and other groups of industrialized countries with high owner-occupation rates appears bound up with both ideology and the structure of the welfare regime. Anglo-Saxon homeowner countries typically demonstrate forms of liberal welfare regime in which the dominant element of the welfare mix is the market. There have been suggestions that home ownership systems are 'socially produced', with the characteristic feature in Anglo-Saxon cases being the social production of home ownership through 'market channels' (Poggio, 2006). In this case the welfare regime and social production of tenure are easily related with liberal capitalist orientations towards the market supporting a market-orientated system of housing provision (Barlow and Duncan, 1994; Kurz and Blossfeld, 2004). Nevertheless, such integration is rather simplistic, demonstrating a rather unsophisticated conceptualization of tenure ideology, based on assumptions of possessive individualism and the hegemonic influence of capital. Greater consideration of housing policies, practices and discourses suggests that housing relations and ideology are far more embedded in these societies in processes of neo-liberalization.

Kemeny (1981, 1992) pioneered such an embedded conception of housing tenure, identifying the significance of dwelling and spatial practices, housing discourses and the role of myth in the ideological constitution and social impact of tenure. My approach has attempted to illustrate a richer, more discursive picture of ideological relations, paying specific attention to the constitution of housing objects, individual subjectivities and social relations within particular home ownership contexts. Kemeny's recent position (2005) has shifted from an ideological, towards a more materially determined view of the relationship between tenure demand and welfare regimes, where the contraction of the welfare services has stimulated demand for owner-occupied housing in social democratic regimes. Our analysis would suggest that the process of welfare state withdrawal is itself bound up with discursive ideological processes around property ownership, which may be mutually constitutive and reinforcing. Moreover, a comparative consideration of the relationships between ideological processes and housing systems in other homeowner societies reveals that welfare regimes and housing ideologies are intricately bound up with power relations and processes of social change, but in ways less predictable in terms of limited Western conceptualizations of welfare regimes and social policy.

Identifying convergence in the East Asian model

The extent of diversity in contexts, housing systems and policy measures appears particularly extreme between Japan, Hong Kong and Singapore. Nevertheless, my analysis of home ownership systems and ideological structures in East Asian environments also focuses on identifying convergence. There is, essentially, a unifying approach to home ownership that is revealed by considering the housing system in relations among the state, welfare and families. This relationship is divergent from the Anglo-Saxon model, although still bound up with welfare regime practices and ideological relations. There remains a central, yet fundamentally different role of de-commodified housing relations in social and power relations in East Asian societies. As in the previous section, I begin by looking at de-commodification as a home ownership system feature. The following analysis addresses the contrast between social class relations in Anglo-Saxon and East Asian societies, identifying the characteristics and centrality of home ownership in emerging class identities and in relations between individuals and the state in East Asian contexts.

De-commodification

Features of convergence among the East Asian societies considered are evident in the production and consumption of home ownership and structure a particular approach to welfare commodification. To begin with, the nature of housing construction is largely orientated towards the objectives of the developmental state and involves substantial planning and government control, but it seeks to help promote private sector development. The overriding objectives are economic growth. On the consumption side it is important that families are able to purchase housing units which function as containers of family wealth and welfare exchange. Homes are thus largely consumed as commodified goods and market-exchange relations largely stimulate the augmentation of values. The central objective is the facilitation of housing properties which supports the circulation of commodified forms of welfare, primarily through the family.

Although housing policy frameworks are fundamentally diverse across the Tiger group, the overall approach to housing is more consistent (see Table 7.2). This unity is apparent when East Asian housing provision

Table 7.2 Key aspects of East Asian home ownership systems[1]

	Japan	Hong Kong	Singapore
Home-ownership rate	61%	Private 42%, Public (HOS) 16%	Private 9%, Public(HDB) 83%
Public/social rental housing	Local Gov. 4.7%, Public Corp. 2%	29%	7%[2]
Private/other rental housing	Private 26.8%, Company 3.2%	13%	
Mortgage-debt/GDP ratio	38%	39%	71%
Key events for Home ownership policy	1944–1945 housing stock decimated by bombing leading to severe housing shortages 1950–1955 Pillars of housing system established: Government Housing Loan Corp (GHLC), The Public Housing Act, Japan Housing Corporation 1955–1973 High speed economic growth 1973 Oil crisis brings economic growth and house price inflation to a temporary halt 1974–1985 Increasing flow of capital into land and property. Housing policy becomes economic pump-primer.	1973 Hong Kong Housing Authority (HKHA) formed, new town development and 10-year housing redevelopment programme 1977 HKHA Home-ownership Scheme (HOS) and Private Participation Scheme 1987 Public rental housing subsidy restructured to make better-off tenants pay more rent. Long Term Housing Strategy announced 1988 Home Purchase Loan Scheme 1993 Sandwich Class Housing and Housing Loan schemes	1960 Housing Development Board (HDB) established 1964 HDB Home Ownership Scheme (HOS) 1966 Land Acquisition Act enabling the government to cheaply procure land for development 1968 Approval of the use of Central Provident Fund (CPF) savings to support HDB HOS 1971 Resale market established for HOS flats 1979 Restrictions on HOS resale eased 1981 CPF funds become available for private home-ownership purchase

	Japan	Hong Kong	Singapore
	Cycle of house-price inflation begins. 1986–1990 Rise of bubble economy 1991–2000 'The Lost Decade': economic recession, housing market losses of more than 50 per cent 2001–2007 Restructuring of pillars of Housing system: Urban Development Corp becomes Urban Renaissance Agency, Public rental housing residualized, GHLC withdraws and mortgage sector securitized.	1997 Hong Kong becomes SAR with new housing pledges announced. Asian economic crisis begins 1998 Tenants Purchase Scheme, Home Starter Loan Scheme 2000–2002 Home ownership targets dropped, HOS sales suspended and then reduced 2003–2004 Home Loan Schemes restructured	1989 Citizenship requirements and income ceilings for resale flats lifted 1994 CPF housing grants for resale HOS flats 1995 Semi-public executive condominiums introduced 1996 Anti-speculation measures to curb house-prices 1997 Asian economic crisis hits housing market 2002 Caps on CPF withdrawals for housing 2003 HDB downsizes – finance deregulation
Measures to support owner-occupation	– Until 2007, cheap mortgages through GHLC – Mortgage interest relief – Special tax treatment of housing properties in inheritance and intergenerational transfers	– Home Ownership Scheme housing – Sale of public-rental housing to tenants – Government Home Loan Schemes – Rent penalization of well-off public-renters	– Provision of HDB housing units for sale – Supply of mortgage finance through HDB – CPF savings transfers into HDB housing – HDB maintenance and upgrade of older stock

Notes:
[1] Tenure Data for Japan, 2003; Hong Kong, 2006; Singapore, 2003.
[2] The tenure status of rental housing in Singapore is complicated by the uneven inclusion in housing and census data of the large non-resident population, which can comprise as much as 19 per cent of the total population. The majority of rental accommodation is public-rental housing provided by the Housing Development Board (HDB). Most private rental housing units cater for foreign expatriates.

Sources: Japan Statistics Bureau, 2004; Renaud, 2004; GHLC, 2005; Singapore Department of Statistics, 2005; HKHA, 2006; Hirayama, 2007; Lau, 2007; Phang, 2007.

chains are compared with those of other societies (Doling, 1999). The 'housing provision chain' represents the life cycle of housing from construction through to consumption, where the construction and development of housing has substantial effects on the nature of what is available to consume. In each stage of development, the relationship between state and market has discernable outcomes. In economically liberal, Anglo-Saxon homeowner societies, markets rule at each stage of provision largely unfettered by the state. Housing is seen as a private good and primarily sold or rented in a market. In North European societies where integrated rental housing systems dominate, the development stage is strongly determined by the state but construction carried out by the private sector. At the end, housing allocation and rents are often institutionally regulated on the basis of need and social fairness. In Tiger countries, the state normally asserts itself at the developmental stage with highly directive five-year plans and control over the economy, which affects the speed, location and nature of development. Construction is carried out by private companies and housing sold as a market good in terms of ability to pay.

While housing has been critical to welfare systems and relations in East Asian societies, it has been largely misunderstood. Arguably, this is because housing has been considered such an uneven feature in Western welfare contexts. Although Holliday (2000) considers housing systems across productivist welfare regimes as a feature of social policy, it is not regarded as a unifying element. He indeed identifies it as a divergent feature from which he differentiates sub-categories within the regime, particularly Singapore as a special category where public housing is a substitute for social security. However, the state's approach to the housing system within Tiger economies begins with the consideration of housing as a foundation on which growth is built and is more central to welfare systems and the productivist regime overall.

Home ownership has been the preferred tenure for political as well as economic reasons. Politically, it has been perceived to generate greater social stability and demand for new housing has contributed to the legitimation of the 'growth at all costs' approach. Economically, it is perceived as a source of national as well as family security and individual growth (Lee and Yip, 2001). In housing policy, the construction stage is the preserve of private, profit maximizing companies (subject to economic directives asserted by the state), which thus accounts for the absence of considerations of equity or fairness, but rather the ability to pay in housing consumption (Doling, 1999). While this has often been seen to mean that East Asian housing systems follow a market ethos, it is actually the result of the state's control of the market and its influence in the provision of public goods and services.

While East Asian owner-occupation policy appears market driven like in Anglo-Saxon societies, it is primarily state guided, and thus interventionist rather than neo-liberal. Indeed, governments have been policy active and controlling (Johnson, 1982; Morishima, 1982; Wade, 1990; Choudhury and Islam, 1993), and markets have not been given free reign. Essentially, these societies have been strongly managed by governments that have implement carefully laid down targets and resource allocations – often set out in five-year plans – based on pragmatic considerations rather than the ideology of markets and the minimal state. Schaede and Grimes (2003) identify 'guided markets' as characteristic of Japanese capitalism, but are evident across East Asia. Indeed, in developmental states, *managed* competition has proliferated and the nature of markets has been 'illiberal'.

In terms of welfare, the types of social security traditionally provided by Western welfare states appear very different to the provision of public goods which enhance private consumption and economic expansion in East Asian societies. There are, however, comparable outcomes which are mediated by the role of housing policy and homeowner goods in conditions of minimal welfare (Ronald, 2007a). States directly facilitate home ownership – which is achieved in a variety of ways in each society, but with the government inevitably mediating and subsidizing – but deliver it on market terms. In this way governments are able to provide and enhance goods that facilitate the effectiveness of family welfare.

Housing and education have been key forms of public goods. While housing is the biggest reserve of family wealth and facilitates other consumption and welfare practices, education constitutes the build-up of human capital which also enhances the ability of families to consume. Provision of these goods specifically, ameliorates the demand for, or necessity of, de-commodified forms of social welfare or universal citizenship rights. Housing policy in this case has facilitated the development of a home ownership ideology which has not been so bound up with individualism, but rather familialism. Moreover, principles of housing consumption and welfare exchange are still collective, and the state is still conceived as a competent agent of housing provision. Indeed, the system has constituted a means of state provision without de-commodification, and the maintenance of state power without demands for greater welfare rights and democratization.

Convergence

An appreciation of the role of home ownership gives an insight into patterns of convergence within a productivist welfare regime. In the sub-divisions Holliday devises within the regime (2000), housing policy is one element that marks out a 'developmental universalist' type of productivist society from a 'developmental particularist' type with Japan and Singapore, respectively, more ideal types of each. In developmental universalist societies some social rights are extended to productive elements of the population creating a kind of aristocracy of labour, whereas in a developmental particularist society there are no social rights as such, and individual welfare provision is promoted primarily among the more productive elements of society. In both, social policy is significant alongside the market and families. The critical point of convergence, however, is how housing property structures household welfare, which is not as different between societies as Holliday makes out. By not fully integrating housing into the model of an East Asian welfare regime, a critical unifying element is thus missed.

In Singapore, public owner-occupied housing constitutes the basis of social welfare in terms of providing family-assets by which family welfare can be supported. Employees and their employers make compulsory contributions into a Central Provident Fund account which can be either invested in pensions or insurance or, alternatively, into a 'housing account' in the form of an owner-occupied home. The Housing Development Board provides cheap housing finance and ensures a supply of affordable housing which can be consumed as an exchangeable commodity. In Japan, although there is more universal social-welfare cover, private home ownership provides the basis for the accumulation of family-assets which support the function of family welfare and social security. Again, public institutions have been central in ensuring the construction and finance of owner-occupied housing including, most notably, the Urban Development Corporation (now the Urban Renaissance Agency) and the Government Housing Loan Corporation. Both societies therefore structure a similar aristocracy of labour where those with greater income can generate greater housing-assets and, consequently, access better welfare services (Ronald, 2007a).

Although the social security and public home ownership system in Singapore appears very different to Japanese private owner-occupied housing, it functions similarly, supporting family welfare and minimal state accountability for social-security provision. Both owner-occupied housing programmes facilitate citizen's abilities to build and protect their accrued assets. In Hong Kong the HKHA has provided similar structures of supported entry into owner-occupation and regulates a limited public home ownership sector. The Hong Kong system seems to lie somewhere in the middle in terms of the public/private basis of housing support and levels of de-commodified services provided universally. State influence and control in the housing sector seems to vary in degrees with Singapore being a 'state controlled system', Hong Kong a 'state managed system' and Japan a 'state interference system' (Doling and Ronald, 2007). In all three countries, to varying degrees, the promotion of housing-asset building is significant in overall pension and welfare strategies as households not only rely on housing-assets as financial safety-nets but also on the reduction of monthly housing costs after retirement, following repayment of the mortgage. Housing-assets also feature in social contracts between family members with support provided by younger generations for older ones in exchange for cohabitation and property inheritance rights.

Critically, the political morality implied in these systems is based on privilege rather than entitlement. Despite direct involvement in each case, the government is not necessarily held accountable for household welfare, and thus responsibility for providing broader or more substantial welfare cover is diverted. Home ownership systems in other East Asian societies also rely on similar mechanisms of state housing and finance provision and often function along similar lines.

Housing, hegemony and class

While we have established a convergent basis for the understanding of the role of home ownership in productivist welfare systems, there is also a basis for considering convergence within political and hegemonic processes. This implies an East Asian home ownership ideology in terms of political hegemony that is clearly differentiable from the Anglo-Saxon one considered earlier. The hegemonic nature of home ownership ideology orientates class, the state and social power within a different constellation of relations. What connects home ownership and the maintenance of the soft authoritarian, developmental states in Tiger economies is the relationship between rapid economic development, the growth of urban middle classes and social-mainstreams, and wealth accumulation through home ownership consumption. Housing consumption, economic growth and hegemonic formation are strongly integrated elements in these societies and are strongly related to the local dynamics of social class.

Jones' consideration of East Asian regimes (1993) distinguishes them from Western ones in terms of central direction and the sense of individual rights. They are not conservative corporatist or social democratic in terms of Esping-Andersen's categories (1990), as they do not incorporate the interests of the working classes. They are conservative corporatist without worker participation, *laissez-faire* but not liberal. Indeed, the concepts of class and social stratification are fundamentally different from those assumed within 'labour movement' and class conflict theories originating in Western contexts. While structured differences in status, consumption and life chances are evident, these societies have been resistant to analysis in terms of class interests and solidarity. Although they are strongly hierarchical societies, social relations are based on the principle of duty owed upwards and responsibility down, rather than conflict between group interests. This manifests in relationships between the individual and family, company and nation. A key consequence has been an apparent insensitivity to issues of social inequality and class differences, and the underdevelopment of public social security networks.

There are a number of common conditions East Asian societies have experienced which provide a point of origin for class relations and the evolution of governance. First, leading up to 1945, all these societies were involved in social and military conflict and experienced damage to infrastructure. In the following period each society underwent a national political crisis or radical transformation of some form. These conditions necessitated substantial efforts by the state to engage in nation building, both materially and ideologically. At the same time, immigration and urbanization put pressure on resources. The lack of natural resources also meant that many societies had to rely upon the expansion of manufacturing in order to expand economically (see Agus, Doling and Lee, 2002; Lee, 2002). Also critical in the early post-war period was the desire to 'catch up' with the level of economic growth in Western societies. In the background was the presence of communist China which made rapid socio-economic development exigent.

Tiger economies experienced substantial pressure to industrialize, urbanize and modernize in a short period of time. Consequently, the governments which emerged were authoritarian, nationalistic and plan orientated with little concern for social inequalities and injustices. The mutual influence between politics and business corporations has been direct, facilitating speed and coherence in economic development strategies. In Japan, for example, the relationship between former *zaibatsu* and *keiretsu* industrial affiliations and the state has been particularly strong, especially in the construction sector. Principles of free market forces and democratic freedom have not been a central concern. The success of East Asian governments has been measured in the levels of economic growth they have achieved, which facilitate the accumulation of wealth at the family level. Most East Asian societies now enjoy a substantial level of affluence and new social classes and urban groups have emerged which have redefined practices of social reproduction.

Home ownership plays a substantial role in mediating these social relationships which reflect the pattern of class relationships and consumption of public and private goods in East Asian social regimes. Clammer (2003) identifies how, in the emerging shape of urban class and consumption, growing affluence, immigration, modernization and urbanization in recent decades has interacted with indigenous cultures, identities and social networks. A central feature has been the emergence of a new urban middle class which has developed new social and spatial patterns. A critical factor for this new group is the ability to consume which is necessary for both the construction of status and identity as well as for security and family welfare. In this case enhanced private consumption and the desire for the expansion of consumption of public goods go hand in hand. The new middle classes most vigorously demand the provision of public-goods which facilitate the freedom and security of private consumption (pp. 406–407).

The consumption of housing becomes central to the extent that differential access strengthens status divisions and erodes dependence on public welfare goods among the middle-class groups potentially most powerful in demanding social change. Owner-occupied housing also stimulates and enhances consumption based privatism. Consumption in this environment makes the middle classes dependant on the state for pro-market policies, which undermines other social solidarities and depoliticizes them. The perception becomes that social stability and macroeconomic prosperity are necessary to ensure the effectiveness of housing-assets which are the basis of family welfare and security as well as private consumption. The state, by providing housing (a public good) but by distributing it as a 'market good' ensures middle-class preferences for a strong state or economy rather than greater democratization.

In many East Asian countries, the government has acted to control civil society and strongly monitors the public expression of political and social needs. Clammer proposes that private consumption is encouraged to create a sense among urban populations of largely provincial-immigrant origin that they have socially 'arrived', at the same time the state itself maintains a virtual monopoly on the provision of public goods, which are consequently highly politicized as mechanisms of government policy and means of social control (p. 410). New East Asian middle classes have largely diluted the old exclusive elites, although they do not constitute a unified entity, but rather a class 'for themselves'. As a group they bring pressure to bear on the state for the provision of public goods rather than real social change. They thus coexist passively with semi-authoritarian regimes and have been reluctant to challenge the status quo as long as the state continues to come up with the goods (fruits of economic development). The culture of the new middle class is thus said to consist of cynicism and indifference regarding the public sphere (Mulder, 1998, p. 100).

Central in understanding East Asian regimes, therefore, and their collective divergence from power relations seen in Anglo-Saxon, liberal regimes, is the relationship between ideology, hegemony and the power of the state. We identified that in Anglo-Saxon societies, home ownership has been seen to support patterns of privatism and citizenship via ownership which serve to undermine universal citizenship rights and the influence of collectivist class-power in the public sphere. These ideological considerations prove more difficult to apply in East Asian societies, who have not relied on homeowners, as committed small-scale property owners to support the status quo, or on owner-occupation to undermine the clarity of class lines and social class interests. Authoritarian parties have held power supported by corporate elements, which have coordinated economic growth together. Governments have thus been freer in their economic activities and have received consistent public support despite the underdevelopment of public welfare programmes. In Singapore, for example, Chua (1997) identifies that public protests are resisted by a normative logic asserted by the government of 'the greater good', which has given the PAP freer reign and legitimated its authority. The citizenry have been unlikely to resist this normative logic as long as it has been backed up by economic growth, which has supported the augmentation of family-held housing-assets that meet security needs and enhance the perceived capacity to consume. The state has also been able to shore up electoral support by exercising its power to withhold subsidies for neighbourhood upgrades that maintain property values in constituencies where it receives least support (Chua, 1997).

The primary means by which social conditions have been understood to improve is through overall economic growth, which reinforces the development of goods that enhance individual consumption, like increases in housing values and greater access to education. Leading political parties have, historically, turned this to their advantage by suggesting that they alone are able to deliver the goods, and only under stable political and social conditions. The neglect of social housing, resistance to development of a welfare state and the underdevelopment of citizenship rights has thus not eroded political support as much as would be expected under European conditions of class interest and conflict.

Left-wing movements and trade unions have not been as evident in the formation of welfare capitalism as in Western societies. In strong welfare state societies, it has been in the interests of citizens to elect the party which is most able to maintain high levels of state provision. However, as dependency on state services is not evenly distributed, as many can and will pay for services such as education, healthcare and housing themselves, there exists a dual mode of consumption. The position of the state has consequently been strengthened where it can play the interests of one group of private consumers against the other group of public ones (Dunleavy, 1979). Essentially, in East Asian societies, the development of home ownership has played a critical part in ideologically orientating citizens towards welfare arrangements which favour economic growth over the extension of democratic rights and public goods. However, the contradiction between private and collective interests has not been central ideologically. Owner-occupied housing has been used to resist the emergence of de-commodified relations, and unified social classes in ways that have supported paternalistic regimes orientated primarily towards economic interests.

A new course

Recent developments in industrialized East Asian societies, however, have indicated substantial shifts in the dynamics of housing consumption, welfare provision and political power. The implication is that approaches to, and the function of, housing systems and home ownership have begun to transform and, to some extent diverge. Since the 1990s, there have been a number of changes associated with the socio-economic maturation of societies as well as a more intensified era of globalization, which have resulted in social welfare and political realignment (see Goodman and White, 1998; Peng and Wong, 2004). The end of a 'golden era' of house-price inflation was also a catalyst for change as the economic destabilization of housing-assets in the late-1990s challenged the basis of the welfare mix that had supported the legitimacy of growth orientated, productivist regimes. The effect has been an escalation in the socialization of welfare policies and welfare spending. In the last decade a series of social security policies have been initiated across developed East Asian societies, including national pension schemes, elderly-care programmes and other income insurance and healthcare benefits. Many are distributed on the basis of need rather than income or contributions, and cover greater numbers of women and the elderly. At the same time, the role of state intervention in economic development has also been reduced and greater emphasis put on deregulation and the function of markets. Approaches to home ownership and welfare, however, have become more uneven.

Historically, while there have been similar social and economic objectives, conditions and social policy pathways have been quite different. Whereas Japanese policy has always been more sensitive to spatial distribution and how to manage urbanization in-line with the decline of rural areas, the concern of city-states like Hong Kong and Singapore has been rapid immigration and supporting the urban, low-income workforce. There have thus been important differences in social-policy formations. Japan has in the past directed considerable public funds to rural areas and was quick to build up more universal health and pension (but was not a big spender compared to European societies). Hong Kong and Singapore focused on public housing measures and have only recently begun to consider more universal benefits. Nevertheless, the legacies of economic development in Tiger economies made the deepening of public welfare, and reduced reliance on family-based networks, more viable.

Another feature of socio-economic development is the achievement of relatively equal distributions of income. In Japan especially, enterprise unionism has helped equal income distribution across occupations. This has now made it easier for policy makers to begin considering redistributive social policy as a way of maintaining growth and social equity. The economic costs of redistribution are lower because the amounts involved are less onerous. The political costs associated with reform are also lower as chances of one class benefiting more than others are less. The influence and scale of social-mainstream and middle-class identities formed during rapid economic growth and structured by patterns of owner-occupied housing consumption are also important in this respect. Compared to Western societies, class-consciousness and class-conflict have been effectively muted. Collective labour-movements during the 1960s and 70s forced some redistributive policies through, although these were largely realized in developmental corporatist terms, meaning that money often went into public projects (such as redevelopment and construction) which benefited the private sector and drove economic growth. Nevertheless, increasing affluence, combined with feelings of social unity, are argued to have strengthened the normative basis of social equity and eventually become a brake on the growth-at-all-costs ethos (Peng and Wong, 2004). No matter how much policy makers may now emphasize economic growth people only tolerate so much economic disparity.

For Peng and Wong (2004) developments in social policy are being stimulated by a political de-alignment in East Asian regimes. The direction of change, they contend, is towards welfare-state-deepening and away from the principle of economic 'growth-at-all-costs'. This involves social policies couched in terms of social protection as a state responsibility. What is surprising is that this has emerged in societies orientated towards minimal welfare state, in the absence of any programmic political parties or strong labour union mobilization. The achievement of high levels of national wealth and social equality has supported the rise of public and political opposition. There is an emerging scramble for new issues with which to gain political advantage. New issues have energized political competition, and in this context social welfare has gained prominence as it cuts across social differences.

Another catalyst of change may have been housing condition transformations. For Dymski and Isenberg (1998) the new 'global age' is characterized by low inflation, weakened social-protection, reduced state subsidies for homeowners, and a greater mix of households and dwellings. The instability demonstrated in East Asian housing property assets in the late 1990s may well have brought pressure to bear on entrenched welfare ideologies. The effects may be enhanced by the rapid levels of social-ageing in the region. While Japan is a world leader in social-ageing, other East Asian societies are set to catch up in the coming decades. The prospect of a growing dependent population relying primarily on insecure assets for their retirement may have had a considerable impact on discourses in favour of broader mechanisms of social provision. This appears the inverse response to the 'global age' in Western homeowner societies where there has been a greater shift in risks from institutions to households, greater emphasis on housing property assets as a hedge against insecurity and a weaker state safety-net for those becoming casualties (Diamond and Lea, 1992).

Social, political and economic changes have constituted a new basis of housing relations in East Asian homeowner societies. There are some substantial differences between societies. Singapore and Hong Kong have retained more of the productivist model while developing a longer-term outlook on approaches to state-intervention (Groves et al., 2007; Phang, 2007). Japan, however, has yielded further to the market, appearing to follow a path more similar to the residualized housing systems of Anglo-Saxon homeowner societies. More universally, the function of owner-occupied properties as asset-based welfare has been eroded by the withdrawal of governments from finance and provision, and the further deregulation of housing sectors. Housing is increasingly seen as a means to stimulate the market base of society and government withdrawal. Housing systems have been a target of reforms, and are playing central roles in the restructuring of welfare systems. It appears that home ownership systems have entered a new phase in which social, economic and political dimensions are shifting. While the function of home ownership has become less predictable, there is resilience in state commitment to owner-occupied housing as the primary tenure.

Comparing home ownership regimes

East is east and West is west

At the outset of this book I suggested that the East Asian homeowner societies I examine form a particular type of housing regime. I have tried to illustrate that the role and function of home ownership differs substantially from the one identified in Anglo-Saxon societies. Moreover, I have attempted to relate home ownership systems with features of both liberal and productivist welfare regimes and show how housing provision approaches interact with hegemony and welfare structures in different ways. Despite system differences in East Asian housing systems, unifying qualities may be identified by focusing on the specific role of housing in the welfare system. The situation is essentially the inverse of Western contexts where housing has traditionally been considered the 'wobbly pillar' of the welfare state.

What is significant about East Asian systems of home ownership is that they demonstrate that the state's role in housing provision is more important than in previous considerations of the welfare state. At the same time, while housing has been too market influenced to have been considered a welfare system feature in Anglo-Saxon societies, the increasing alignment and orientation of Anglo-Saxon social and welfare systems around owner-occupied property assets, and social policy around building up home ownership and individual security in terms of it, belie greater convergence around a pattern identifiable in East Asia. However, to suggest there is a pattern of convergence in these terms between Anglo-Saxon and East Asian homeowner societies is misleading as ideologies, hegemonic structures, housing systems and welfare trajectories are fundamentally different.

In East Asian regimes housing has been more central to an established system, reliant on the accumulation of wealth through housing investments and welfare exchanges within the family. Here, housing has a stronger dual nature as welfare-good and exchange-commodity. While such a system is similar to many Southern European approaches to home ownership and family-welfare, as well as 'workfare' and emergent asset-based welfare discourses in Anglo-Saxon societies, the role of the state in Asian contexts is much more decisive. Diverse but intensive measures have been taken to ensure that rapid take-up in owner-occupation can be achieved. This has involved, for example, interventionist institutional frameworks (Japan) or, alternatively, a total orientation of the housing system around the public provision of home ownership (Singapore).

Significantly, the role of home ownership as a means to contain and build assets appears to have been a primary source of security to many families due to low expectations that governments will provide welfare-goods or financial support. This has made self-reliance and the accumulation of financial security through housing-assets a principal means of contending with potential family needs and future instability. Housing market volatility in the last decade has illustrated economic vulnerability within these societies. Although volatility is a shared feature of Eastern and Western home ownership systems, East Asian homeowners have had poor access to public welfare safety-nets when their assets fail, and limited recourse to the state. The 1997 Asian crisis put this vulnerability into sharp focus. In terms of globalization, housing systems in East Asia demonstrate that the increased force of international markets, economic flows and the logic of neo-liberalism have not had uniform effects or led to market or system convergence, contradictory to strong globalization theories. The pressures of ageing societies and intensified global economic pressures have been a force for a shift in discourse and for governments to begin to build up welfare services rather than dismantle them.

In terms of home ownership ideology, the state has come to recognize the development of the owner-occupied housing sector as a mechanism for economic growth, which has been more critical in East Asain societies in maintaining socio-political stability than propagating homeowner conservatism and economically liberal ideologies. Anglo-Saxon liberal regime systems follow market discourses more comprehensively at each stage, through provision to consumption. East Asian systems are, alternatively, often dominated by the state at the planning and provision stage, and it is has only been important that consumption is commodified. How systems diverge in both system and social terms is summarized in Table 7.3.

In the East Asian societies considered, political power, social cohesion and social hegemony are not maintained by neo-liberal market ideologies of individual freedom and choice, but rather by consumption and the ability of the state to deliver the goods of modernization and economic growth to an increasing number of middle-class households. This is what has made home ownership central to state planning and

Table 7.3 Divergent features of East Asian and Anglo-Saxon home ownership models

	East Asian model	Anglo-Saxon model
Social System		
State power	Dominated by single conservative or soft authoritarian party. Housing sector considered primarily in economic terms, with economic growth forming the basis of state legitimacy.	Politico-ideological, balanced between main competing parties. Property ownership considered a conservative social force that enhances individualism and market-reliance.
Social structure	Symbolically collectivistic societies but paternal-hierarchical structure. Dominated by middle-class mainstream. Weak citizenship rights and developing civil society.	Stratified social classes with increasingly fragmented divisions and affiliations. Active civil society and, decreasingly, trade unions.
Development pathway	Intensive, high-speed economic growth, industrialization and urbanization. Sustained pressure on resources and urban space.	Sustained process of industrialization and urbanization. More recently globalization orientated and post-industrial.
Welfare approach	Productivist welfare capitalist: low spending on social welfare, provision focused on economically productive groups. Emphasis on public goods which enhance self-reliance and private consumption. Established traditions of family (and sometimes company-based) welfare provision.	Liberal welfare capitalist: developed but residualized welfare states with higher welfare spending and social-security-nets. Past pressure on governments to improve housing and social conditions. Increasing marketization and re-commodification of public services.
Capitalism	Plan rational or developmental: based on bureaucratic-corporate elite. Often substantial government intervention.	Market rational and neo-liberal: based on entrepreneurial elites.

Housing System

Housing policy	Subsidy and tax bias towards home ownership. Relatively underdeveloped social-rental sectors (except Hong Kong). Focus on 'state provision' in Hong Kong and Singapore, and 'selective intervention' in Japan, Korea and Taiwan. Top-down approach coordinated by public corps. Strong support of construction sector.	Tax system bias towards home-owners. Residualized social-rental sectors, and focus on the market and construction sector to drive housing production. Growing number of assisted equity programmes for low-income homeowners.
Finance	Normally state mediated housing loan system supplemented by family loans and developing private loan sectors. Primarily middle-class access.	An increasingly competitive private-sector loan system with broad class access. Increasing transfer of risks from lenders to borrowers. Growing sub-prime sector, secondary mortgage market and international flows of finance.
Housing market and stock	Urban market, driven by rapid development and supply of new build units.	Integrated property market dominated by speculative developers as well as second hand stock.
Housing provision chain	Tiger type: state asserts itself at development stage (via 5-year plans) and often controls land supply (directly or via land adjustment) along with speed, location and nature of development. Construction by private companies and housing sold as market good based on ability to pay.	Liberal type: land supply and construction dominated by private landowners and developers. Consumption based on market principles and ability to pay.
Family housing practices	Mostly vertically extended families but increasingly nucleated. Home-owner privatism based on family interdependence and self-reliance.	Predominantly nucleated families but increasingly fragmented. Home-owner privatism based on principles of individualism and autonomy.

policy discourses in these contexts. While there are numerous systems, there are shared characteristics in power relationships, social-solidarities and reproduction of the state.

Arguably, East Asian societies do not truly represent property-owning-democracies. Although home ownership has been used as a way to encourage the development of social capital and build up attachments between individuals and society, and even strengthen nationalism, it has not been an explicit means to enhance the political rights of property-owners. The power base of these societies has encouraged passivity not participation. Levels of association between home ownership and social participation vary across the group, and while democratic associations between property-ownership and social participation in Japan have been explicit (following the constitution devised under post-war US occupation), Singaporean owner-occupiers have become more dependant on a single party (Chua, 1997). In Anglo-Saxon societies the assertion is that a sense of rights based on property ownership has been nurtured in an attempt to supersede the sense of rights based on universal rights (Kemeny, 1981, 1992; King, 1996, 2006). This socio-political dimension is absent in most East Asian contexts where universal rights have always been suppressed, but where collectivism has not constituted a contradiction to capitalism. Moreover, home ownership has not been seen as a means to develop individualistic sensibilities and ideologies. It has, rather, been used to enhance a sense of interdependency within kinship-networks and a sense of solidarity with a middle mainstream. The ideological or discursive constitution of individual subjects and housing objects also appear to follow this divide. In Anglo-Saxon societies housing is constituted as a private market object and individuals as market-investor subjects, which has eroded the social nature of housing goods and viability of the state in provision. Whereas, in East Asian countries, although housing objects manifest a market salience, their consumption is more collectively mediated through the family and the state remains central as an agent of provision and facilitation.

East meets West?

There remain however, several key points of convergence between East Asian and Anglo-Saxon approaches to home ownership. These include, first, the significance of political sponsorship in successfully establishing a home ownership system, although ways and means vary. Second, the normative construction of a society as naturally predisposed to individually owned housing, connected to a cultural owner-occupier heritage is a common feature of modern homeowner societies. As owner-occupier value systems and housing cultures are not similar between Eastern and Western homeowner societies it appears that homeowner ideologies may not be as important as the normalization of home ownership itself. Lee (1999) implicates Chinese tradition in home ownership preferences in Hong Kong, while in Japan research has revealed parallel discourses on home ownership 'tradition' (Ronald, 2004, 2008), but these are arguably no more significant than claims of an Anglo-Saxon tradition. Modern home ownership is more the result of state manipulation than a sociocultural predisposition. Third, the tacit connection made between home ownership, conservatism and middle-class formation, and social stability appears a feature of social and political discourses in homeowner societies, although both the function and content of ideology related to middle-class housing consumption is different. In Anglo-Saxon society, homeowner status structures individualization and separation from the public sphere, and in East Asia, greater attachment and social inclusion.

We must also be cautious of an over-assertion of market-liberalism in Anglo-Saxon home ownership policy systems. Governments have strongly subsidized private housing purchase and intervened in the market to ensure the growth of the owner-occupied sector. The market liberalism of liberal regimes in respect of housing policy and home ownership should thus not be overemphasized. The point of convergence is therefore, a trend for Anglo-Saxon societies (particularly in relation to welfare residualization and commodification) to follow an East Asian pattern (Groves et al., 2007). Indeed, recent political discourses in Anglo-Saxon societies suggest that governments are considering the substantial financial resources owner-occupying households have built up and the growing tangibility of housing-assets as a means to support the reduction of welfare services, erode state-pension-provision and undermine universal welfare rights.

The reduction of state control over housing provision and housing markets, and the extension of social security in East Asian societies on one side and the greater orientation towards housing-assets as a means to commodify welfare consumption and reduce state responsibility and accountability for individual welfare in Anglo-Saxon societies on the other, make it appear that Eastern and Western social and policy trajectories may eventually meet somewhere in the middle. The growth of home ownership would thus constitute a force for social convergence. However, such a conclusion poorly accounts for the diversity of housing and welfare systems, different socio-historic conditions and the socio-political dynamics of each society. It is arguably more useful to consider the alignment of different policy and social systems around home ownership as a single, although potentially critical factor in the development of welfare and capitalism in each society. Also important is the consideration of features of housing systems and social organization which may be attributable, but not reduced, to different, identifiable home ownership regimes.

8
The Future of Home Ownership and the Consequences of Tenure

Introduction

There are questions identified at the beginning of this book concerning the relationship between housing and society. These specifically addressed relations between tenure ideologies and social power relations, housing systems and welfare regimes, and differences in the constitution of home ownership and social structures in different societies. Each chapter has attempted to answer one or more of these questions with the intention of developing empirical and theoretical understanding of the role of housing in societies orientated towards home ownership. I begin making conclusions by summarizing the main arguments and addressing how home ownership should be understood as a dimension of social structure and social relations. This is followed by a more considered appraisal of home ownership ideology, identifying the progress made by the book in developing theory and establishing how policies and discursive housing practices constitute social conditions which appear related to social power relations in different societies. I finally look forward to the implications of potential growth in home ownership across a broader group of societies as well as the emerging features of existing homeowner societies which seem to have been destabilized and socially polarized by their over-dependency on housing markets. Owner-occupied housing systems and practices now appear embedded in socio-economic structures and definitive in how individuals deal with risk and insecurity over the life-course. How governments deal with housing will thus become more central to the evolution of welfare systems and patterns of social development.

Home ownership has long been considered in terms of its ideological significance, although how tenure exerts a social influence and what the effects are have not been so clear. Housing as a dimension of the social structure was poorly addressed until the 1960s. Subsequent debates dwelt on the salience of Marxist of Weberian notions of class and how they related to different types of residents. In recent decades the sociological understanding of home ownership has been increasingly couched in terms of consumption, with a growing emphasis on the owner-occupied home as locale of processes of individualization. Essentially, the shift in focus on ideology and tenure has been from a Marxist notion on false consciousness and bourgeois ideologies of property ownership to postmodern conceptions of symbolic consumption. The suggestion made was that such approaches were either deterministic or fundamentally neglected the divisive aspects of the promotion of owner-occupied housing. The literature on the meaning of housing and tenure suggests that tenure discourses have a substantial impact on the orientation of individuals and households towards security, autonomy and family life, and are strongly normative in these terms. Another specific feature of housing discourses is their constitution of housing objects and housing users in more or less social terms, which summons or constructs particular types of commodified relations between individuals, the market and the state.

Advancing globalization has stimulated debates on the relationship between housing and welfare systems in explaining different patterns of social development. Housing has historically been considered the wobbly pillar of the welfare state and moreover, housing systems have seemed to poorly align with the existing models of welfare regimes which dominate explanations of differences between advanced capitalist societies. However, the growth of owner-occupation rates and housing-property values, along with increased commodification, neo-liberalization and residualization of welfare provision, have seen housing play a more central role in welfare and retirement strategies in some societies. The suggestion has been that home ownership may be playing a part in building an asset-based welfare approach in some countries, especially those where neo-liberal governance and markets are most advanced.

The empirical section of this book addressed two groups of homeowner societies. The emergence of an institutional orientation towards home ownership policy and practice was first considered in three cases of economically (neo-)liberal Anglo-Saxon countries: Britain, the United States and Australia. Substantial diversity in development pathways was identified although also evident was a growing convergence around a

Home Ownership and the Consequences of Tenure 241

neo-liberal, market-orientated housing system model. A specific role of home ownership was illustrated in this model, related to processes of social transformation towards a leaner form of welfare state, market-based welfare provision and an individualistic, asset-building, investor subject. In the East Asian context too, a group of three home ownership ideological societies were identified (Japan, Singapore, Hong Kong) which also demonstrated different pathways and radically diverse housing systems. These countries too betrayed core similarities within the group in how home ownership practices and policy contributed to the constitution of social relations under a particular type of capitalist state and a productivist form of welfare regime. In this model the link between individualism and the neo-liberalization of sociopolitical relations was not so significant, although the housing system was important to a commodified welfare orientation of families. Eastern and Western groups of homeowner societies finally were contrasted, which provided a means to consider the centrality of housing and tenure relations in the constitution of social conditions in these contexts, and the significance of housing ideology in the discursive practice of power relations.

Ideological concerns

While the arguments in the book have often been broad, we can now begin to address the concept of an ideology of home ownership more reflexively. The unravelling of home ownership ideology reveals diverse ways in which housing tenure systems have interacted with society and political relations. Since the late nineteenth century, home ownership has been understood to play a part in social class relations and has been perceived as a means to subdue the working classes. However, the evidence that housing tenure has significant outcomes on political attitudes has not been convincing, nor has the simple association between political parties and tenure approaches. Indeed, in the Australian case the political left has often fought for improved access into owner-occupation for workers and, furthermore, tenure growth has been associated with the extension of a sense of rights rather than a decline of radicalism (Winter, 1994; Troy, 2000).

The more discursive consideration of housing tenure reveals that while home ownership may have a role in strengthening hegemonies around property ownership and market relations, its effect in and on society is deeper. The impact of home ownership in the societies where it dominates is comprehensive as it has come to define the normal, appropriate or ideal ways of organizing domestic life, and how this domestic world intersects with the public one. Owner-occupation appears fundamentally embedded with various discourses which mediate social understandings of critical aspects of social life like citizenship, autonomy, family life and adulthood. Understanding of home ownership as an ideology requires moving beyond a simple notion of dominant ideology and involves more dynamic flows of power and forces of subjugation in which residents are as complicit or active as state institutions or market intermediaries.

The alignment of housing systems and welfare regimes is made clearer by a discursive rather than hegemonic approach to housing and ideology. The consideration of how housing systems fit with social democratic, corporatist or liberal welfare regimes has not been particularly productive. Moreover, it has been difficult to simply reconcile liberal regimes with home ownership orientated systems and social democratic regimes with social-renting (Kurz and Blossfeld, 2004; Kemeny, 2006). Nevertheless, the role of home ownership in supporting the economic structures and social discourses necessary for welfare roll-back and greater neo-liberalization of governance is more apparent. The focus on home ownership and how it situates and orientates individual subjects around the dimensions of welfare providers including the state, the market and the family, reveals an ideological relation between housing and welfare regimes. The ideological dimensions of tenure and housing systems can not be understood in terms of left and right, or collectivistic and individualistic hegemony. They involve complex relations between housing objects, housing providers and individual subjects. Of central importance is how social or private housing objects are discursively constituted which defines either the state or the market as more or less competent providers, making housing more or less commodified and householders more or less constituted as financialized subjects.

With the expansion of home ownership across corporatist and social democratic regimes, along with the considerable advancement of mortgage markets and rapid house-price augmentation, it seems possible that housing systems may play an ever more important role in the restructuring of welfare states and building hegemonies in favour of greater privatization and marketization. As I shall discuss in greater depth shortly, this is already evident in the extent that some social democratic governments have already privatized or deregulated the social rental housing sector and supported increased entry into home ownership. The particular development of home ownership in these societies may thus become central to emerging welfare relations and an important area for future research.

Kemeny (2005) has come to similar conclusions, but arguably for different reasons. In Kemeny's original thesis (1981), high rates of home ownership impacted on society through various forms of privatization, influencing urban form, life-styles, gender roles, systems of welfare and social security as well as other dimensions of social structure. Later on, the ideological aspects of individualism and home ownership became more central to the thesis (1992). However, following Castles (1998), Kemeny has recently suggested the relationship between home ownership and welfare may potentially be reversed with minimalist models of welfare pushing high rates of home ownership. Recent growth in home ownership rates in social democratic societies like Sweden suggest that the global squeeze on the state and the restructuring of welfare may be reorientating households towards tenure, where it appears necessary to build up more financial capacity in early life to provide security in old age. The new position is essentially structural rather than ideological. My approach also identifies the relationship between home ownership and welfare, but supports the maintenance of a discursive consideration of the interaction of social structure, home ownership and ideology. The roll-back of welfare and the deregulation of housing policy have been driven by discourses of globalization and national competitiveness on one side (Clapham, 2006), whereas market discourses and house-price inflation have made home ownership (along with other individual capital building mechanisms) more viable as an alternative to high-tax, maximal welfare on the other.

Beyond addressing home ownership ideology more discursively, this book has taken a substantial and arguably innovative step by trying to deal with tenure and ideology in comparative terms. The methods for looking at such meaningful, qualitative and contextually contingent variables across societies are essentially limited and not yet developed. The hope is that this book contributes to development. The primary focus has been only three of many English-speaking homeowner societies, and the analysis already illustrates the potential or necessity to address differences in policies and discourses even more thoroughly and systematically within this group. The consideration of radical different approaches to housing and more convergent features of tenure-ideology relations in East Asian societies challenges central Anglo-Saxon assumptions about the very nature of tenure and housing systems and how they function in the maintenance or transformation of social conditions. There are also prospective patterns of homeowner society and home ownership ideology in other regions of Southern and Eastern Europe which may potentially provide even greater insight into the nature of interaction between housing and society. Again, this represents an important area for future research.

Comparative housing research has primarily focused on quantifiable features and tangible measures (like GDP, unit outputs, and tax and subsidy mechanisms) in order to discern patterns of convergence and divergence between societies and build understanding of global, socio-economic processes. This has been useful, but has not provided a complete picture. As has been suggested (Dickens et al., 1985; Elsinga et al., 2007; Forrest and Murie, 1995; Haworth et al., 2004), greater sensitivity to different localities and cultures, discursive elements and ideological practices fundamentally enhance understanding. Moreover, they strengthen the effectiveness and expand the scope of comparative housing approaches.

Similarities and differences

My analysis has demonstrated some convergent ideological features across the societies studied. In both Eastern and Western societies there is evident normalization around a polarization of tenure discourses concerning the meanings of tenure. There is substantial evidence of a stigmatization of renting, which may be more extreme in Anglo-Saxon societies, especially in cases of public rental housing estates. In the East Asian countries considered, such estates are rare except in Hong Kong. Here too, however, while public rental housing still constitutes adequate family housing, there are particular 'types' of residents, and those with adequate levels of income have been normatively pressured to become owner-occupiers (Chan, 2000). What may be most salient about tenure polarization and the diminished status of renting is that it legitimates the provision of only a residual sector of social rental housing and supports the owner-occupied market sector overall.

Economic discourses also appear significant, and there is often a similar financial logic to home-owning. This is specifically evident in discourses on renting which normally conjure images of imprudent tenants throwing their 'money down the drain' and is consistently constituted as a 'waste of money'. There are some nuanced divergences in economic meanings between societies however. Entrepreneurial and investor discourses have been more central to the Hong Kong home ownership boom, whereas in Japan and Singapore there has been more emphasis on building family-assets rather than speculatively gambling with them. Across Anglo-Saxon societies the core of meanings and the nature of discourse demonstrate some consistency (see Chapter 3) which belies fundamental differences in housing experiences. A key feature in all societies is the experience at some point of a 'golden age' of rapid house-price inflation which may have embedded particular economic perceptions of housing properties and housing markets.

A fundamental point of divergence in ideologies appears to be the relative significance of individualism and self-identity mediated by the owner-occupied home. In Anglo-Saxon societies there has been an assumption that home ownership preferences are bound up with individualistic propensities or discourses, and research has considered the home as a medium of identity consumption and self-expression (for example, Csikszentmihalyi and Rochberg-Halton, 1981; Miller, 2001). East Asian societies are resistant to the over-assertion of individualistic values, and collective solidarity has been a central social discourse (Walker and Wong, 2005). Home ownership has rarely been sold as a means for individuals to assert their difference from everyone else. Indeed, the home is a medium of interdependent relationships between the family within and society without. More important in East Asian contexts has been the home as a medium of self-reliance and for building up the economic and social capital of the family.

For Kemeny (1992), privatization and individualism are critical ideological features of 'monotenural', homeowner societies and collectivist hegemonies have been similarly embedded in societies with strong social rental sectors. East Asian systems confound the individualistic aspects of an ideological model. Arguably, the process of individual*ization* may be the more important feature of owner-occupied tenure. Families essentially compete in a market for better housing and seek to build up financial resources in order to become self-reliant, the idea being that in this way they will not become dependent or a burden on collective resources. Moreover, self-reliance may seem the logical course in societies with minimal welfare states that provide few de-commodified services. Most crucially, the private family spaces and property assets constituted by owner-occupied housing facilitate practices of family privatism and self-reliance. A more unifying feature across homeowner societies is arguably the marketization and commodification of relations which suits various types of minimal welfare system.

Social-class dimensions are complex but ostensibly important to the rise of tenure systems. In Western societies the state may have convinced itself that home ownership will undermine class conflicts. While the political effects are difficult to measure, it is evident that more households became homeowners across social classes in line with the erosion of traditional class solidarities. In East Asia, government support of owner-occupied housing provision was driven by a concern with building a sense of social solidarity across a middle-class mainstream, rather than the desire for social-class fragmentation. Housing has been intertwined with a particular development pathway in which economic growth has been more important to the legitimacy of the state and the reconciliation of the working classes than the provision of de-commodified services.

It is important to note that despite all the differences in ideologies and the embedding of the housing system in social relations that discourses in all these societies demonstrate a deep conviction concerning a cultural tenure heritage. Although the origins of housing systems are diverse, the future of homeowner societies now seems inextricably bound up with a pathway contingent on developments in housing markets. Indeed governments appear to have structured an overdependence on the type of housing systems which make households most vulnerable to the risks of economic cycles and the flows of international markets. The home ownership pathway may, of course, provide many families with greater security and opportunities to become wealthier. However, housing markets have largely created more inequalities across societies (Hamnett, 1999; Malpass, 2006). I now finally look to the future of home ownership and developments in homeowner societies. First, I deal with the greater international impact the tenure may have, based on the propensity of an increasing number of governments to look towards adjusting housing policies to facilitate social changes fitting with the logic of advancing globalization. Last, I consider the impact home ownership is beginning to have on the features of homeowner societies that appear to be reshaping relations among individuals, families and the state which are increasingly dependant on the market.

More homeowner societies?

As a result of the domination of home ownership and the reconstitution of housing objects as market properties, a form of 'tenure imperialism' has emerged in many homeowner societies, especially Anglo-Saxon, liberal-economic ones. This imperialism has asserted a rather singular view of how to live, what to build and which policies are best. Under conditions of intensified globalization and the deepening and expansion of financial networks, the model of financial marketization and housing investment consumption of homeowner societies appears to be increasing in influence across a broader group of industrialized societies in continental Europe. Doling (2006) identifies how, within the EU, even though housing policy has an independent competency in each member country an EU government agenda has been set out based around a more neo-liberal, deregulated, mortgage market model (see CML, 2005), where integration between national housing systems is enhanced by the interconnectedness and transferability of housing finance products and services. It seems apparent that EU government discourses are beginning to mimic Anglo-Saxon governments which emphasize marketization, deregulation and the expansion of home ownership in response to the emerging imperatives of global competition.

> reducing restrictions on refinancing mortgage debt and offering improved possibilities to finance a larger proportion of the purchase price of property via more generous and cheaper mortgage loans could extend home ownership and also boost consumption. Transaction costs on housing are too high in most member states. More flexible housing markets would encourage labour mobility and the development and efficiency of the financial services sector, empower home-buyers and support more consumer spending. (European Commission, 2004, pp. 25–26)

Inevitably, greater integration of housing finance will only undermine the stability of local housing systems, further open up economies and make more households more vulnerable to international in-and-out-flows of capital. The Anglo-Saxon homeowner society, in these terms, has been considered a threat to the integrity of international housing systems and social democratic hegemonies in other societies (Clapham, 2006).

There is already evidence of shifts in housing policy in social democratic and corporatist countries that suggest a change in the discursive order of housing. In the Netherlands, for example, there has been a marked a shift since 2000 in policy. The ideal of 'choice' and the individual as a consumer, expressing personal desires and preferences for housing, has become the focus of discourse and embodied in policy, reflecting a neo-liberalization of housing. Another outcome has been that demand for home ownership has continued to expand, but has been constrained by a particularly inelastic supply. Critically, governments have not sought to sell off social rental housing units to individual residents, but rather deregulate housing associations as a means of commodifying housing. Sahlin (2004) also identifies a neo-liberal trend in Swedish housing policy which has been ongoing since the early 1990s. There appears a similar shift in policy, with state withdrawal and greater emphasis on the market as a provider. For example, market values have also become central to the calculation of social rents (Turner and Whitehead, 2002), and there has been growing demand for home ownership. Relationships among the state, the market and citizens, in terms of rights, obligations and expectations in housing, are essentially being reconstituted. Although housing policy in Sweden and the Netherlands has neo-liberal aspects, there is not yet such a clear reconstitution of individual subjects as market consumers or polarization of the meaning of tenures.

In Belgium, Germany and France, alternatively, state withdrawal from housing provision is not so evident. Shifts in housing policy have placed more emphasis on the market, but may be regarded as policy evolutions rather than fundamental alterations (Busch-Geertsema, 2004). Systems are being 'restyled' rather than being rolled back (de Decker, 2004). Essentially there has been more emphasis on 'enabling' housing policy, with markets being an important part of this.

For Atterhög (2005), Western European governments in societies with low rates of home ownership have been more effective in stimulating home ownership rates than Anglo-Saxon societies in recent years. This may be because there is more potential to do so, but also may reflect a realignment in housing policy around the globalization agenda and neo-liberal ideologies. The differences between countries in the marketization of housing policy arguably reflect different approaches to home ownership as a mechanism of social and economic change. Dodson's suggestion (2007) is that governments have perceived a change in global conditions and the need to adjust the state approach to how it perpetuates itself. Governments have thus had choices concerning how they approach neo-liberalization. Some have been more conservative (Belgium, Germany and France) while others more radical (Netherlands and Sweden) in their shift towards the logic of market discourses and the 'choice' of the citizen as a consumer. The latter may come to constitute a group of potential or 'pre-homeowner' societies.

Compared to Anglo-Saxon societies, the objectives of ensuring fair and adequate shelter for all with a strong role for rental housing still appears central in the policy systems of European social democratic and corporatist regimes. However, the marked shifts towards home ownership and market choice in policy, in some societies, resemble steps once taken in Anglo-Saxon homeowner nations which began a process of total re-centring of tenure.

A process of reconstitution has begun with the privatization of social housing objects, and the market replacing the state as the most suitable or capable provider. The further deregulation of finance networks across borders, and the growing exposure of employment markets in potential homeowner societies, may encourage both governments and individual households to look more and more to housing-property ownership and the potential to build assets through the market as a hedge against growing economic exposure and insecurity.

There is an alternative scenario that the expansion of home ownership and mortgage markets may be reversed. The history of housing systems and property markets demonstrates considerable dynamism and unpredictability suggesting we should expect further change. Although owner-occupation may be the form of housing most aligned with the interests of contemporary capitalism, the features and orientation of capitalism historically fluctuates. Post-war home ownership has certainly been a golden age for homeowners. However, the latest drive of house-price inflation has demonstrated considerable instability and unsustainability while the neo-liberalized shifts in employment, markets and welfare have formed a far more hazardous context for homeowners. The recent collapse in US sub-prime housing finance sent out unsettling financial waves that vibrated across global markets. The queues of worried British savers outside the Northern Rock bank (the most neo-liberalized and globalized of UK mortgage providers) in the summer of 2007 illustrated the considerable lack of confidence in housing and mortgage finance that has developed in the most recent years of housing market expansion. It is possible, if the security and prosperity of owner-occupation was challenged by policy and market shifts, that the alignment between home ownership and neo-liberal capitalism would be undermined leading to a considerable downturn in home ownership.

Beyond home ownership

While some countries seem to be rushing to build broader populations of homeowners, established homeowner societies seem to be entering a new stage. Anglo-Saxon housing systems in particular appear to be developing systematic problems. Fundamental questions are emerging regarding sustainability and suggest the need for a substantial restructuring in housing and social policy. The most rapid growth in home ownership in Anglo-Saxon countries occurred during the post-war period of economic growth, under Fordist socio-economic conditions. In these circumstances stable employment, the expansion of social security and mortgage-based home-purchase formed a mutually supporting network. In recent decades this network has been fundamentally destabilized by the undermining of secure labour markets and the atrophy of social security-nets which have eroded the income stability necessary for secure home ownership (Ford et al., 2001). This breakdown has unfolded in an environment of amplified individual economic risk and the disintegration of traditional communities and family networks (Beck, 1992). Households have arguably responded to the individualization of conditions by embracing home ownership which, as long as house-prices have increased, appeared to provide a hedge against individual economic instability and against pension and welfare shortfalls in old age. However, things appear to be happening in the housing systems of homeowner societies which may be the inevitable outcome of sustained policy dependency and house-price inflation.

A central feature of post-home ownership housing regimes has been 'exhaustion'. This refers to both the exhaustion of homeowners in terms of affordability and the exhaustion of the housing market in terms of sustaining stable value increases. The numbers of younger homeowners and first-time-buyers have been falling dramatically. This has led to significant readjustments in government policy, lending practices and family support networks (see Chapter 5). At the same time there has been a growth in the number of buy-to-let mortgages, multiple owners and a build-up of housing wealth among older homeowners. A fundamental divide is emerging between those in or outside the tenure, and between different groups of homeowners who entered the market at different points in the market cycle, with subsequent disparities in capital gains. Among homeowners, younger or marginal households have greatest exposure to the risks of market downturn, while older owner-occupiers and those with higher and more secure incomes have least. The outcome is growing striations across society based on positions relative to the housing market. For Groves et al. (2007) there is evidence across homeowner societies of emerging generational and inherited wealth inequalities, as well as a new private landlord class.

> One of the implications of this is that there are new divisions of interest, and new patterns of dependency and stratification emerging in these countries. Political demands around the housing question now relate to differences in position in relation to the property market: differences between renters and owners; differences between owners in different positions in relation to the value of their property and the nature of their investment; and differences related to the number of properties owned. These legacies are likely to have some influence on the pattern of development of housing policy and welfare systems. (p. 213)

While on one hand affordability is a central problem on the other the long-term maintenance of price increases is necessary to the maintenance of the system. If property values fail to consistently grow faster than inflation, the ability of home ownership to generate the assets necessary to support retirement and welfare needs will be undermined. Owner-occupied housing may continue to ensure minimal housing costs in old age, but may become much less attractive than other investments. If house-prices do not appear to generate considerable gains, demand may drop. This may feed a cycle of price erosion and undermine the equity that many households have built up. The Singapore housing system has demonstrated the hazard of universal home ownership and the increasing pressure that develops under such conditions to maintain a flow of buyers at the bottom end of the market to maintain the assets of those at the top (Chua, 2003).

At this moment in Anglo-Saxon societies, house-prices appear to be stabilizing, but at a very high level. Governments are having to take measures to sustain the system and are caught between ostensibly contradictory demands: to make housing more affordable to greater numbers of people *and* to make sure house-prices go up in order to build capital equity amongst existing property owners. One of the purposes of expanding the tenure has been to enhance social mobility and flexibility in the employment market. The current system appears to have the opposite effect. Households now have to stay in properties longer than is suitable as prices have made it difficult to trade up.

Despite the unsustainable price increases already evident, many governments intend to expand home ownership even further. In Britain the target is for more than a million more homeowners and to achieve 75 per cent home ownership. In Australia and the United States too, governments have an eye on increasing property ownership. Under current circumstances, the likelihood of pushing more home ownership is low, although there is potential across other developed societies (Atterhög, 2005). Potential homeowner societies are likely to develop similar problems however, unless they are able to keep a stronger policy balance and are prepared to rein in house-price booms. East Asian societies appear more cautious. The 1990s Asian currency crisis revealed the over-exposure of housing markets to global economic trends, which were particularly hard felt in environments where families rely on their property assets for security and welfare needs. Governments have largely sought to deregulate home ownership and reduce their role in the market while also putting a brake on over-investment in housing-property and dependency on housing assets to support retirement and welfare needs.

Where do we go from here?

It may be easy to present a doom and gloom picture of housing markets in homeowner societies. The intention is not to generate doubt and panic, but to draw attention to the perils of tenure imbalance and to establish greater resistance to the neo-liberal logic that more home ownership is intrinsically good. The intention is to identify the increased centrality of housing systems in social relations more broadly, and the significance of home ownership discourses that assert an ideological view of tenure. Home ownership has become so culturally embedded in many societies that it seems odd, for most, to question it. Most academic and policy discourses too, seem reactionary to the logic of home ownership. A path of social development, orientated towards building up individual asset-bases through providing greater access to property ownership, has been explicitly identified (Retsinas and Belsky, 2005), while pulling away, or let fall, networks of welfare and employment security.

Owner-occupied property assets may yet provide good parachutes and safety-nets for households who find themselves in financial difficulties in the future. A lot relies on the willingness and ability of governments to stabilize the system, or at least not further destabilize, as well as greater prudence on the part of individuals. With the greying of society and the further encroachment of market relations into the life-world, it is likely that there will be even greater pressure on property ownership in the future and even stronger socio-economic divisions between types of residents.

The ability of a broader spread of home ownership and increases in housing equity to compensate for welfare state withdrawal is questionable. Greater individual housing wealth cannot compensate for all the various kinds of services and security provided by the traditional welfare state. Moreover, home ownership as a welfare strategy is based on assumptions about future housing markets and socio-economic conditions. Owner-occupied housing is a long-term investment involving considerable risk and a sustained and expensive period of indebtedness. It makes households and economies highly vulnerable to economic fluctuations. As a strategy for retirement and welfare provision in later life it is a gamble, for both individual households and governments seeking to build asset-based welfare, on the condition of housing equity and market increases in 20 or 30 years' time. Even if markets do well, housing wealth may be an inadequate or ineffective compensation for the roll-back of pensions and welfare services that post-war welfare states have provided.

One answer to the growing insecurities and inequalities generated by homeowner housing regimes involves an ideological reorientation. Other than providing a more stabilizing framework for housing markets, governments need to readdress the role of rental housing. The current strategy of finding different ways to get households into hybrid forms of owner-occupied tenure only perpetuates the home ownership mythology. Such approaches simply support greater flows of capital into the sector which feed housing unaffordability and the precariousness of marginal owner-occupiers. A more effective strategy may be to rehabilitate renting and reverse the discursive prejudices that have built up against it. This requires a seismic ideological shift and a symbolic reconstitution of rental housing. In countries like Germany and Switzerland, much urban rental housing is highly desirable and there is no discursive contradiction between being successful or living an independent family life, and rented accommodation. If housing policies can redeem rental 'homes' in homeowner societies, it will provide a real housing 'choice' and mitigate the imbalances generated by over-dependency and over-investment in owner-occupied housing. There is thus a fundamental need for research that will identify the kind of practices that will normalize renting in the same way that government policies helped establish owner-occupation as the default tenure. Greater understanding of housing discourses and tenure ideologies in societies with attractive rental sectors is, therefore, as important as understanding home ownership ideology in homeowner-societies.

At the moment, a reversal in home ownership policy and the tide of neo-liberalization and welfare commodification seems implausible. The ideological force of owner-occupation is now overwhelming and it appears that neither residents nor policy makers are capable of thinking beyond its normative boundaries. Inevitably, governments will have to get more involved and innovative with schemes that get households from outside the system, inside. For individual households, home ownership may prove a source of a sense of security and a good capital asset in a milieu of ever advancing risk. It will also, as a locus of economic and ontological security, sensitize households and make them more vulnerable to the vicissitudes of markets. There will be a number of consequences for the development of welfare systems which will be increasingly determined by government approaches to the housing system. If and when house-prices become unstable, political pressure will be such that governments will have to take drastic market regulatory steps due to levels of dependency on individual housing-property, which was, ironically, created by deregulation and promotion of the free market. While many households may be able to rely on their housing assets to cover social security and retirement needs, a significant part of the population will still require government assistance. Essentially, the scope of welfare roll-back and the establishment of an asset-based system are limited. Governments are likely to be faced with contrary interests. These include, first, supporting those excluded from home ownership, second, assisting the market position of large groups of marginal home-buyers, and third, propping up market price increases. Governments therefore, may well become the victims of the very policies, discourses and ideologies they have sought to advance.

Bibliography

Abercrombie, N., S. Hill and B.S. Turner, 1980, *The Dominant Ideology Thesis*, London, Allen and Unwin.
Abercrombie, N., S. Hill and B. S. Turner, 1986, *Sovereign Individuals of Capitalism*, London, Allen and Unwin.
ABS, 2001, Australian Bureau of Statistics, http://www.abs.gov.au/Ausstats/abs@.nsf/Previousproducts/1301.0Feature%20Article172001?opendocument&tabname=Summary&prodno=1301.0&issue=2001&num=&view
ABS, 2002, Australian Bureau of Statistics, Australian National Accounts, http://www.abs.gov.au/AUSSTATS/abs@.nsf/Previousproducts/5232.0Feature%20Article290Mar%202002?opendocument&tabname=Summary&prodno=5232.0&issue=Mar%202002&num=&view
Adams, J.S., 1984, The meaning of housing in America (Presidential Address), *Annals of the Association of American Geographers*, 74 (4), pp. 151–526.
Agnew, J., 1981, Home-ownership and identity in capitalist societies, in: J.S. Duncan (ed.), *Housing and Identity*, London, Croom Helm.
Agus, M.R., J. Doling and D-S. Lee, 2002, *Housing Policy Systems in South East Asia*, London, Macmillan.
Allen, G. and G. Crow (eds), 1989, *Home and Family: Creating the Domestic Sphere*, London, Macmillan.
Allen, J., J. Barlow, J. Leal, T. Maloutas and L. Padavani, 2004, *Housing and Welfare in Southern Europe*, Oxford, Blackwell.
Althusser, L., 1984, *Essays on Ideology*, London, Verso.
Andrews, M., 2006, Housing tenure choices by the young, *Housing Finance*, June, London, CML.
Anily, S.J., J. Hornik and M. Israeli, 1999, Inferring the distribution of households' duration of residence from data on current residence time, *Journal of Business and Economic Statistics*, 17 (3), pp. 373–381.
Arias, E., 1993, Introduction, in: E. Arias (ed.), *The Meaning and Use of Housing*, Aldershot, Avebury.
Atterhog, M., 2005, *Importance of Government Policies for Home Ownership Rates – an International Survey and Analysis*, Working Paper No. 54, School of Architecture and the Built Environment, Stockholm, Royal Institute of Technology.
Bachelard, G., 1994, *The Poetics of Space*, Boston, Beacon Press.
Baker, T. and J. Simon, 2002, *Embracing Risk: The Changing Culture of Insurance and Responsibility*, Chicago, Chicago University Press.
Ball, M., 1986, *Home Ownership: A Suitable Case for Reform*, London, Shelter.
Ball, M., M. Harloe and M. Martens, 1988, *Housing and Social Change in Europe and the USA*, London, Routledge.
Banks, J., R. Blundell and J.P. Smith, 2004, Wealth portfolios in the UK and the US, in: *NBER Working Papers*, Cambridge, MA.
Barker, K., 2004, *Delivering Stability: Securing our Future Housing Needs*, London, HM Treasury.
Barker, K., 2006, *Review of Land Use Planning*, London, HM Treasury.

Barlow, J. and Duncan, S., 1994, *Success and Failure in Housing Provision: European Systems Compared*, Oxford, Pergamon Press.
Baudrillard, M., 1994, *Simulacra and Simulation*, Michigan, Michigan University Press.
Baudrillard, M., 1998, *The Consumer Society: Myths and Structures*, London, Sage Publications.
Bauman, Z., 1992, *Imitations of Postmodernity*, London, Routledge.
Bauman, Z., 1997, *Postmodernity and its Discontents*, Cambridge, Polity Press.
Bauman, Z., 1998, *Work, Consumerism and the New Poor*, Buckingham, Open University Press.
Baxter, J. and P. Macdonald, 2005, *Why is the rate of home ownership falling in Australia?* AHURI Research Centre, http://www.ahuri.edu.au/publications/download/10081_fr
Beck, U., 1992, *Risk Society*, London, Sage.
Beck, U., 2000, *The Brave New World of Work*, Cambridge, Cambridge University Press.
Beer, A. and B. Blair, 2000, *Home Truths: Property Ownership and Housing Wealth in Australia*, Melbourne University Press.
Berger, P. and T. Luckman, 1966, *The Social Construction of Reality: A Treatise in the Sociology of Knowledge*, Middlesex, Penguin Harmondsworth.
Berry, M., 1986, Housing provision and class relations under capitalism, *Housing Studies*, 1 (2), pp. 109–121.
Berry, M., C. Whitehead, P. Williams and J. Yates, 2006, Involving the private sector in affordable housing provision: Can Australia learn from the United Kingdom?, *Urban Policy and Research*, 24 (3), pp. 307–323.
Bhaskar, R., 1979, *The Possibility of Naturalism*, Brighton, Harvester Press.
Bhaskar, R., 1994, *Dialectic: The Pulse of Freedom*, London, Verso.
Bhaskaran, M., 2003, *Re-inventing the Asian Model: The Case of Singapore*, Singapore, Eastern Universities Press for the Institute of Policy Studies.
Bocock, R., 1993, *Consumption*, London, Routledge.
Boddy, M., 1980, *The Building Societies*, London, Macmillan.
Boelhouwer, P., 2002, Trends in Dutch housing policy and the shifting position of the social rented sector, *Urban Studies*, 39 (2), pp. 283–302.
Boelhouwer, P. and H. van der Heijden, 1992, *Housing Systems in Europe: A Comparative Study of Housing Policy*, Part 1., Delft, Delft University Press.
Boelhouwer, P. and H. van der Heijden, 2005, Relationship between Reduction in Pension Provision and Growth in Homeownership, *Housing, Theory and Society*, 22 (2), pp. 76–79.
Boleat, M. and A. Coles, 1987, *The Mortgage Market*, London, Allen and Unwin.
Bondi, L., Christie, H., Munro, M. and Smith, S.J. (2000) *Anatomy of a housing boom*, ESRC End of Award Report R000222902, www.regard.ac.uk
Bootle, R., 1996, *The Death of Inflation. Surviving and Thriving in the Zero Era*, London, Nicholas Brealey.
Bounds, M., 1989, *False expectations and derivative policies: Analysing tenant participation*, Paper presented at the Australian Sociological Association, Melbourne, La Trobe University.
Bourassa, S., A. Greig and P. Troy, 1995, The limits of housing policy and home ownership in Australia, *Housing Studies*, 10, pp. 83–104.
Bourassa, S.C. and W.G. Grigsby, 2000, Income tax concessions for owner-occupied housing, *Housing Policy Debate*, 11 (3), pp. 521–546.

Bourdieu, P., 1984, *Distinction: A Social Critique of the Judgment of Taste*, London, Routledge.
Bratt, R.G, 1989, *Rebuilding a Low Income Housing Policy*, Philadelphia, Temple University Press.
Bratt, R.G. 2007, Homeownership for low income households: A comparison of the Section 235, Nehemiah, and Habitat for Humanity programs, in: W.M. Rohe and H.L. Watson (eds), *Chasing the American Dream: New Perspectives on Affordable Homeownership*, New York, Cornell University Press.
Brett, J., 1992, *Robert Menzies' Forgotten People*, Sydney, Macmillan.
Bridges, S., R. Disney and A. Henley, 2004, Housing wealth and the accumulation of financial debt: evidence from UK households, in: Bertola, G., R. Disney and C. Grant (eds), *The Economics of Consumer Credit*, Massachusetts, MIT Press.
Buchholz, T.G., 2002, *Safe at Home: The New Role of Housing in the U.S. Economy*, Washington, DC, Home Ownership Alliance.
Burr, V., 1998, Overview: realism, relativism, social constructionism and discourse, in: I. Parker (ed.), *Social Construction, Discourse and Realism*, London, Sage.
Burrows, R., 2003, *Poverty and Home Ownership in Contemporary Britain*, UK, Policy Press.
Busch-Geertsema, V., 2004, The changing role of the state in German housing and social policy, *European Journal of Housing Policy*, 4 (3), pp. 303–321.
Bush,G.W.,2002,http://www.whitehouse.gov/news/releases/2002/06/20020618-1.html
Butlin, N.G., 1964, *Investment in Australian Economic Development*, 1861-1900, Cambridge, Cambridge University Press.
Cabinet Office, 2004, Public Opinion Survey, Tokyo.
Campbell, C., 1995, The sociology of consumption, in: D. Miller (ed.), *Acknowledging Consumption: A Review of New Studies*, London, Routledge.
Castells, M., L. Goh, and R.Y.-W. Kwok, 1990, *The Shek kip Mei Syndrome: Economic Development and Public Housing in Hong Kong and Singapore*, London, Pion.
Castles, F.G., 1985, *The Working Class and Welfare: Reflections on the Political development of the Welfare State in Australia and New Zealand 1890-1980*, Wellington, Allen and Unwin.
Castles, F.G., 1998, The really big trade-off: Home ownership and the welfare state in the new world and the old, *Acta Politica*, 33 (1), pp. 163–185.
Castles, F.G. and M. Ferrera, 1996, Home ownership and the welfare state: Is Southern Europe different, *South European Society and Politics*, 1 (2), pp. 163–185.
Cerny, P., 1990, *The Changing Architecture of Politics: Agency, Structure and the Future of the State*, London, Sage.
Cerny P.G. and M. Evans, 2004, Globalisation and public policy under New Labour, *Policy Studies*, 25 (1), pp. 51–65.
Chan, K.W., 2000, Prosperity or inequality: Deconstructing the myth of home ownership in Hong Kong, *Housing Studies*, 15, pp. 29–44.
Chaney, D., 1993, *Fictions of Collective Life*, London, Routledge.
Chang, C.O., 1991, Research on residential issues and policy framework, *Journal of National Cheng Chi University*, 63, pp. 263–292.
Chapman, T., 1999, Spoiled home identities and the experience of burglary, in: T. Chapman and J. Hockey (eds), *Ideal Homes*, London, Routledge.
Cheng, Chi Ho, 1997, A study of the speculative behaviours of young people in Hong Kong (Department of Applied Social Studies, Hong Kong Polytechnic

University) Cited in: K.W. Chan, 2000, Prosperity or inequality: Deconstructing the myth of home ownership in Hong Kong, *Housing Studies*, 15, pp. 29–44.
Cheung, J., 2000, Fresh action unneeded, *South China Morning Post*, 27 June.
Chiu, R.L.H., 2006, Globalisation and localisation: Performance of the housing markets of the Asian Tigers since the financial crisis, *Housing Finance International*, XX (3), pp. 12–17.
Choudhury, A. and I. Islam, 1993, *The Newly Industrialised Economies of East Asia*, London, Routledge.
Chua, B.H., 1997, *Political Legitimacy and Housing: Stakeholding in Singapore*, London, Routledge.
Chua, B.H., 2000, Public housing residents as clients of the state, *Housing Studies*, 15 (1), pp. 45–60.
Chua, B.H., 2003, Maintaining housing values under the condition of universal home ownership, *Housing Studies*, 18 (3), pp. 765–780.
Clammer, J., 1995, *Difference and Modernity: Social Theory and Contemporary Japanese Society*, NY, London, Kegan Paul International.
Clammer, J., 2003, Globalisation, class, consumption and civil society in South-East Asian cities, *Urban Studies*, 40 (2), pp. 403–419.
Clapham, D., 2005, *The Meaning of Housing*. Bristol, Policy Press.
Clapham, D., 2006, Housing policy and the discourse of globalization, *European Journal of Housing Policy*, 6 (1), pp. 55–76.
Clark, G.L., 2000, *Pension Fund Capitalism*, Oxford, Oxford University Press.
Clark, G.L., and N. Whiteside, 2003, Introduction, in: G.L. Clark and N. Whiteside (eds), *Pension Security in the 21st Century: Redrawing the Public–Private Debate*, Oxford, Oxford University Press.
Clarke, S. and N. Ginsberg, 1976, The political economy of housing, *Kapitalistate*, summer(4/5), pp. 66–99.
Clinton, B., 1994, letter to Henry Cisneros, secretary of the department of Housing and Urban Development, 3rd November, cited in S.A. Gabriel., and S. S. Rosenthal , 2005, Homeownership in the 1980s and 1990s: aggregate tends and racial gaps, *Journal of Urban Economics*, 57, pp. 101–127.
CML, 1996, Negative equity: Outlook and effects, *Council of Mortgage Lenders Research*, No 8, London.
CML, 2005, Mortgage credit in the EU: the EU Commission Green Paper, *Council of Mortgage Lenders*, London.
CML, 2007, Home-ownership at a crossroads, *Housing Finance*, Issue 2, London.
Coates, I., 2001, Capitalist models and social democracy: The case of New Labour, *British Journal of Politics and International Relations*, 3 (3), 284–307.
Collin, F., 1997, *Social Reality*, London, Routledge.
Colton, K.W., 2002, *Housing Finance in the United States: The Transformation of the US Housing Finance System*, Joint Center for Housing Studies, Harvard University, http://www.jchs.harvard.edu/publications/finance/W02-5_Colton.pdf
Coontz, S., 1988, *The Social Origins of Private Life: A History of American Families, 1600–1900*, London, Verso.
Costello, P., 2006, Australian Government, The Treasury, The Great Australian Dream Project, http://www.treasurer.gov.au/DisplayDocs.aspx?pageID=&doc=speeches/2006/016.htm&min=phc

Cox, K., 1982, Housing tenure and neighbourhood activism, *Urban Affairs Quarterly*, 18 (1), pp. 107–129.
Cox, K. and J. McCarthy, 1982, Neighbourhood activism as a politics of turf, in: K. Cox and R. Johnston (eds), *Conflict, Politics and the Urban Scene*, London, Longman.
Craib, I., 1992, *Modern Social Theory: From Parsons to Habermas*, 2nd edn, Hemel Hempstead, Harvester Wheatsheaf.
Craik, J., 1989, The making of the mother: the role of the kitchen in the home, in: G. Allen and G. Crow (eds), *Home and Family*, Basingstoke, Macmillan.
Crompton, R., 1993, *Class and Stratification*, Cambridge, Policy Press.
Csikszentmihalyi, M. and E. Rochberg-Halton, 1981, *The Meaning of Things; Domestic Symbols of the Self*, Cambridge, Cambridge University Press.
Czischke, Darinka, 2005, *Social Housing in the EU: Time for legal certainty for local authorities, social housing providers and millions of European households*, Report to the European Commission, Cecodhas, Brussels.
Daunton, M., 1983, Public place and private space. in: D. Frazer, and A. Sutcliffe (eds), *The Pursuit of Urban History*, London, Edward Arnold.
Davidoff, L. and C. Hall, 1987, *Family Fortunes*, London, Hutchinson.
DCLG, 2006, *Survey of English Housing*, London, Communities and Local Government.
Decker, J.L., 1992, *Made in America: Self-styled Success from Horatio Alger to Oprah Winfrey*, Minnesota, University of Minnesota Press.
Decker, P. de, 2004, Dismantling or pragmatic adaptation? On the restyling of welfare and housing policies in Belgium, *European Journal of Housing Policy*, 4 (3), pp. 261–281.
De Leon, R., 1992, *Left Coast City: Progressive Politics in San Francisco, 1975–1991*, USA, University Press of Kansas.
De Neufville, J. and S. Barton, 1987, Myths and the definition of policy problems: An exploration of home ownership and public–private partnerships, *Policy Sciences*, 20, pp. 181–206.
Department of Environment, 1971, *Fair Deal for Housing*, London, HMSO, Cmnd 4728.
Derrida, J., 1998, *On Grammatology*, Baltimore, John Hopkins University Press.
Després, C., 1991, The meaning of home: Literature review and directions for future research and theoretical development, *The Journal of Architectural and Planning Research*, 8 (2), pp. 96–115.
Deverson, J. and K. Lindsay, 1975, *Voices from the Middle Classes*, London, Hutchinson.
Deyo, F.C., 1992, The political economy in social policy formation: East Asia's newly industrialised countries, in: R.P. Applebaum and J. Henderson, (eds), *States and Development in the Asia Pacific Rim*, Newbury Park, CA, Sage.
Diamond, D.B. and M.J. Lea, 1992, The decline of special circuits in developed country housing finance, *Housing Policy Debate*, 3 (3), pp. 747–777.
Dickens, P., S. Duncan, S. Goodwin, and F. Grey, 1985, *Housing State and Localities*, London, Methuen.
DiPasquale, D. and E.L. Glaeser, 1997, Incentives and social capital: Are homeowners better citizens?, *Journal of Urban Economics*, 45, pp. 354–384.
Dodson, J., 2007, *Government Discourse and Housing*, Aldershot, Ashgate.

Doling, J., 1997, *Comparative Housing Policy: Government and Housing in Advanced Industrialized Countries*, London, Macmillan.
Doling, J., 1999, Housing policies and the little Tigers: How do they compare with the other industrialised countries?, *Housing Studies*, 14 (2), pp. 229–250.
Doling, J., 2002, The South East Asian housing policy model, in: M.R. Agus, J. Doling, and D-S. Lee (eds), *Housing Policy Systems in South East Asia*, London, Macmillan.
Doling, J., 2006, A European housing policy?, *European Journal of Housing Policy*, 6 (3), pp. 335–349.
Doling, J., J. Ford and B. Stafford, 1991, The changing face of homeownership: Building societies and household investment strategies, *Policy and Politics*, 19 (2), pp. 109–118.
Doling, J. and J. Ford, 2003, *Globalisation and Home Ownership: Experiences in Eight Member States of the European Union*, Delft University Press.
Doling, J. and N. Horsewood, 2003, Home ownership and early retirement: European experience in the 1990s, *Journal of Housing and the Built Environment*, 18 (4), pp. 289–308.
Doling, J. and R. Ronald, 2007, *Housing and asset-based welfare in the West: Some lessons from the East*, Paper presented at the ENHR Comparative Housing Policy Workshop, Dublin, April.
Donoghue, J., B. Tranter, and R. White, 2002, *Australian dreams: Home ownership, share ownership and Coalition policy*, Paper presented at the Jubilee conference of the Australasian Political Studies Association, Australian National University, Canberra, October.
Dovey, K., 1985, Home and homelessness, in: I. Altman and C. Werner (eds), *Home Environments*, New York, Plenum Press.
Dunleavy, P., 1979, The urban basis of political alignment: Social class, domestic property ownership and state intervention in consumption processes, *British Journal of Political Science*, 9 (4), pp. 409–443.
Dunleavy, P., 1980, *Urban Political Analysis*, London, Macmillan.
Dunleavy, P., 1987, Class de-alignment in Britain revisited, *West European Politics*, 10, pp. 400–419.
Dunn-Haley, K., 1995 The house that Uncle Sam built: The political culture of federal housing policy 1919–1932, PhD diss., Stanford University.
Dymski, G. and D. Isenberg, 1998, Housing finance in the age of globalisation: From social housing to life cycle risk, in: D. Baker, G. Epstein and R. Pollin, (eds), *Globalisation and Progressive Economic Policy*, Cambridge, Cambridge University Press.
Eades, J.S., T. Gill and H. Befu, 2000, *Globalisation and Social Change in Contemporary Japan*, Melbourne, Trans Pacific Press.
Economist, The, 2005, The global housing boom: In come the waves, June.
Economist, The, 2006, Gimme shelter: Now that the party is over, how bad will the hangover be? August.
Elshtain, J., 1981, *Public Man, Private Women: Woman in Social and Political Thought*, Oxford, Martin Robertson.
Elsinga, M., P. de Decker, J. Toussaint, and N. Teller (eds), 2007, *Beyond Asset and Insecurity: On (In)security of Home Ownership in Europe*, Amsterdam, IOS Press.
Engelen, E., 2003, The logic of funding European pension restructuring and the dangers of financialisation, *Environment and Planning A*, 35, pp. 1357–1372.
Engels, F., 1970, *The Housing Question*, (1873), Moscow, Progress Publishers.

Esping-Andersen, G., 1990, *The Three Worlds of Welfare Capitalism*, Cambridge, Polity Press.
Esping-Andersen, G., 1996, *Welfare States in Transition*, London, Sage.
Esping-Andersen, G., 1997, Hybrid or unique? The Japanese welfare state between Europe and America, *Journal of European Social Policy*, 7 (3), pp. 179-189.
Esping-Andersen, G., 1999, *Social Foundations of Post Industrial Economies*, Oxford, Oxford University Press.
ESRI, 2006, http://www.esri.ie/
European Commission, 2004, *Facing the Challenge: The Lisbon Strategy for Growth and Employment*, Report from the High Level Group chaired by Wim Kok, Luxembourg: Office for Official Publications of the European Communities.
European Mortgage Federation, 2005, http://www.hypo.org/Content/Default.asp?PageID=159
Ewald, F., 1991, Insurance and risk, in: G. Burchell, C. Gordon and P. Miller (eds), *The Foucault effect: Studies in Governmentality*, Hemel Hempstead, Harvester Wheatsheaf.
Fairclough, N., 1992, *Discourse and Social Change*, London, Polity Press.
Fairclough, N., 1995, *Critical Discourse Analysis: The Critical Study of Language*, London and New York, Longman.
Featherstone, M., 1991, *Consumer Culture and Postmodernism*, London, Sage.
Featherstone, M., 1992, Postmodernism and the aetheticization of everyday life, in: S. Lasch and J. Friedman (eds), *Modernity and Identity*, Oxford, Blackwell.
Field, W., 1997, Policy and the British voter: Council housing, social change, and party preference in the 1980s, *Electoral Studies*, 16 (2), pp. 195-202.
Finch, J., 1989, *Family Obligations and Social Change*, Cambridge, Policy Press.
Flood, J. and J. Yates, 1987, *Housing Subsidies Study*, Australian Housing Research Council, Canberra, Australian Government Printing Service.
Folsom, M.W., 1922, *A Home of Your Own*, Chicago, National Association of Real Estate Boards.
Ford, J., R. Burrows and S. Nettleton, 2001, Home ownership in a risk society: A social analysis of mortgage arrears and possessions, UK, Policy press.
Forrest, R., 1983, The meaning of home ownership, *Society and Space*, 15 (1), pp. 205-216.
Forrest, R. and P. Williams, 1984, Commodification and housing: Emerging issues and contradictions, *Environment and Planning A*, 16, pp. 1163-1180.
Forrest, R., A. Murie and P. Williams, 1990, *Home Ownership: Differentiation , and Fragmentation*, London, Unwin Hyman.
Forrest, R. and A. Murie (eds), 1995, *Housing and Family Wealth: Comparing International Perspectives*, London, Routledge.
Forrest, R., P. Kennett and P. Leather, 1999, Home ownership in crisis? The British experience of negative equity, Aldershot, Ashgate.
Forrest, R. and J. Lee, 2003, *Housing and Social Change: East West Perspectives*, London, Routledge.
Forrest, R. and J. Lee, 2004, Cohort effects, differential accumulation and Hong Kong's volatile housing market, *Urban Studies*, 41 (11), pp. 2181-2196.
Foucault, M., 1970, *The Order of Things: An Archaeology of the Human Sciences*, New York, Pantheon.
Foucault, M., 1977, *Discipline and Punish: The Birth of the Prison*, London, Allen Lane.

Foucault, M., 1980, Truth and power, in: C. Gordon (ed.), *Power/Knowledge: Selected Interviews and Other Writings 1972–1977*, Brighton, Harvester Wheatsheaf.
Franklin, A., 1986, *Owner occupation, privatism, and ontological security: A critical reformulation*, Working Paper, SAUS Publications, University of Bristol.
Franklin, B. and D. Clapham, D., 1997, The social construction of housing management, *Housing Studies*, 12 (1), pp. 7–26.
Freidman, M., 1962, *Capitalism and Freedom*, Chicago, University of Chicago Press.
Frey, W.H., 2001, *Melting Pot Suburbs: A Census 2000 Study of Suburban Diversity*, Washington, DC, Brookings Institution Center on Urban and Metropolitan Policy.
Fukuyama, Francis, 1999, *The Great Disruption: Human Nature and the Reconstitution of Social Order*, Newyork, Touchstone.
Gamble, A., 1988, *Free Economy and the Strong State: The Politics of Thatcherism*, Basingstoke, MacMillan.
Geertz, C., 1973, *The Interpretation of Cultures: Selected Essays*, New York, Basic Books.
Gerth, H. H., C. Wright Mills, and B.S. Turner, 1991, *From Max Webber: Essays in Sociology*, 2nd edn, London, Routledge.
Giddens, A., 1981, *A Contemporary Critique of Historical Materialism, 1. Power, Property and the State*, London, Macmillan.
Giddens, A., 1984, *The Constitution of Society*, Cambridge, Polity Press.
Giddens, A., 1990, *The Consequences of Modernity*, Cambridge, Polity Press.
Giddens, A., 1991, *Modernity and Self Identity: Self and Society in the Late Modern Age*. Stanford, Stanford University Press.
Goffman, E., 1959, *The Presentation of Self in Everyday Life*. New York, Doubleday.
Goldthorpe, D., D. Lockwood, F. Bechhofer, and J. Platt, 1969, *The Affluent Worker in the Class Structure*, Cambridge, Cambridge University Press.
Goodman, R. and K. Refsing (eds), 1992, *Ideology and Practice in Modern Japan*, London and New York, Routledge.
Goodman, R. and I. Peng, 1996, The East Asian welfare states: Peripatetic learning, adaptive change, and national building, in: G. Esping-Andersen (ed.), *Welfare States in Transition: National Adaptations in Global Economies*, London, Sage.
Goodman, R. and G. White, 1998, Welfare orientalism and the search for an East Asian welfare model, in: R. Goodman, H. Kwon and G. White (eds), *The East Asian Welfare Model*, London and New York, Routledge.
Gouldie, E., 1974, *Cruel Habitations*, London, George Allen and Unwin.
Government Housing Loan Corporation, 1999, *Housing Statistics of Japan 1998*, Tokyo, Housing Loan Progress Corporation.
Gramsci, A., 1971, *Selections from the Prison Notebooks*, in Q. Hoare and G. Nowell-Smith (eds), London, Lawrence and Wishart.
Granovetter, M., 1985, Economic action and social structure: The problem of embeddedness, *American Journal of Sociology*, 91 (3), pp. 481–510.
Grigsby, W.G., 1990, Housing finance and subsidy in the United States, *Urban Studies*, 27 (6), pp. 831–845.
Groves, R., A. Murie and C. Watson, 2007, *Housing and the New Welfare State: Examples from East Asia and Europe*, Aldershot, Ashgate.

Gulbrandsen, L., 2004, Home ownership and social inequality in Norway, in: K. Kurz and H. Blossfeld (eds), *Home Ownership and Social Inequality in Comparative Perspective* (Studies in Social Inequality), Stanford University Press.
Gurney, C., 1996, Meanings of home and homeownership: Myths, histories and experiences, PhD thesis, Bristol University, UK.
Gurney, C., 1999a, Lowering the drawbridge: A case study of analogy and metaphor in the social construction of home ownership, *Urban Studies*, 36 (10), pp. 1705–1722.
Gurney, C., 1999b, Pride and prejudice: Discourses of normalisation in private and public accounts of home ownership, *Housing Studies*, 14 (2), pp. 163–183.
Habermas, J., 1973, *Legitimation Crisis*, Boston, Beacon Press.
Habermas, J., 1976, Problems of legitimation in late capitalism, in: P. Connerton (ed.), *Critical Sociology*, Harmondsworth, Penguin.
Haddon, R., 1970, A Minority in a Welfare State Society, *New Atlantis*, 2, pp. 80–133.
Haffner, M., 2005, Secondary mortgage markets in the United States and the Netherlands, Paper presented at European Network for Housing Research Conference on Housing in Europe: New Challenges and Innovations in Tomorrow's Cities, Iceland, June–July.
Hamilton, F. E. I., 1999, Transformation and space in Central and Eastern Europe, *The Geographical Journal*, 165, pp. 135–144.
Hamnett, C., 1991, A nation of inheritors? Housing inheritance, wealth and inequality in Britain, *Journal of Social Policy*, 20 (4), pp. 509–536.
Hamnett, C., 1999, *Winners and Losers: Home Ownership in Modern Britain*, London, UCL Press.
Hansard, 1951, Vol. 493, Cols 846–847, 13 November; London, HMSO.
Hansard, 1980, Vol. 967, Cols 79–80, 15 May; London, HMSO.
Harloe, M., 1995, *The People's Home? Social Rented Housing in Europe & America*, Oxford, Blackwell.
Harloe, M. and M. Maartjens, 1983, Comparative housing research, *Journal of Social Policy*, 13 (3), pp. 255–277.
Harmes, A., 2001, Mass investment culture, *New Left Review*, 9, pp. 103–124.
Harris, N., 1973, *Competition and the Corporate Society*, London, Methuen.
Harvey, D., 1978, Labour, capital and class struggle around the built environment in advanced capitalist societies, in: K. Cox (ed.), *Urbanisation and Conflict in Market Societies*, Chicago, Macroufa Press.
Häusermann, H. and W. Siebel, 1996, *Soziologie des Wohnens: Eine Einführung in Wandel und Ausdifferenzierung des Wohnens*, Weinheim, Juventa.
Haworth, A., T. Manzi and J. Kemeny, 2004, Social constructionism and international comparative housing research, in: K. Jacobs, J. Kemeny and T. Manzi (eds), *Social Constructionism in Housing Research*, Aldershot, Ashgate Press.
Hay C., 2005, Too important to leave to the economists? The political economy of welfare retrenchment, *Social Policy and Society*, 4 (2), pp. 197–205.
Hayakawa, K., 1990, Japan, in: Van Vliet (ed.), *International Handbook of Housing Policies and Practices*, Westport, CT, Greenwood Press.
Heidenheimer, A., H. Heclo and C. Adams, 1975, *Comparative Public Policy: The Politics of Social Choice in Europe and America*, London, Macmillan.
Henderson, J. and R.P Appelbaum, 1992, Situating the state in the East Asian development process, in: R.P. Appelbaum and J. Henderson (eds), *States and Development in the Asia Pacific Rim*. Newbury Park, CA, Sage.

Hein, C., J.M. Diefendorf and Y. Ishida, 2003, *Rebuilding Urban Japan After 1945*, New York, Palgrave Macmillan.
Helleiner, E., 1995, Explaining the financialization of financial markets, Bringing the state back, *Review of International Political Economy*, 2 (2), pp. 315–341.
Heskin, A.D., 1983, *Tenants and the American Dream: Ideology and the Tenant Movement*, New York, Praeger.
Hill, M.R., 1959, *Housing Finance in Australia 1945–1956*, Melbourne, University Press.
Hirayama, Y., 2003, Home ownership in an unstable world: The case of Japan, in: R. Forrest and J. Lee (eds), *Housing and Social Change: East and West Perspectives*, London, Routledge.
Hirayama, Y., 2005, Running hot and cold in the urban home-ownership market: The experience of Japan's major cities, *Journal of Housing and the Built Environment*, 20 (1), pp. 1–20.
Hirayama, Y., 2007, Reshaping the housing system: home ownership as a catalyst for social transformation, in: Y. Hirayama and R. Ronald (eds), *Housing and Social Transition in Japan*, London, Routledge.
Hirayama, Y and K. Hayakawa, 1995, Home ownership and family wealth in Japan, in: R. Forrest and A. Murie (eds), *Housing and Family Wealth: Comparing International Perspectives*, London, Routledge.
Hirayama, Y. and R. Ronald, 2007 (eds), *Housing and Social Transition in Japan*, London, Routledge.
HMSO, 1939, *About Housing*, 2279, London.
HMSO, 1977 *Housing Policy: A Consultative Document*, 6851, London.
Hoekstra, J., 2005, Is there a connection between welfare state regime and dwelling type? An exploratory statistical analysis, *Housing Studies*, 20 (3), pp. 475–495.
Holliday, I., 2000, Productivist welfare capitalism: Social policy in East Asia, *Political Studies*, 48, pp. 706–723.
Holmans, A., 1987, *Housing Policy in Britain*. London, Croom Helm.
Holme, A., 1985, *Housing and Young Families in East London*, London, Routledge.
Hong Kong Economic Journal, 2000, 19 June.
Hong Kong Housing Authority, 1993, *Review to the Ad Hoc Committee to Review the Housing Subsidy Policy*, Hong Kong, HKHA.
Hong Kong Housing Authority, 2006, *Housing in Figures*, The Government of Hong Kong, http://www.housingauthority.gov.hk/en/aboutus/resources/statistics/0,,,00.html.
Horsewood, N. and P. Neuteboom, 2006, *The Social Limits of Growth: Security and Insecurity Aspects of Home Ownership*, Amsterdam, IOS Press.
Housing and Land Survey of Japan, 1998, 2003, http://www.stat.go.jp/English/data/jyutaku/index.htm
Housing Authority, 1997, *Annual Report, 1996/97*, The Government of Hong Kong.Hulse, K., 2002, *Demand Subsidies for Private Renters: A Comparative Review*, Melbourne, Australian Housing and Urban Research Institute.
Hurd, M. and S. Kest, 2003, Fighting predatory lending from the ground up: an issue of economic justice, in: G.D. Squires (ed.), *Organizing Access to Capital: Advocacy and the Democratization of Financial Institutions*, pp. 119–134, Philadelphia, Temple University Press.
Izuhara, M., 2002, Care and inheritance: Japanese and English perspectives on the generational contract, *Ageing and Society*, Vol. 22, pp. 61–77.

Izuhara, M., 2007, Turning stock into cash flow: Strategies using housing assets in an ageing society, in: Y. Hirayama and R. Ronald (eds), 2007, *Housing and Social Transition in Japan*, London: Routledge.
Jacobs, K. and T. Manzi, 1996, Discourse and policy change: The significance of language for housing research, *Housing Studies*, 11 (4), pp. 543–560.
Jacobs, K. and T. Manzi, 2000, Evaluating the social constructionist paradigm in housing research, *Housing Theory and Society*, 17, pp. 35–42.
Jacobs, K., J. Kemeny and T. Manzi (eds), 2004, *Social Constructionism in Housing Research*, Aldershot, Ashgate Press.
Jager, M., 1986, Class definition and the aesthetics of gentrification: Victoriana in Melbourne, in: N. Smith and P. Williams (eds), *Gentrification of the City*, London, Allen and Unwin.
Japan Real Estate Institute, 2006, http://www.reinet.or.jp/e/index.htm
Japan Statistical Association, 2001, *Tokei de Miru Nihon* (Japan in Statistics), Tokyo, Japan Statistical Association.
Jessop, B., 1996, Post-fordism and the state, in: B. Greve (ed.), *Comparative Welfare Systems: The Scandinavian Model in a Period of Change*, London, Macmillan.
Johnson, C.A., 1982, *Miti and the Japanese Miracle: The Growth of Industrial Policy, 1925–1975*, Tokyo, Charles E. Tuttle.
Jones, C., 1993, The Pacific challenge: Confucian welfare States, in C. Jones (ed.), *New Perspectives on the Welfare State in Europe*, London, Routledge.
Kanemoto, Y., 1997, The housing question in Japan,. *Regional Science and Urban Economics*, 27, pp. 613–641.
Kemeny, J., 1981, *The Myth of Home Ownership: Public Versus Private Choices in Housing Tenure*, London, Routledge.
Kemeny, J., 1986, The ideology of home ownership, in: B. McLoughlin and M. Huxley (eds), *Urban Planning in Australia: Critical Readings*, Longman, Cheshire.
Kemeny, J., 1992, *Housing and Social Theory*, London, Routledge.
Kemeny, J., 1995, *From Public Housing to the Social Market: Rental Policy Strategies in Comparative Perspective*, London, Routledge.
Kemeny, J., 2001, Comparative housing and welfare: Theorising the relationship, *Journal of Housing and the Built Environment*, 16, pp. 53–70.
Kemeny, J., 2002, Reinventing the wheel? The interaction basis of constructionism, *Housing Theory and Society*, 19 (3–4).
Kemeny, J., 2005, The really big trade-off between home ownership and welfare: Castles' evaluation of the 1980 thesis, and reformulation 25 years on, *Housing, Theory and society*, 22 (2), pp. 59–75.
Kemeny, K., 2006, Corporatism and housing regimes, *Housing, Theory and Society*, 23(1), pp. 1–18.
Kemeny, J. and S. Lowe, 1998, Schools of comparative housing research: From convergence to divergence, *Housing Studies*, 13 (2), pp. 161–176.
King, P., 1996, *The Limits of Housing Policy: A Philosophical Investigation*, Middlesex University Press.
King, P., 2001, Was Conservative housing policy really conservative?, *Housing Theory and Society*, 18 (3–4), pp. 98–126.
King, P., 2004, Relativism, subjectivity and the self: A critique of social constructionism, in: K. Jacobs, J. Kemeny and T. Manzi (eds), 2004, *Social Constructionism in Housing Research*, Aldershot, Ashgate Press.

King, P., 2006, *A Conservative Consensus: Housing Policy Before 1997 and After*, Exeter, Imprint Academic.
Kingston, P.W., L.P. Thompson and M.E. Douglas, 1984, The politics of home-ownership, *American Politics Quarterly*, 12, pp. 131–150.
Knight, D., 2002, The biographical narratives and meanings of home of private tenants, PhD thesis, University of Wales.
Knight Frank, 2006, http://www.knightfrank.co.uk/press/2006_news_stories/KnightFrankGlobaLHpi.aspx
Knorr-Cetina, K.D. and A. Preda (eds), 2000, *The Sociology of Financial Markets*, Oxford, Oxford University Press.
Koyano, W., 1996, Filial piety and intergenerational solidarity in Japan, *Australian Journal on Ageing*, 15 (2), pp. 51–56.
Krause, L., A.T. Koh and T.Y. Lee, 1987, *The Singapore Economy Reconsidered*, Singapore, Institute of South East Asian Studies.
Kurz, K. and H. Blossfeld (eds), 2004, *Home Ownership and Social Inequality in Comparative Perspective* (Studies in Social Inequality), Stanford University Press.
Lacan, J., 2002, *Ecrits: A Selection*, London, Norton and Company.
Langley, P., 2006, The making of investor subjects in Anglo-American pensions, *Society and Space*, 24, pp. 919–934.
Langley, P., 2007, *The financialisation of Anglo-American mortgages*, Paper presented at Think Tank on the Management and Governance of Housing Wealth, Durham University, UK, February.
Larraine, J., 1979, *The Concept of Ideology*, Hutchinson, London.
Lasch, C., 1984, *The Minimal Self: Psychic Survival in Troubled Times*, Picador.
Lau, K.Y., 2007, The state managed housing system in Hong Kong, in: R. Groves, A. Murie and C. Watson (eds), *Housing and the New Welfare State: Examples from East Asia and Europe*, Aldershot, Ashgate.
Lawrence, R., 1987, What makes a house a home?, *Environment and Behaviour*, 19, pp. 154–168.
Lea, M.J., R. Welter and A. Dubel, 1997, *Study on Mortgage Credit in the European Economic Area*, San Diego, CA, Postdam and Bonn: European Commission, Directorate General XXIV and Empirica.
Lee, J., 1999, *Housing, Home Ownership and Social Change in Hong Kong*. Hampshire, UK, Ashgate.
Lee, J., 2002, *Is there an East Asian housing culture? Contrasting housing systems of Hong Kong, Singapore, Taiwan and South Korea*, Paper presented at ENHR Conference, Vienna University, July.
Lee, J. and N.M. Yip, 2001, Homeownership under economic uncertainty: The role of subsidised flat sales in Hong Kong, *Third World Planning Review*, 23, (1), pp. 61–78.
Lee, J., R. Forrest and W.K. Tam, 2003, Home ownership in East and South East Asia, in: R. Forrest and J. Lee (eds), *Housing and Social Change: East-West Perspectives*, London, Routledge.
Lee, K.Y., 2000, *From Third World to First: The Singapore Story 1965–2000*, Singapore, Singapore Press Holdings.
Le Grange, A. and N.M. Yip, 2001, Social belonging, social capital and the promotion of home ownership: A case study of Hong Kong, *Housing Studies*, 16 (3), pp, 291–310.
Leisering, L. and R. Walker (eds), 1998, *The Dynamics of Modern Society: Poverty, Policy and Welfare*, Bristol, Policy Press.

Levett, T., 1983, The globalisation of markets, *Harvard Business Review*, May, pp. 92–102.
Lijphart, A. and M.L. Krepaz, 1991, Corporatism and consensus democracy, *British Journal of Political Science*, 21, pp. 235–246.
Lim, K.L., 2001, Implications of Singapore's CPF scheme on consumption choices and retirement, *Pacific Economic Review*, 6, pp. 361–382.
Lin, K.C. and A. Tyabji, 1987, *An analysis of the 100 per cent home ownership policy in Singapore*, Paper presented at the 15th International Association of Housing Science World Congress on Housing, Singapore.
Lipset, S.M., 1991, American exceptionalism reaffirmed, in: B.E. Shafer (ed.), *Is America Different: A New Look at American Exceptionalism*, Oxford, Clarendon Press.
Listokin, D., 1991, Federal housing policy and preservation: Historical evolution, patterns and implications, *Housing Policy Debate*, 2 (2), pp. 157–185.
Littlewood, J., 1986, Is home ownership for renters?, in: T. Booth and T. Crook (eds), *Low Cost Home Ownership*, Aldershot, Gower.
Lodziak, C., 1986, *The Power of Television: A Critical Appraisal*, London, Pluto Press.
Lodziak, C., 1996, *Manipulating Needs*, London, Pluto Press.
Lodziak, C., 2002, *The Myth of Consumerism*, London, Pluto Press.
Low, L. and T.C. Aw, 1997, *Housing a Healthy, Educated and Wealthy Nation through the CPF*, Singapore, Times Academy Press for the Institute of Policy Studies.
Lowe, S., 1992, The social and economic consequences of the growth of home ownership, in: J. Birchall (ed.), *Housing Policy in the 1990s*, London, Routledge.
Lowe, S., 2004, *Housing Policy Analysis: British Housing in Cultural and Comparative Context*, London, Palgrave.
Lundqvist, L.J., 1998, Property owning and democracy – Do the twain ever meet?, *Housing Studies*, 13 (2), pp. 217–231.
Lux, M, 2007, The context-sensitive methodology for comparative housing research in transition countries, Paper presented at ENHR Comparative Housing Seminar, European Network of Housing Research, Dublin, April.
MacGregor, J., 1965, *Strategy for Housing, in The Conservative Opportunity*, London, Batsford.
Maclennan, D., G. Meen, K. Gibb and M. Stevens, 1997, *Fixed Commitments, Uncertain Incomes*, York, Joseph Rowntree Foundation.
Madge, J. and Brown, C., 1981, *First Homes: A Survey of the Housing Circumstances of Young Married Couples*, London, Policy Studies Institute.
Madigan, R., 1988, *A new generation of homeowners?* Discussion Paper, Glasgow, Centre for Housing Research, University of Glasgow.
Madigan, R. and M. Munro, M., 1996, House beautiful: Style and consumption within the home, *Sociology*, 32, pp. 1609–1622.
Malpass, P., 2005, *Housing and the Welfare State*, London, Palgrave Macmillan.
Malpass, P., 2006, Housing policy in an opportunity society, in: J. Doling and M. Elsinga (eds), *Home Ownership, Getting in, Getting from, Getting out, Part 2*, Amsterdam, IOS Press.
Management and Coordination Agency, 1998, *Jutaku Toukei Chousa* (Housing Survey of Japan), Tokyo, Statistics Bureau.
Mandic, S. and D. Clapham, 1996, The meaning of home ownership in the transition from socialism: The example of Slovenia, *Urban Studies*, 33, pp. 83–97.

Marcuse, P., 1987, The other side of housing: Oppression and liberation, in B. Turner, J. Kemeny and L. Lundqvist (eds), *Between State and Market: Housing in the Post Industrial Era*, Stockholm, Almqvist and Wiksell International.
Martin, R., 2002, *Financialization of Daily Life*, Philadelphia, PN: Temple University Press.
Marx, K. and F. Engels, 1965, *The German Ideology*, New York, International Publishers.
Masnick, G.S., 2004, Home ownership and social inequality in the United States, in: K. Kurz and H. Blossfeld (eds), *Home Ownership and Social Inequality: In Comparative Perspective* (Studies in Social Inequality), Stanford University Press.
Mason, J., 1989, Reconstructing the public and the private: The home and marriage in later life, in: G. Allan and G. Crow (eds), *Home and Family: Creating the Domestic Sphere*, Basingstoke, Macmillan.
McAllister, I., 1984, Housing tenure and party choice in Australia, Britain and The United States, *British Journal of Political Science*, 14, pp. 509–522.
McCarthy, D., O.S. Mitchell and J. Piggott, 2002, Asset rich and cash poor: Retirement provision and housing policy in Singapore, *Journal of Pension Economics and Finance*, 1, pp. 197–222.
McGuire, C., 1981, *International Housing Policies: A Comparative Analysis*, Toronto, Lexington Books.
McKay S., 2001, The savings gateway: 'Asset-based welfare' in practice, *Benefits*, 10 (2), pp. 141–145.
Merleau-Ponty, M., 1969, *Tegn: Udvalgte essays*, København, Rhodos.
Merrett, S., 1979, *State Housing in Britain*, London, Routledge and Kegan Paul.
Merrett, S., 1982, *Owner Occupation in Britain*, London, Routledge and Kegan Paul.
Miles, D., 2004, *UK Mortgage Market: Taking a Longer Term View*, London, HM Treasury.
Miller, D., 1998, Conclusion: a theory of virtualism, in: J.G. Carrier and D. Miller (eds), *Virtualism*, Oxford, Berg.
Miller, D., 2001, *Home Possessions: Material Culture Behind Closed Doors*, New York and Oxford, Berg.
Ministry of Construction, 1995, *Minkan Juutaku Kensetsu Shikin Jittai Chousa* [Survey on the Financial Situation in Private Home Construction], Tokyo.
Ministry of Health and Welfare, 1941, *Housing Statistics Survey of Large Cities*, Tokyo.
Ministry of Land, Infrastructure and Transport, 2003, *Tochi Hakusyo* [Government White Paper on Land], National Printing Bureau, Tokyo.
Ministry of Land, Infrastructure and Transport, 2007, http://www.mlit.go.jp/english/index.html
Miyake, J. (1985) Jutaku shijo ron [On the housing market], in *Shin Kenchikugaku Taikei Henshu Iinkai* [Committee on New Architectural Theories] (ed.) *Shin Kenchikugaku Taikei Vol.14: Haujingu [New Theories of Architecture Vol.14: Housing]*, Tokyo, Shokoku Sha, pp.73–153.
Mizuoka, F., 2004, Japan: The economic consequences of the fetish of space, *Urban Policy and Research*, 22 (1), pp. 93–99.
Morishima, M., 1982, *Why has Japan Succeeded?* Cambridge, Cambridge University Press.
Morishima, M., 1988, Confucianism as a basis for capitalism, in: D.I. Okimoto and T.P. Rohlem (eds), *Inside the Japanese System: Readings on Contemporary Society and Political Economy*, Stanford University Press.

Mulder, N., 1998, The legitimacy of the public sphere and the culture of the new urban middle class in the Philippines, in: Dradsbaek Schmidt et al. (eds), *Social Change in South East Asia*, Harlow, Longman.
Mulder, C.H., 2005, Home ownership and family formation, *Journal of Housing and the Built Environment*, 21 (3), pp. 281–298.
Munro, M., R. Madigan, and C. Memery, 1998, Choices in owner-occupation, in: P. Taylor-Gooby (ed.), *Choice in Public Policy*, Basingstoke, Macmillan.
Munro, M. and P. Leather, 2000, Nest-building or investing in the future? Owner-occupiers' home improvement behaviour, *Policy and Politics*, 28 (4), pp. 511–526.
Munro, M., J. Ford, C. Leishman and K. Karley, 2005, *Lending to Higher Risk Borrowers*, York, JRF.
Murie, A., 1998, Secure and contented citizens? Home ownership in Britain, in: A. Marsh and D. Mullins (eds), *Housing and Public Policy*, Open University Press.
Mythen, G., 2005, Employment, individualization and insecurity: Rethinking the risk society perspective, *The Sociological Review*, 53 (1), pp. 129–149.
Nationwide, 2006, http://www.nationwide.co.uk/hpi/
Noguchi, Y., 1988, *Souzoku no Jittai to Eikyo ni Kansuru Chousa Kenkyu* [Study on the Facts and Effects of Inheritance], Keizai Sesaku Kenkyu Sho.
Nomisma, 2006, http://www.nomisma.it/index.php?id=4&L=1
Norris, M. and D. Redmond, 2007, *Housing Contemporary Ireland : Policy, Society and Shelter*, UK, Springer.
NVM, 2006, Nederlandse Vereniging van Makelaars, http://www.nvm.nl/nvm/index.jsp?navid=_nvmvooru_3&doelgroep=woningmarkt
Oakley, A., 1976, *Housewife*, Harmondsworth, Penguin.
ODPM, 2000, *Quality and Choice, A Decent Home for All: The Way Forward for Housing*, London, Office of the Deputy Prime Minister.
ODPM, 2005a, *Planning for Housing: A Consultation Paper*, London, Office of the Deputy Prime Minister.
ODPM, 2005b, *Home for All*, London, Office of the Deputy Prime Minister.
ODPM, 2005c, *Housing in England, Part 1: Trends in Tenure and Cross Tenure Topics*, London, Office of the Deputy Prime Minister.
OECD, 1999, *Coping with population ageing in Australia*, Economics Department Working Papers, No. 217, Paris.
OECD, 2004, Economic Outlook, No. 81, Paris.
Offe, C., 1984, *Contradictions of the Welfare State*, Massachusetts Press.
OFHEO, 2006, http://www.ofheo.gov/HPI.aspx
Oizumi, E., 2007, Transformations in housing construction and finance, in Y. Hirayama, and R. Ronald, 2007 (eds), *Housing and Social Transition in Japan*, London: Routledge.
Oxley, M., 2001, Meaning, science, context and confusion in comparative housing research, *Journal of Housing and the Built Environment*, 16 (1), pp. 89–106.
Pannell, B., 2007, Improving attitudes to home ownership, *Housing Finance*, March, London, CML.
Papadakis, E. and P. Taylor-Gooby, 1987, *The Private Provision of Public Welfare*, Wilmslow, Wheatsheaf.
Paris, Chris, 1993, *Housing Australia*, Melbourne, Macmillan.
Parker, I. (ed.), 1998, *Social Constructionism, Discourse and Realism – Inquiries in Social Construction*, London, Sage.
Pawley, M., 1978, *Home Ownership*, London, Architectural Press.

Paxton, W., 2001, Assets: A third pillar of welfare, in: S. Regan (ed.), *Asset-Based Welfare: International Experiences*, London, IPPR.
Peck, J. and A. Tickell, 2002, Neoliberalising space, antipode, 34 (3), pp. 380–404.
Peng, I. and J. Wong, 2004, *Growing out of the developmental state: East Asian welfare reform in the 1990s*, Paper presented at the RC19 Annual Conference on Welfare State Restructuring: Processes and Social Outcomes, Paris 2–4, September.
Pensions Commission, 2004, *Pensions: Challenges and choices*, http//pensioncommission.org.uk/publications/2004/annrep/index.asp
Perin, C., 1977, *Everything in Its Place*, Princeton, NJ, Princeton University Press.
Perkins, H. and D. Thorns, 2003, The making of a social world: Aotearoa/New Zealand as an exemplar, in: R. Forrest and L. Lee (eds), *Housing and Social Change: East West Perspectives*, London, Routledge.
Peters, M.A., 2001, *Post-structuralism, Marxism and Neo-liberalisation: Between Theory and Politics*, Lanham, MD, Rowman and Littlefield.
Phang, S.Y., 2001, Housing policy, wealth formation and the Singapore economy, *Housing Studies*, 16 (4), pp. 443–459.
Phang, S.Y., 2007, The Singapore model of housing and the welfare state, in R. Groves, A. Murie and C. Watson, *Housing and the New Welfare State: Examples from East Asia and Europe*, Aldershot, Ashgate.
Pickvance, C., 1999, *Four varieties of comparative analysis*; Paper presented at the Netherlands Graduate School of Housing and Urban Research International Workshop on Cross-national Comparison, Amsterdam, December.
Poggio, T., 2006, *Different patterns of home ownership in Europe*, Paper presented at the ENHR Home Ownership and Globalisation Working Group conference on Home ownership in Europe: Policy and research issues, Delft University of Technology, The Netherlands, November.
Poole, William, 2003, Housing in the macroeconomy, speech at OFHEO Symposium on House Prices in the US Economy, Washington, DC, 10 March.
Pooley, C. (ed.), 1993, *Housing Strategies in Europe 1880–1930*, Leicester University Press.
Pratt, G., 1982, Class analysis and urban domestic property: A critical reexamination, *International Journal of Urban and Regional Research*, 6 (4), pp. 481–501.
Pratt, G., 1986, Against reductionism: The relations of consumption as a mode of social structuration, *International Journal of Urban and Regional Research*, 10 (3), pp. 377–399.
Pratt, G., 1987, Class, home and politics, *Canadian Review of Sociology and Anthropology*, 24, pp. 39–57.
Productivity Commission, 2003, Australian Government, http://www.pc.gov.au/inquiry/housing/draftreport/mediarelease.html
Putnam, T., 1990, Introduction, in: T. Putnam and C. Newton (eds), *Household Choices*, London, Futures Publications.
Rainwater, L., 1966, Fear and the house as haven in the lower class, *AIP Journal*, 32 (1), pp. 23–31.
Rakoff, R., 1977, Ideology in everyday life: The meaning of the house, *Politics and Society*, 7, pp. 85–104.
Rapoport, A., 1981, Identity and environment: A cross cultural perspective, in: S. Duncan (ed.), *Housing and Identity: Cross-cultural Perspectives*, London, Croom Helm.

Real Estate Institute of Australia, 2005, *Home ownership, superannuation and self-funded retirement: Proposal made to the Federal Government*, http://www.reia.com.au/documents/REIA_Submission_on_People_under_40yo.pdf
Regan, S. (ed.), 2001, *Asset-Based Welfare: International Experiences*, London, IPPR.
Renaud, B., 2004, *Performance and change: East Asain housing policies after fifty years*, Paper presented at the International Housing Conference on Housing in the 21st century: Challenges and commitments, Hong Kong, February.
Retsinas, N.P. and E.S. Belsky (eds), 2005, *Building Assets – Building Credit*, Washinton, DC, Brookings Institution Press.
Rex, J. and R. Moore, 1967, *Race, Community and Conflict*, Oxford, Oxford University Press.
Riceour, P., 1981, *Hermeneutics and the Human Sciences: Essays on Language, Action and Interpretation*, J.B. Thompson (ed.), Cambridge, Cambridge University Press.
Richards, L., 1990, *Nobody's Home: Dreams and Realities in a New Suburb*, Melbourne, Oxford University Press.
Rohe, W., S. van Zandt and G. McCarthy, 2002, Home ownership and access to opportunity, *Housing Studies*, 17 (1), pp. 51–61.
Ronald, R., 2004, Home ownership, ideology and diversity: Re-evaluating concepts of housing ideology in the case of Japan, *Housing, Theory and Society*, 21 (2), pp. 49–64.
Ronald, R., 2006, Meanings of property and home ownership consumption in divergent socio-economic conditions, in: J. Doling and M. Elsinga, *Home Ownership: getting in, getting out, getting from - Part 2*, Amsterdam, IOS Press.
Ronald, R., 2007a, Comparing homeowner societies: Can we construct an East-West model?, *Housing Studies*, 22 (4), pp. 473–493.
Ronald, R., 2007b, The Japanese home in transition: Housing, consumption and modernization, in Y. Hirayama and R. Ronald (eds), *Housing and Social Transition in Japan*, London, Routledge.
Ronald, R., Forthcoming 2008, Between investment, asset and use consumption: the meaning of home ownership in Japan, *Housing Studies*, 23(2).
Ronald, R. and Y. Hirayama, 2006, Housing commodities, context and meaning: Transformations in Japan's urban condominium sector, *Urban Studies*, 43 (13), pp. 2467–2483.
Rose, D., 1980, *Towards a Re-evaluation of the Political Significance of Home Ownership in Britain*, Conference of Socialist Economists, Housing Construction and the State, London, Political Economy of Housing Workshop.
Rose, R. and R. Shiratori, 1986, *Welfare State: East and West*, Oxford, Oxford University Press.
Rosow, I., 1948, Homeownership motives, *American Sociology Review*, 13, pp. 751–756.
Rowlands, R. and C. Gurney, 2001, Young people's perceptions of housing tenure: A case study in the socialisation of tenure prejudice, *Housing, Theory and Society*, 17 (3), pp. 121–130.
Rowse, T., 1978, Heaven and a hills hoist: Australian critics on suburbia, *Meaning*, 37(1), reprinted in R. White and P. Russell (eds), *Memories & Dreams*, Sydney, Allen and Unwin.
Rubin, L.B., 1976, *Worlds of Pain: Life in The Working Class Family*, New York, Basic Books.
Rudd, C., 1994, Japan's welfare mix, *The Japan Foundation Newsletter*, 22 (3), pp. 14–17.

Ruonavaara, H., 1988, *The Growth of Urban Home Ownership in Finland*. Sociological Studies Series A, No. 10, University of Turku.
Ruonavaara, H., 1993, Types and forms of housing tenure: Towards solving the comparison/translation Problem, *Scandinavian Housing and Planning Research*, 10, pp. 3–20 .
Rybczynski, W., 1986, *Home: A Short History of an Idea*, London, Heinemann.
Sahlin, I., 2004, Central state and homelessness in Sweden: New ways of governing, *European Journal of Housing Policy*, 4 (3), pp. 345–367.
Saito, A. and A. Thornley, 2003, Shifts in Tokyo's world city status and the urban planning response, *Urban Studies* 40 (4), pp. 665–685.
Sand, J., 1998, At home in the Meiji Period, in: S. Vlastos (ed.), *Mirror of Modernity*, Berkley, University of California Press.
Sato, I., 2007, Welfare regime theories and the Japanese housing system, in: Y. Hirayama and R. Ronald (eds), 2007, *Housing and Social Transition in Japan*, London, Routledge.
Saunders, P., 1978, Domestic property and social class, *International Journal of Urban and Regional Research*, 2, pp. 233–251.
Saunders, P., 1979, *Urban Politics: A Sociological Interpretation*, London, Hutchinson.
Saunders, P., 1990, *A Nation of Home Owners*. London, Unwin Hyman.
Sayer, A., 2000, *Realism and Social Science*, London, Sage.
Scanlon, K. and Whitehead, C. (2004), *International Trends in Housing Tenure and Mortgage Finance*, London, Council for Mortgage Lenders.
Schaede, U. and W. Grimes, 2003, *Japan's Managed Globalization: Adapting to the Twenty First Century*, Armonk, M.E. Sharpe.
Schmidt, S., 1989, Convergence theory, labour movements, and corporatism: The case of housing, *Scandinavian Housing and Planning Research*, 6 (2), pp. 83–101.
Searle, B. and S. Smith, 2006, De-materialising money: the ebb and flow of wealth between housing and other things, Paper presented at the ENHR Housing Finance Workshop, Ljubljana, Slovenia, June.
Seeley, J., 1956, *Crestwood Heights*, Toronto, Toronto University Press.
Sherraden, M. 1991, *Assets and the Poor: A New American Welfare Policy*, New York, M E Sharpe.
Sherraden, M., 2003, Assets and the social investment state, in: W. Paxton (ed.), *Equal Shares: Building a Progressive and Coherent Asset Based Welfare Policy*, London, IPPR, pp. 28–41.
Shiratori, R., 1986, The future of the welfare state, in: R. Rose and R. Shiratori (eds), *The Welfare State: East and West*, Oxford, Oxford University Press.
Shlay, A.B., 2006, Low-income homeownership: American Dream or delusion, *Urban Studies*, 43 (3), 511–531.
Siltanen, J. and M. Stanworth, 1984, The politics of private woman and public man, in: J. Siltanen and M. Stanworth (eds), *Women and the Public Sphere*, London, Hutchinson.
Singapore Department of Statistics, 2005, http://www.singstat.gov.sg/
Singapore Government, 2007, Statistical Highlights, http://www.singstat.gov.sg/pubn/reference/toc-sh.pdf
Smith, S., 2006, Home ownership: Managing a risky business, in: J. Doling and M. Elsinga (eds), *Home Ownership: Getting in, Getting from, Getting out*, Delft, Delft University Press.
Smith, S., M. Munro and H. Christie, 2006, Performing (housing) markets, *Urban Studies*, 43 (1), pp. 81–98.

Snooks, G., 1994, *Portrait of the Family Within the Total Economy*, Sydney, Cambridge University Press.
Somerville, P., 1994, On explanations of housing policy, *Scandinavian Housing and Planning Research*, 11 (4), pp. 211–230.
Somerville, P., 1997, The social construction of home, *Journal of Architectural and Planning Research*, 14 (3), pp. 226–245.
Somerville, P., 2005, A skeptic looks at Housing Theory, *Housing, Theory and Society*, 22 (2), pp. 59–75.
Somerville, P. and B. Bengsston, 2002, Constructionism, Realism and Housing Theory, *Housing Theory and Society*, 19 (3), pp. 121–136.
Sorensen, A., 2002, *The Making of Urban Japan*, London, Routledge Curzon.
Stephens, M., 2003, Globalisation and housing finance systems in advanced and transitional economies, *Urban Studies*, 40 (5–6), pp. 1011–1026.
Statistics Bureau (Japan), 1986–2003, http://www.stat.go.jp/english/
Steger, M., 2003, *Globalisation*, Oxford, Oxford University Press.
Sternberg, E., 2000, An integrative theory of urban design, *Journal of the American Planning Association*, 66, pp. 265–278.
Sternlieb, G. and J.W. Hughes, 1982, Housing of the poor in a post shelter society, *Annals of the American Academy of Political and Social Sciences*, 465 (1), pp. 109–122.
Stretton, H., 1970, *Ideas for Australian Cities*, Melbourne, Georgina House.
Survey of English Housing, 2006, Communities and Local Government, http://www.communities.gov.uk/housing/housingresearch/housingsurveys/surveyofenglishhousing/
Swiss National Bank, http://www.snb.ch/
Tatch, J., 2006, Will the real first time buyers please stand up, *Housing Finance*, September, London, CML.
The Straits Times, 2005, Singapore, 19th February.
Thompson, J.B., 1984, *Studies in the Theory of Ideology*, Cambridge, Polity Press.
Thorns, D.C., 1976, *The Quest for Community*, London, Allen and Unwin.
Thorns, D., 1981, Owner-occupation: Its significance for wealth transfer and class formation, *Sociological Review*, 29 (4), pp. 705–728.
Thorns, D., 1989, The impact of homeownership and capital gains upon class and consumption sectors, *Environment and Planning D, Society and Space*, 7, pp. 293–312.
Thorns, D., 1992, Fragmenting society: A comparative analysis of regional and urban development, London, Routledge.
Titmuss, R., 1958, *Essays on the 'Welfare State'*, London, Allen and Unwin.
Torgersen, U., 1987, Housing: The wobbly pillar of the welfare state, in: B. Turner, J. Kemeny and J. Lundqvist (eds), *Between State and Market: Housing in the Post-industrial Era*, Stockholm, Almqvist and Wiskell.
Tosics, I. and J. Hegedus, 1998, Centrally planned housing systems, in: W. Van Vliet (ed.), *The Encyclopaedia of Housing*, pp. 42–44, London, Sage.
Tremewan, C., 1994, *The Political Economy of Social Control in Singapore*, London, St. Martins Press.
Troy, P., 2000, Suburbs of acquiescence, suburbs of protest, *Housing Studies*, 15 (5), pp. 717–738.
Turner, B. and C. Whitehead, 2002, Reducing housing subsidy: Swedish housing policy in an international context, *Urban Studies*, 39 (2), pp. 201–217.

UN, 2005, http://www.un.org/esa/population/publications/WUP2005/2005wup. htm
US Census Bureau, 2007, http://www.census.gov/
US Department of Housing and Urban Development, 2004, The influence of household formation on home ownership rates across time and space, Office of Policy Developments and Research.
Vale, L.J. 2007, The ideological origins of affordable homeownership efforts, in: W.M. Rohe and H.L. Watson (eds), *Chasing the American Dream: New Perspectives on Affordable Homeownership*, New York, Cornell University Press.
Victorian Parliament, 1943, (House of Assembly) Parliamentary debates, Hansard, Vol. 216, Melbourne, Government Printer.
Wade, R., 1990, *Governing the Market: Economic Theory and the Role of Government in East Asian Industrialisation*, Princeton, NJ, Princeton University Press.
Walker, A. and C.K. Wong, 1996, Rethinking the Western Construction of the welfare state, *International Journal of Health Services*, 26 (1), pp. 67–92.
Walker, A. and Wong, J.C.-K., 2005, *East Asian Welfare Regimes in Transition, From Confucianism to Globalization*, Britsol, The Policy Press.
Warde, A., 1992, Notes on the relationship between production and consumption, in: I. Burrow and C. March (eds), *Consumption and Class: Division and Change*, London, Macmillan.
Waswo, A., 2002, *Housing in Postwar Japan: A Social History*, London, Curzon Press.
Waters, M., 1995, *Globalisation*, London, Routledge.
van Weesep, J. and H. Priemus, 1999, The dismantling of public housing in the USA, *Journal of Housing and the Built Environment*, 14 (1), pp. 3–12.
Weiss, L., 1998, *The Myth of the Powerless State; Governing the Economy in a Global Era*, Cambridge, Polity Press.
White, M., 1996, Labour market risks, in: P. Meadows (ed.), *Work-in or Work-out?*, New York, Joseph Rowntree Foundation.
White, S., 2001, Asset-based egalitarianism: Forms, strengths and limitations, in: S. Regan (ed.), *Asset-Based Welfare: International Experiences*, London, IPPR.
Whitehead, C., 1993, Privatising housing: An assessment of the UK experience, *Housing Policy Debate*, 4 (1), pp. 101–139.
Wilcox, S., 1997, *Housing Finance Review 1997/1998*, York, JRF.
Wilcox, S., 2000, *Housing Finance Review 2000/2001*, London, CIH/CML.
Wilcox, S., 2005, *Affordability and the Intermediate Housing Market: Local Measures for All Local Authority Areas in Great Britain*, York, JRF.
Wilensky, H.L., 1975, *The Welfare State and Equality: Structural and Ideological Roots of Public Expenditure*, Berkley, University of California Press.
Williams, N., 1989, Housing tenure political attitudes and voting behaviour, *Area*, 21 (1), pp. 117–126.
Williams, P, 1984, The Politics of property: Home ownership in Australia, in: J. Halligan and C. Paris (eds), *Australian Urban Politics: Critical Perspectives*. Melbourne, Longman Cheshire.
Williams, P., 1987, Constituting class and gender: A social history of the home, 1700–1901, in: N. Thrift and P. Williams (eds), *Class and Space: The Making of Urban Society*, London, Routledge and Kegan Paul.
Williams, R., 1983, Problems of the coming period, *New Left Review*, 4, p. 16.

Wilmot, P. and M. Young, 1971, *Family and Class in a London Suburb*, London, Routledge and Kegan Paul.
Winnick, L., 1954, *American Housing and its Use*, New York, Wiley.
Winter, I., 1994, *The Radical Home Owner: Housing Tenure and Social Change*, Melbourne, Gordon and Breach.
Wong, Alink A.K and S. Yeh (eds), 1985, *Housing a Nation: 25 Years of Public Housing in Singapore*, Singapore, Housing and Development Board.
Yamada, Y., 1999, Affordability crisis in housing in Britain and Japan, *Housing Studies*, 14 (1), pp. 99–110.
Yap, M.T., 2002, *Employment insurance: a safety net for the unemployed*, in Institute of Policy Studies, Report Prepared for the Remaking Singapore Committee.
Yates, J., 2003, The more things change?, An overview of Australia's recent home ownership policies, *European Journal of Housing*, 3 (1), pp. 1–33.
Young, M. and P. Wilmot, 1957, *Family and Kinship in East London*, London, Pelican.
Yu, W.K., 1997, The Hong Kong government's strategy for promoting home ownership – an approach to reducing the de-commodifying effects of public housing services, *International Journal of Urban and Regional Research*, 21 (4), pp. 537–553.

Index

adulthood, 2, 57, 73
advanced societies, 5
affluent workers, 156
affordability, 160, 175
affordable, 132
Althusser, 25–7
American Dream, 6, 150
   Down-payment Programme, 103, 149
   home ownership dream, 138
Anglo-Saxon homeowner model, 61, 215
   societies, 8, 10, 14–15, 44, 46, 49, 106, 117–19, 211
Asian crisis
   currency, 107, 180, 251
   economic, 178, 189
asset(s), 53, 149, 174
asset-based, 12, 100–5, 111, 194, 198
   social system, 132
   welfare, 95, 196, 204, 231
asset-building, 189
Attlee, 123
Australia(n), 61, 87
   dream, 152
authoritarian, 228
autonomy, 2, 35, 50, 56, 104

Barker Reports, 137
Beck, 22
Belgium, 95, 248
Better Homes in America movement, 140
Better Housing Programme, 141
Beverage report, 123
black, 144, 148
Blair, 111, 131
bolshevism, 29, 122
   see also Red Scare
bourgeois, 16
Brown, 131–2, 136, 137
building societies, 122, 154
   Act, 128

Bush, 138, 149, 150
buy-back scheme, 197
buy-to-let, 136, 250

capital
   gains, 22
   led corporatism, 94
   losses, 56
capturing ideology, 36, 60
   see also ideology
Central Provident Fund (CPF), 194–7, 202, 225
Child Trust Fund, 103
Chinese, 187, 189
choice, 108
Chua, 195, 200, 228
citizen(s), 76, 104, 113, 127
   citizenry, 145
   citizenship, 61, 122, 131, 157, 160, 163, 173, 217
civic
   participation, 33
   privatism, 65
civil
   rights, 144
   society, 64
class, 52, 71
   see also middle-class; social; working-class
clients of the state, 199
Clinton, 148, 149
collective, 24
collectivism, 35, 89
collectivist, 7, 112
collectivity, 184
commodification, 73, 107, 115, 208, 216
commodified, 113, 179
commodifying agents, 114
commodities, 40, 53, 67, 73, 100, 157, 160, 195
   see also de-commodification; re-commodification

Commonwealth Housing Act, 154
Commonwealth Housing
  Commission, 155
Commonwealth State Housing
  Agreements, 155
company
  housing, 173
  welfare, 173, 177
comparative, 13, 43, 206
competitive states, 95
Confucian, 165
conservatism, 32, 34–5, 120, 156,
  202, 233
  conservative, 33, 125, 162, 169
  Conservatives, 122, 124, 192
consumption, 14, 17, 19, 23, 27, 32, 67,
  68, 71, 72, 155, 164, 167, 227, 233
control, 56, 57
convergence, 5, 105, 162, 214, 223,
  233
corporatism, 166
  corporatist regimes, 94; societies,
  90; theory, 94

debt, 56, 159
de-commodification, 14, 73, 88–9, 93,
  103–4, 113–14, 142, 158, 166,
  179, 182, 194, 208, 219
  see also commodification;
    re-commodification
decorating, 57, 70, 72
demography, 101, 139, 144, 192
Department of Housing and Urban
  Development, 145
deregulation, 202
development
  particularist, 224
  universalist, 224
developmental state, 165
Direct Assistance Scheme, 159
discourse(s), 25–8, 39, 41, 43, 47, 48,
  79, 91, 125, 138, 210, 240
discursive, 43, 74, 242
dominant ideology, 25–7, 30, 91
dualist, 90

East Asia(n), 8, 106
  model, 219
  productivist, 44
  Tigers, 14, 86–7, 163, 188, 203, 205
  welfare regimes, 165
Eastern Europe, 7
economic
  bubble, 175
  nationalism, 166
  rationality, 56
  security, 55
Eden, 124, 211
enterprise society, 173
equity release, 102
Esping-Andersen, 85, 88, 91, 115, 165
EU, 247
exchange-commodity, 232
executive condominium, 197
exotic loans, 150
  see also mortgage(s)

false consciousness, 8, 31, 240
family
  banking, 188
  building, 72
  formation, 4
  life, 11
  self-reliance, 170
  -based welfare, 164, 198, 227
  -vocational privatism, 65
Fannie Mae, 141, 145, 148
fertility rates, 4, 177
FHA, 141, 148, 150
financial asset, 49
  see also asset(s)
financial security, 53
Financial Services Act, 128
financialization, 80
  financialized, 242
First Home Owners Grant, 103, 159
first-time-buyers (FTB's), 133–4, 136,
  149, 158, 161, 250
Foucault, 40, 41
fragmentation, 21
France, 61, 248
Freddie Mac, 146, 148
free market, 147

gambling, 55
generations, 15, 135, 179
  see also family
Germany, 6, 248

Giddens, 23
Ginnie Mae, 146
global age, 231
globalization, 9, 28, 45, 83, 95, 96–8, 107, 112, 206, 216, 233, 243
golden era, 229, 245
Government Housing Loan Corporation, 170, 174, 176, 178
Government Sponsored Enterprises (GSE), 147
Gramsci, 25, 26, 27
The Great Australian Dream, 152
Greece, 6
growth-at-all-costs ethos, 204, 231
guided markets, 223
Gurney, 55, 58, 60, 75, 77

Habermas, 84, 113
Hamnett, 21
hedge, 101, 109
hegemony, 8, 26, 27, 65, 76, 89, 157, 164, 210, 225
  hegemonic, 28, 162
  hegemonies, 9, 91, 112, 116, 153, 163, 241
Herbert Hoover, 139
high-rise flats, 203
home ownership
  ideologies, 9, 42–3, 48, 74, 81
  ideology, 8, 31, 35, 42–3
  rate, 3
  regimes, 238
  societies, 7, 61, 81, 118, 163
Home Ownership Scheme, 184–5, 190
HomeBuy, 103, 132
home-buyers, 135, 190
homeland, 76
Homestead Act, 138
homogeneity, 58, 171
Hong Kong Housing Authority (HKHA), 182, 183, 184, 185, 190, 224
HOPE programme, 148
house-prices, 132, 152, 197, 242
  boom, 152
  euphoria, 5, 126
  increases, 200

inflation, 1, 54–5, 69, 129, 172, 174
  values, 190
housing
  account, 196
  classes, 18, 19
  discourses, 80
  finance, 102
  groups, 18
  market(s), 20, 22, 102
  policy, 12, 27, 41, 98, 119, 179;
    cycle, 214
  provision chain, 221
  studies, 13
  system(s), 2, 45, 47, 93, 95, 136, 204, 241
  -assets, 228
  -debt, 3
  -equity, 3
  -ladder, 1, 38, 177, 197, 198
Housing, Town Planning Act, 121
The Housing Act, 122
Housing Choice voucher, 146
Housing Corporation, 169
Housing Development Board (HDB), 195–7, 199, 202, 224
housing-property assets, 203
Howard, 159
HUD, 148

identity, 34, 52, 70
ideology, 7, 24–9, 31, 37, 47, 63, 71, 91, 92, 108, 116, 206, 210, 218, 241
ie, 169, 172
immigration, 139, 153, 158, 181
independence, 49, 57, 104
Individual Development Account, 103
individualism, 4, 6, 19, 26, 33, 62–6, 69, 80, 92, 104, 110, 124, 205
individuality, 57
individualization, 22, 63, 67–9, 72, 78, 109, 112–13, 117, 217, 245
individualized, 152
inequalities, 21
inheritance, 179, 201
insurance, 110
interest rate(s), 130, 146, 152, 159, 185, 198

investment(s), 59, 74, 78–9, 102, 110, 126, 130, 184, 202, 244
Ireland, 95

Japanese style welfare, 174

Keiretsu, 226
Kemeny, 9, 19, 33, 35, 64–5, 88–9, 91–2, 94, 106, 114–15, 153, 155, 218, 243

labour
   markets, 96
   movement theory, 85
   movements, 91, 230
   -led corporatism, 94
Labour, 120, 126, 156–7
Land Acquisition Act, 195
land myth, 172
Landlord Tenant Act, 155
landlords, 138, 155, 170, 250
   see also private
Lee Kuan Yew, 193
Liberal Democratic Party, 173
Liberal Party, 156, 159
liberal regimes, 7, 93, 96, 208
life cycle, 59
lifestyle(s), 11, 32, 53, 67, 69
lost decade, 175, 177–8
Low Cost Ownership task-force, 131

Macmillan, 211
Malpass, 21, 105, 111
marginal homeowners, 22
market(s), 79, 105, 108–9, 112, 115, 129, 133, 142, 157, 160, 184
   crash, 130
   good, 12
   marketization, 16, 131, 178, 202
   rational, 139
   -investor subject(s), 216, 236
Marx and Engels, 24, 25, 26
Marxist, 17–19, 28, 29, 30, 31, 46, 62, 240
meanings, 49, 50, 59, 73
Menzies, 154, 156
merit good, 12
metaphor, 55
methodology, 36, 39

middle-class, 20, 52, 64, 169, 171, 173, 178, 189, 225
middle-class-feeling, 173
   see also class
Miles Report, 131
minority, 149, 152
mobile privatism, 66
   see also private
Modern Conservative, 128, 131
   see also conservatism
modernity, 24, 168
modernization, 164
'moratorium in state support', 215
mortgage(s), 54, 128, 135, 150, 153, 159, 190, 196
   debt, 3, 133
   guarantees, 186
   securitization, 146
   tax-relief, 125, 142
   -baked securities (MBS), 147
   -interest tax deduction(s), 144, 151
myth, 38, 186

nation building, 154
National Association of Real Estate Boards (NAREB), 140
national capitalisms, 96
negative equity, 55, 130
Negotiated Order Theory, 38
neighbourhood, 52
neo-liberalism, 9, 12, 28, 61, 79, 84, 96, 100, 104–5, 107–8, 110, 112, 117, 132, 137, 151, 160, 202, 204, 240
   governance, 215
Netherlands, 99, 107, 247
New Deal, 141
New Labour, 131, 208
New Zealand, 87
non-white, 148
normalization, 40, 50, 74, 75, 77, 157, 163, 237
normalized, 74, 172
Northern Rock Bank, 249
Norway, 1, 7, 95

ODPM, 131, 132
ontological security, 22, 68, 70

Index   281

opportunity society, 111, 131
opportunity, 137
Own-Your-Own-Home campaign, 140

path dependency, 95
pathway(s), 112, 153, 164, 246
pension, 84, 92, 101–2, 230
  'time-bomb', 101
People's Action Party (PAP), 192, 199, 201
personalization, 70
polarization of tenure, 51
policy hegemony, 217
political
  attitudes, 25, 33
  opinions, 77
positivism, 37–8
possessive individualism, 113
postmodern, 7, 23
power relations, 13, 25, 36, 40
powerlessness, 64, 66
pre-homeowner societies, 248
privacy, 50–1
private
  landlords, 120–1, 154
  privatism, 19, 62–3, 65, 69, 89, 91, 117
  privatization, 9, 12, 16, 100, 107, 114
  rental 133, 155
Private Sector Participation Scheme (PSPS), 185
productivist welfare regime, 164, 166, 207
  see also welfare
proper path(s), 58, 60, 77
property, 51, 74, 129, 160
  owning democracy, 29, 48, 131, 173, 233
  'propertized', 113
  -based citizenship, 106
  -based welfare, 104
public
  housing, 24, 137, 139, 142, 183–4
  owner-occupation, 6, 182, 191, 194, 203
  rental housing, 123–4, 130, 133, 170, 180, 181–2
Public Works Act, 142

pump-primer, 204
Purchase Loan Scheme, 185

re-commodification, 104, 214
  see also commodification; de-commodification
Red Scare, 139
Rent Control Ordinance, 170
rental
  controls, 121
  housing, 144–5, 169
  renters, 2, 59, 93
  renting, 2, 51, 93, 121
  systems, 90
repossessions, 99
retirement, 87, 99, 101, 161, 197, 202
Rex and Moore, 18
right-to-buy, 111, 127, 129
risk(s), 12, 20, 21, 79, 80, 96, 98–9, 108–10, 135, 143, 178
Roosevelt, 141

safety-net(s), 99, 109, 133, 174, 191, 201, 252
Sandwich Class, 185
Saunders, 18, 22, 32–3, 43, 59, 128
saving, 102, 149
Saving Gateway, 103
Savings and Loans, 140
scrap and build, 176
Section 8 vouchers, 146
Section-235, 145
Section-502, 143
securitization, 147
security, 53–5, 57, 74, 105
self, 50
  -identity, 23, 66, 68–9, 71
  -maintaining privatism, 66
  -reliance, 188, 194, 245
Self-help Home ownership Opportunity Programmes (SHOP), 149
Sherraden, 100, 103–4
slum
  clearance, 143
  dwellings, 121
Small Families Improvement Scheme, 199

social
  class(es), 11, 19, 21, 22, 51, 67, 225, 245; *see also* class
  constructionism, 8, 37–9, 40, 42
  democratic, 90, 93, 112
  housing, 10
  inequality, 5, 20
  mainstream, 168, 171, 177, 205, 225
  rental housing, 89, 111, 116, 190
  reproduction, 27, 28
  security, 184, 207
  status, 5, 53, 74
  -flow, 171
Sociological Realism, 41
South European, 7, 86
Spain, 6
Special Administrative Region, 180
speculative, 160
standard
  life-course, 179
  -family model, 172
state
  controlled system, 225
  managed system, 225
Step Repayment System, 174
stigmatization, 53, 136, 210
stock market crash, 140
subjugation, 74
sub-prime, 105, 150, 152, 249
subsidization, 139, 145
  mortgage system, 151
suburban, 143, 153, 156, 158
sweat equity, 150
Sweden, 248
Switzerland, 6
symbolic consumption, 67, 73

Tenant Purchase Scheme, 186
tenure, 45, 50, 75, 120
  discourse, 77; *see also* discourse polarization, 78
  preferences, 189

systems, 13
'tenure imperialism', 246
Thatcher, 64, 127, 186
theories, 13, 17, 45–6
'total home ownership policy', 215
trade unions, 34, 166
trickle down, 198
Tung Chee-hwa, 189
Two-Generation Mortgage, 175

unemployment, 177, 189
unitary, 90
universal citizenship, 228
universal home ownership, 192
Urban Renaissance Agency, 224
Urban Renaissance Policy, 178
urbanization, 164, 181

voting, 34

Waiting List Income Limit, 182
War on Poverty, 144
Weberian, 17
welfare
  capitalism, 164
  good, 11
  mix, 95, 167, 207, 229
  provision, 86
  regime(s), 13, 14, 85, 91, 93, 100, 106, 115, 163, 218
  state(s), 83–5, 87, 95, 104, 113, 116, 123, 165, 167, 194
  -state hegemonies, 108
wobbly pillar, 231
workfare, 87, 153, 158, 161, 167, 210
working man's paradise, 153
working-class, 16, 20, 65, 85, 121–3, 153–4, 156–7
  see also class

zaibatsu, 226

CPSIA information can be obtained
at www.ICGtesting.com
Printed in the USA
BVHW030214281119
565074BV00004B/17/P